FIVE PLAYS

FIVE PLAYS

PETER USTINOV

An Atlantic Monthly Press Book

LITTLE, BROWN AND COMPANY · BOSTON · TORONTO

PR
6041
.S73
F5
1965

The Love of Four Colonels is reprinted by permission of the
Dramatists Play Service. The amateur acting rights of *The
Love of Four Colonels* and *Romanoff and Juliet* in the United
States and Canada are controlled exclusively by Dramatists
Play Service, Inc., 440 Park Avenue South, New York,
N.Y. 10016. No amateur performance of the plays in such
territory may be given without obtaining in advance the
written permission of the Dramatists Play Service, and paying
the requisite fee.

Photo credit—Halsman

*Published simultaneously in Canada
by Little, Brown & Company (Canada) Limited*

CONTENTS

INTRODUCTION: 'PETER USTINOV SPEAKING'
An interview with Henry Brandon
page 1

ROMANOFF AND JULIET
page 11

THE MOMENT OF TRUTH
page 79

BEYOND
page 161

THE LOVE OF FOUR COLONELS
page 175

NO SIGN OF THE DOVE
page 249

INTRODUCTION

WELL, yes—I'm a great believer in beginner's luck, and that's probably why I try so many things. There are times when I feel slightly envious of the kind of writer, for instance, who was born in the docks of Liverpool and protects himself by writing about nothing else and is the greatest expert in the world on the docks of Liverpool. I'd find that extremely difficult. In fact, I'm one of those people who are so hopelessly mixed in breeding that they cannot be emotionally involved in the fate of any particular country. In other words, my foot doesn't really start tapping to any particular anthem or military march.

My father was British, his brother is Canadian, his other brother is Argentinian, and his sister is Egyptian—and that's all merely in one family. My wife is Canadian, my daughters are American, my son has a British passport (of course, I'm talking in terms of passports now). The irony is that we're all of the same family, or blood, if you like. And I also find relatives in every country I go to, so that I really feel perhaps more emotionally involved in the United Nations than in any individual country. All the same, emotionally I'm very European, certainly.

It seems likely that my Russian origin has contributed a great deal to my work. I find that I write in a manner which reveals itself to the Russian in that the Russian literary tradition was the first important one which didn't have its roots in any concept of the classical; from the beginning of Russian literature there are elements of comedy and tragedy hopelessly and irrevocably entangled. I think that's why Shakespeare is so popular in Russia and Racine is not. A man playing Hamlet very well in the French Conservatory would get a first prize for comedy, because *Hamlet* is unacceptable as a tragedy in the French sense. Chekhov? I have a sneaking suspicion that Chekhov approved, up to a point, of the restraint with which his plays were done, but he really thought they should be slightly funnier than Western critics are willing to admit. Or funnier than the way that they're played now even by the Moscow Art Theatre.

Yes, my mother was French, but she lived in Leningrad, which, as I had occasion to find out recently, is very much more cosmopolitan than Moscow. I had read about that, but when you go to Russia you really feel that if Moscow is the heart of Russia, Leningrad is its aspiration. I was naturally rather moved by my trip to Moscow for the film festival last July—it was my first visit to Russia. It did seem to

Grateful acknowledgment is made to Mr Henry Brandon for permission to reprint this interview with Peter Ustinov which first appeared in THE SUNDAY TIMES.

me that so many things which are believed by the West to be sinister inventions of the Soviet government are in point of fact Tsarist elements which the Soviet regime has never succeeded in quashing.

In Moscow, I may tell you, a very beautiful girl came rushing up to me with tears in her eyes and called me "uncle"—and I also met my aunt for the first time. I'd never seen her before. And she behaved with that kind of rather suspect dignity which one got used to in British films during the war. In fact, she said exactly what I had seen in a British film and never really believed. When the door opened, there she was, aged eighty-one. I said who I was, and she said, "Oh, come in, I've just made some coffee." It was uncomfortably near that kind of thing when a man comes home after five years in a German prison camp, knocks at the door, and is greeted by a woman who says, "Oh, hello, Tom—tea's on."

My English education influenced me in that I was forced—at least for the better part of it—to walk to school every day through a virtual slum, of a type which hardly exists any more, dressed in a top hat and tailcoat and with a furled umbrella in my hand. The school prospectus said that the umbrella was essential to differentiate us from City of London bank messengers. Certainly, passing through that slum every day with monotonous regularity was the most useful part of my education. And if you believe that education ends when you leave school, then you're fitted only for certain kinds of work which happen, unfortunately, to be extremely important. But if, on the other hand, you believe, as I do, that school is only the place where you learn to learn, then, of course, it's a very useful pastime at a period of life when the mind needs such a pastime.

But I might easily have been educated in Germany or Holland. My father was a representative of the German News Agency in Holland, and it was after my mother was, I think, about seven months pregnant that his immediate boss decreed that he should be moved to London, where he eventually became press attaché at the German Embassy— until 1935, when he couldn't stand it any more and became British. (He was a German officer in the First World War, though he was never very explicit about all that.) But I know that when he left the German Embassy and became British he got a cable from the German Foreign Office telling him to report at once in Berlin, followed by a cable from some representative of the German general staff, about half an hour later, telling him on no account to return. And then in 1938— it all seems very odd now—he got a call from a phone booth from the German military attaché in London begging him to use his contacts to try to arrange a meeting between the German and British general staffs in order to force the British to stand firm at Munich. But the British didn't dare risk a meeting.

INTRODUCTION

The argument which raged at the German Embassy was not absent in my school, because I sat at the desk next to young Von Ribbentrop. He was rather discreet when my father adopted British nationality, but then I suppose he couldn't say very much because on the other side of him was the son of the Jordanian minister, and he, of course, was by Ribbentrop's terms of reference a Semite. So his attentions were divided.

I wasn't very good at anything at school. I got two out of ten, usually; the son of the Jordanian minister, one out of ten; and Ribbentrop, in the middle, frustrated, usually got no marks at all but was kept on because of the important necessity of giving the son of the representative of a powerful and somewhat aggressive nation a place in the sun. He had been refused, I believe, by Eton, which meant that he automatically came to us at Westminster, where the clothes were similar but the reputation perhaps not quite as giddy, and where there were much smaller playing fields for battles to be won or lost on.

In retrospect, I'd say what I've said somewhere before—it's a joke but there's an element of truth in it—that English education is probably the best in the world if you can survive it; if you can't, there's really nothing left for you but the diplomatic corps or something like that.

For that matter, I firmly believe that any child worth his salt will learn more by reaction against than by obedience to. I remember certain cases of injustice at Westminster which were horrible in themselves, although on a very small scale; but they did make a child, or rather they did make me, aware of injustice, which is a very good thing. For instance, I was asked on one occasion to name the greatest composer of all time. I said Bach, and was told that the correct answer was Beethoven. When I was heard to mutter that I preferred Mozart to Beethoven I was made to write out a hundred times, "Beethoven is the greatest composer who ever lived." Arrant injustice, you see. Then, too, the musical subject for the year when I was about seven or eight was Tchaikovsky, and at the end-of-term exam one of the questions was "Name a Russian composer." I put down "Rimski-Korsakov" and was upbraided in front of the whole school for showing off.

Also I got a school report which I wouldn't have believed if my mother hadn't actually shown it to me the other day. It said: "He shows great originality, which must be curbed at all cost."

Still, from that point of view school was less dangerous than the Army, which, after all, is a return to school. It came to me at a very, very dangerous moment in my life, when I had tasted the first fruits of

[3]

liberty and had left home—I had an apartment of my own. I had learned to take pleasure in personal gain on a very small scale, though I had also learned what it was like to have no money at all. And just when I was enjoying freedom to the full, I was back in the Army again—it really was like going back to school. I stayed in it for four and a half years, surviving by my wits as much as by anything else. Beginning at school, I detested cricket; I've no aptitude for it. The click of the ball on the bat has certainly inspired great and important Englishmen to rhapsodies of abstract satisfaction; it made even a man like the late Lord Birkett, whom I admired a great deal, write books about it. But I hate that noise almost more than anything else I know —it puts my teeth on edge.

As for soccer, I liked it very much, but I've always been rather heavily built, and although I could run quite fast over a short distance, the pursuit of the ball right across the field made me lose courage about halfway to it when I saw out of the corner of my eye other, fleeter people racing for the same thing. I was therefore put in goal, the theory being that as the stoutest boy there it would be extremely difficult for me to get out of the ball's way quickly enough for me *not* to be a good goalkeeper.

So with cricket and soccer at school I got by by learning—or perhaps it was germane to me—to make people laugh. Just as in the Army, I was not in hot water when anybody else would have been simply because I became almost a kind of mascot. During those ghastly kit inspections they like to have in the Army, where you have to fold your socks in a certain shape—I was incapable of doing that once my feet had stretched them—I managed to lay out the kit in such a way that, although the sergeant might happen to be horrified, the officer was amused by it, it was so ridiculous.

So again, as at school, I usually escaped trouble by employing the technique of the melancholy clown, the sad sack. I didn't do it consciously, but I see in retrospect what happened. And once you do that, of course, or if you have the kind of personality that lends itself to that, things begin breaking your way in some mysterious fashion.

I should have said that after Westminster I went to a thing called the London Theatre Studio. My mother was instrumental in arranging that because she belonged to one of those immense artistic families, like the Dolmetschs, in which everybody did something. It was almost a kind of artistic collective, or kibbutz, if you like. I'll spare you the details and merely say that my mother is a painter and my cousin the artistic director of La Scala. Another cousin is Tcherepnin, who is professor of music at De Paul University in Chicago.

Anyway, if I'd decided to become a stockbroker or something

[4]

like that there would have been repercussions in my mother's family, as if I'd selected a profession in which there was no future for a boy. It was accepted as completely natural that I should gravitate toward one of the arts as the only serious kind of thing for a man to do—lucrative, safe, and honourable.

But the drama school was really a last resort. My father had almost washed his hands of me. I had been bottom in everything at school except French, history, and geography and, as is the way with fathers (I know it myself), he grew more and more disappointed with the reports I brought home. Eventually he accepted the situation with a kind of resignation, and I went into the theatre as a ne'er-do-well. Or, rather, I went to drama school.

Everything went wrong for me there. They said I was—well—not exactly arrogant, but that I knew my own mind too well, that I wouldn't learn and that I was unrelaxed; that in all the more athletic activities of the drama school I was stiff and unbending and hopeless. My father then got into a really disgusted mood with me; how on earth was I to be launched in the world? I couldn't find a job, and he grew more and more sour. Then I managed to pass an audition at the Players' Club, giving a turn as the Bishop of Limpopo. I remember my father saying, "Not even drama—vaudeville," although he liked to laugh more than anything else.

Suddenly I made a kind of hit with what amounted to a female impersonation of a German lieder singer giving her final farewell performance. I got marvellous notices. And despite my father's denigration of vaudeville, I used to see him in the audience with a few friends, though he'd leave before the end so that I shouldn't know he'd been present. His pride had become rather ill disguised by this time, and toward the end of his life he couldn't really understand what had happened, because my whole career was all contrary to what *his* father had told him about things.

Those Players' Club days were a long time ago. Now I consider myself a writer first and foremost. Acting is intrinsically easier than writing. To act well is, of course, difficult, but I think it's more difficult to write a bad play than to give a bad performance, to put it at its lowest level. I think acting is in many ways the most powerful outlet for observation—and a most economical one, too, because you can suggest things with a fraction of a movement of an eyebrow, which would need much more extensive treatment in literature.

Yes, it's true, I'm tempted to abandon acting now and concentrate on writing. Occasionally a part comes along which allows me to take a sabbatical and is fun to do—it's a form of holiday that I don't mind doing at all. But acting in the theatre in a long run is absolute torture; it doesn't do the theatre any good either, because I don't think the audience gets its money's worth after a certain time. I can't think that the human frame and the human mind are made for a repetition of the same thing, day in, day out, for a year or two years or more.

Television? I don't find it at all fascinating at the time. It's really the medium of intimacy. That's why politicians so often go wrong on it when they're told by their advisers that at that particular moment eleven million people are watching—They very often talk as if they knew eleven million people were indeed watching, whereas those eleven million are in units of four, three, two, or, most probably, one. You are in fact really talking, or revealing yourself, to a single person. If you talk to that single person as though he were eleven million, he will turn the set off, and quite rightly.

I think television has changed the face of politics much more than it has affected the arts, even if it has made certain arts really accessible. Politics it has transformed completely. I think that if, say, Eden had lived a hundred years ago, he would, despite all his unfortunate illnesses, have managed to maintain power, because at the time when an infuriated crowd was there to break the windows of his residence, he would have been in Scotland, like the Duke of Wellington, and would have come back three weeks later when the incident was closed and forgotten.

This is no longer possible, because now the television camera is everywhere. Very few people, for instance, would deny that Kennedy's victory over Nixon was really fathered by their television debates. The television camera is not exactly a lie-detector—that's putting it too strongly—and in any case one isn't actually trying to find out the truth. But one can find out the truth about a person; not whether a man is telling the truth but whether his personality on television is a true one or not.

The first play I wrote (apart from juvenilia) had a kind of spontaneity, a freshness, which I can never reproduce now because I know too much. I gave that play to Herbert Farjeon in whose revue I was appearing then in 1941. I wrote it between 1940 and 1941, in pencil, in school exercise books (I remember those English exercise books with "danger don'ts" on the back: "Don't follow a rolling ball into the street without looking both ways"—that sort of business). Farjeon never said anything, though I saw him practically every day. At last I broached the subject and asked if I could have it back, but he was very evasive.

Then—it was the day Russia was attacked by the Germans—I went down to the country to see my parents, who were living in Gloucestershire, and we got all the Sunday papers to devour the news. There was tremendous excitement. We listened to the radio and tried to pick up Russian stations on the shortwave, and this went on until well after lunch. Then I read James Agate's column in the *Sunday Times*, and the headline was "A New Dramatist." I remember having a pang of jealousy. I started reading it, and, goodness me, it was all about my own play, which Herbert Farjeon had had typed, at his own expense, and given to Jimmy Agate. So now came this rave notice about an unperformed play. It ended: "A new dramatist has arrived and the play will be seen."

Well, it wasn't seen until about eighteen months later. But Agate's notice did make a big difference. Shortly after that, I went into the Army, and when my play came on I was transferred to the Army kinematograph service. Since then I've made a living by playwriting, acting, and directing; I've directed five films all told.

Acting is the quickest way of making a living. Writing is a longer-term thing. It is also, from the purely day-to-day angle, a kind of insurance policy as you begin to acquire what the French call an "*œuvre*". This has a certain value because they keep on playing one's work in repertory, and so on, in obscure countries.

Yes, I may have mentioned Chekhov, but I'm not really conscious of being influenced by any writer at all. There's none that I really dote on; to that extent I'm much more influenced by abstract things. I'm very much influenced by Mozart, for instance, which sounds like an awfully pretentious thing to say. Yet I'm very, very keen on a light touch which can reveal itself on close scrutiny to be profound. Again, there's something in the way I write which owes allegiance to Russianism, and that means that I'm not afraid to be a square. There is something essentially square about Russian writing—it's so square that it becomes octagonal, which is something that people who use the word "square" hadn't really bargained for. There is a quality in the film of *Billy Budd*, if I say so myself, which is an attempt to be so honest that it is absolutely without artifice. If it has a quality, and I think it has, it's a quality I'm most proud of: it looks you straight in the eye, or as straight as it can, and says, "Here I am—take me or leave me—*boom!*" And there isn't even one trick of the camera to try to bamboozle you into a feeling that it's smart or modern or streamlined.

Yes, my new play is about capital punishment. I hate capital punishment. It was more humane when it was public, not done with this present vile ritual, and God knows we are full of vile rituals—It is enough to make one retch with anger when one reads in the newspaper that two Spanish anarchists have been sentenced to be garrotted because a military tribunal of baleful idiots has decided that they're not fit to be shot. I hate to think that Goya, of all people, lived in vain. I believe we've reached the stage when it is the duty of writers with strong convictions to say what they think.

INTRODUCTION

I love watching the Theatre of the Absurd as a member of the public. But I can't write that way because I don't believe many big themes can be tackled with that technique. And I think it's a time when big themes are tremendously important. We've recently seen, for example, how fallible our great constructions of legal systems are. Wasn't the whole time-honoured structure of English law made an absolute fool of by a handful of ladies of easy virtue?

I've always thought that the English were really an extremely romantic, violent, and tempestuous nation by nature. As it happened, the long, the unexpectedly long, reign of Queen Victoria turned them aside from all this. But I think the English are in search now, after Victorianism and its aftermath, of their lost violence, and this, unfortunately, often seems to take the form of petulance, and flatulence as well. I mean the Angry Young Men, for instance. No, I don't think they've ended already—I mean, "Damn you, England!" and all that kind of thing—which seems to me, by the way, to be really a form of narcissism.

Of course, I think any revolution (I suppose one can call what's going on in England a sort of revolution) only really gets under way when the opposition is on the run anyway. The Russian Revolution looks romantically as though it had started overnight; so does the French Revolution. But they didn't start overnight at all. They started with intellectuals and thinkers who had mobilized the crowd very cunningly.

The Russian government at the moment is very careful not to make the mistake of underestimating the influence of the intellectuals —that's why they're continually either cosseted or reprimanded. In England, on the other hand, revolution or no revolution, the intellectual is ignored, because England has invented a great safety valve: in the words of the psychiatrist in my latest play, you "are consulted in order to be ignored". There is nothing more frustrating than to sit on the board of, say, the Arts Council and present all the façade of allocating inadequate moneys, which, after they've consulted you, they do exactly what they like with. By "they" I mean the permanent officials. You can very easily sit on advisory board after advisory board in England and find they are really just safety valves on the boiler of state.

All right—women. Have they influenced my life and outlook and all that? Well, it's a bit early for stocktaking. But I don't mean by that that I intend to have three more wives! Women have played an important part in my life, children certainly too.

I think an only child, as I was, develops more quickly because he is able much sooner to realize the value of meditation and being left alone. He can also become negligent toward the feelings of others simply through lack of practice. Because we are creatures of habit, and everything is habit-forming, even being alone, I found it rather difficult to adapt myself to the exigencies of marriage, simply because it meant sharing, up to a point, thoughts and even actions which I had formed the habit of dealing with in isolation. And it never occurred to me that it might be construed as being slightly unfriendly to continue like that. And when I'm left alone and work for two or three weeks by myself—because I cannot drag the whole family with me—I find I very quickly relapse into those early habits with a kind of relief, and then have to readapt myself.

But I do miss them after a week or two—I miss them a great deal. What I miss is the fascination of watching creatures develop and the kind of pride you take if something you're responsible for suddenly makes an individual decision. Because, you know, I think it's fatal to think that children are there for your own amusement. They are a kind of confirmation of life, the only form of immortality that we can be sure of. There's an element of my great-great-great-great-great-great-great-grandfather walking about now in myself. I mean there's a gene which belongs to him, and he's still here in that sense; at least, he's represented by a chargé d'affaires!

I was going to say that the structure of society interests me a good deal, too, but perhaps I'll just say that I'm fascinated by the practice of dressing up on formal occasions. I find the launching of a battleship or something like that an irresistibly comic spectacle. Why people have to put on hats with feathers blowing in the wind—I see no difference, really, between that and the African jungle.

And I find it extremely amusing to go into the shower bath after a game of tennis and see a man with no clothes on but wearing an expression on his face as if he were dressed. Sometimes at a place like the Royal Automobile Club you get four generals who've just played squash, and the generals' clothes and hats are hung up and they're absolutely purple in the face, with a line around their necks and the rest of them as white as a sheet—and they're looking into the distance and clearing their throats and discussing things as though they were dressed. It's these moments in life that I think indicative of the follies and pretensions of human beings. Yet I'm inspired by the effort of man to get away from his nakedness and build something solid and reliable and worthy, even if it means abandoning such ridiculous rituals as battleships and their firing salutes to each other.

ROMANOFF AND JULIET

A Comedy in Three Acts

ROMANOFF AND JULIET was presented by Linnit and Dunfee Ltd. at the Piccadilly Theatre on 17 May 1956, with the following cast:—

FIRST SOLDIER	Joe Gibbons
SECOND SOLDIER	David Lodge
THE GENERAL	Peter Ustinov
HOOPER MOULSWORTH	John Phillips
VADIM ROMANOFF	Frederick Valk
IGOR ROMANOFF	Michael David
JULIET	Katy Vail
THE SPY	David Hurst
BEULAH MOULSWORTH	Josephine Barrington
EVDOKIA ROMANOFF	Marianne Deeming
JUNIOR CAPTAIN MARFA ZLOTOCHIENKO	Delphi Lawrence
FREDDIE VANDERSTUYT	William Greene
THE ARCHBISHOP	Edward Atienza

The Play directed by
DENIS CAREY

The American production of ROMANOFF AND JULIET was presented by David Merrick on 10 October 1957, at the Plymouth Theatre in New York City. The production was staged by George S. Kaufman. The setting was by Denis Malcles. Settings and Lighting were supervised by Howard Bay. The cast was as follows:—

FIRST SOLDIER	Phil Leeds
SECOND SOLDIER	Jack Gilford
THE GENERAL	Peter Ustinov
HOOPER MOULSWORTH	Fred Clark
VADIM ROMANOFF	Henry Lascoe
IGOR ROMANOFF	Gerald Sarracini
JULIET	Elizabeth Allen
THE SPY	Carl Don
BEULAH MOULSWORTH	Natalie Schafer
EVDOKIA ROMANOFF	Marianne Deeming
JUNIOR CAPTAIN MARFA ZLOTOCHIENKO	Sylvia Daneel
FREDDIE VANDERSTUYT	William Greene
THE ARCHBISHOP	Edward Atienza

SYNOPSIS OF SCENES

The Main Square in the Capital City of the Smallest Country in Europe.

ACT I: *Dawn to Morning.*
ACT II: *Noon to Afternoon.*
ACT III: *Evening to Night.*

AUTHOR'S NOTE

In the original production, the two Embassies were constructed on trucks which were fixed to the stage at one point, so that the entire buildings could be pivoted on stage and off easily and at will. This scheme proved eminently satisfactory, as it enlarged the acting area considerably when the interiors of the Embassies were not in use. It also enabled the General to seem to push the Embassies out of his mind at the end of the second act, when, at the climax of his Herculean labour in the devious world of diplomacy, he discovers that at last he has told the American Ambassador a piece of news which the latter had not yet gleaned from tapped wire or grapevine. This careless gesture of apparently Samsonesque strength added to the meaning of the play by its simple symbolism.

The crowd effects, fireworks, and musical numbers in the third act were, on the whole, left out in the London production, but have been left in the script to give the reader an impression of what was in the author's mind before the realities of a theatrical budget cast their shadow over his hopes. In fact, some of these diversions might only have confused the issue, and the play is a perfectly practical proposition without them.

November, 1956

ACT I

Dawn to morning.

*The Main Square in the Capital City of the Smallest Country in Europe.
It is dawn. Sombre building on the left with a balcony. Sombre
building on the right with a balcony. In the background, a cathedral,
with an illuminated clock, on which a great many unsteady saints
frequently appear together with Father Time, Death the Reaper,
and other allegorical figures, to hammer out fractions of the hour.
The sky is expansive, and has the crystalline purity of early dawn
in the south.* SOLDIER *left.* SOLDIER *right. Both in the shadows.*

FIRST SOLDIER: Your turn to start.

SECOND SOLDIER: T.

FIRST SOLDIER: R.

SECOND SOLDIER: T.R . . . A.

FIRST SOLDIER: N.

SECOND SOLDIER: T.R.A.N . . . S.

FIRST SOLDIER: U.

SECOND SOLDIER: U? No such word.

FIRST SOLDIER: Yes, there is.

SECOND SOLDIER: Well, if there is, it's not spelled that way.

FIRST SOLDIER: Yes, it is.

SECOND SOLDIER: Ah!

FIRST SOLDIER: Ah . . .

SECOND SOLDIER: T.R.A.N.S.U.B.

FIRST SOLDIER: S.

SECOND SOLDIER: T.

FIRST SOLDIER: A.

SECOND SOLDIER: N.

FIRST SOLDIER: T.

SECOND SOLDIER: I.

FIRST SOLDIER: A.

SECOND SOLDIER: T.

FIRST SOLDIER: I. Oh, damn.

SECOND SOLDIER: You should have foreseen that O. (*Long pause.*)
I said O.

FIRST SOLDIER: I still don't think it's spelled that way.

SECOND SOLDIER: Go on. Say it. N.

FIRST SOLDIER: Transubstantiation? I'm sure it's got three esses somewhere.

SECOND SOLDIER: I gave you Rhododendron just now, although I'm damn sure there's only one H in it.

FIRST SOLDIER: All right, all right. What's that make the score?

SECOND SOLDIER (*consulting a bit of paper awkwardly in the dark*) Eight twenty-four to seven sixty-seven.

FIRST SOLDIER: Who's eight hundred and twenty-four?

SECOND SOLDIER: I am.

FIRST SOLDIER: Bastard.

SECOND SOLDIER: Well, I was eight twenty-three before. Stands to reason.

FIRST SOLDIER: I won't argue. It only goes to show that the night's too long.

SECOND SOLDIER: It's nearly over. (*He consults his watch.*) Death's late.

FIRST SOLDIER: Death? They don't know how to oil him properly.

SECOND SOLDIER: Your turn to start.

FIRST SOLDIER: Oh, hell. Z.

SECOND SOLDIER: That's easy. E.

FIRST SOLDIER: I suppose you're thinking of Zebra?

SECOND SOLDIER: How did you guess?

FIRST SOLDIER: Well—A.

SECOND SOLDIER: What? A? Nonsense. Oh——

FIRST SOLDIER: Ah.

SECOND SOLDIER (*mumming*): Zeaa, Zeab, Zeac, Zead, Zeae, Zeaf, Zeag.

FIRST SOLDIER (*cruelly*): Take your time.

A FIGURE *appears in the uniform of an operetta general, sky blue and silver. He wears a carnival mask round his neck.*

SECOND SOLDIER: Zeah, Zeai, Zeaf. Cave. A General.

GENERAL: Take your time. Finish your game.

SECOND SOLDIER: I give up. L. What's that?

FIRST SOLDIER (*leering*): Eight twenty-four to seven sixty-eight. Now, where's my bloody rifle? It was here a moment ago.

SECOND SOLDIER: My turn to give the order.

[16]

FIRST SOLDIER: O.K., but hang on, let me find the—where the hell is it?

GENERAL: Getting warmer . . . warmer . . .

The rifle drops with a clatter as the SOLDIER *walks into it.* Ah!

FIRST SOLDIER: Got it. Fire ahead.

SECOND SOLDIER (*colloquial*): Regiment. Regiment, pre-sent—are you ready?

FIRST SOLDIER: Yes, only hurry, it's heavy.

SECOND SOLDIER: Pre-sent—ahms!

They do so, with insulting untidiness, in their own time.

GENERAL (*saluting*): Thank you very much. That was a kind thought.

FIRST SOLDIER: Don't mention it.

GENERAL (*takes out a heavy gold watch*): Any sign of Death yet?

SECOND SOLDIER: No, sir.

GENERAL: I make him ten minutes late.

There's a strange sound of creaking machinery. Listen!

They all look at the clock. The wobbling figure of Death the Reaper emerges, and hits a bell with sickening force. The sound produced, however, is dull and unresonant.

FIRST SOLDIER: He's getting old.

GENERAL (*shrugging*): Fourteenth century. Hardly adolescent by our standards.

FIRST SOLDIER (*bitterly*): Our standards.

GENERAL (*reasonably*): You must be a Socialist, young man.

FIRST SOLDIER: Socialist Agrarian Reform Peasants' Industrial Party.

GENERAL: I've never heard of it.

FIRST SOLDIER: I'm a founder member.

GENERAL: Do you vote?

FIRST SOLDIER: Nearly every day.

GENERAL: That's what I like to hear. A true democrat.

FIRST SOLDIER: We get time off to vote.

GENERAL: Yes, yes, of course. So do I.

SECOND SOLDIER: I don't hold with his views, General.

GENERAL: Oh, perhaps you belong to my party?

[17]

SECOND SOLDIER: The National Iron Fist. The Nif. (*He salutes strangely.*) We wear orange shirts . . . or we would do if we could afford them.

GENERAL: No, I'm afraid I don't know that either. I'm Rally of Unionist Separist Extremes, sometimes known as the R.U.S.E. Anyone——?

FIRST SOLDIER }
SECOND SOLDIER } No. Sorry . . .

GENERAL: How strange. It's the party at present in power.

FIRST SOLDIER: There hasn't been a party in power since the ultimate dictatorship of last year's season.

GENERAL: I stand corrected. Of course, you are quite right. We govern by coalitions. What I meant to say is that we hold the casting vote in the present coalition. In fact, I am President of the Republic.

SECOND SOLDIER: At the moment?

GENERAL: Yes. I have been for some ten hours.

FIRST SOLDIER: You're doing well. (*Extends his right hand.*)

GENERAL: May I? (*Shakes* FIRST SOLDIER'S *hand.*) Thank you very much. (*With a sigh.*) Yes. We judge a dog's life as being roughly one-seventh that of a man. But a president doesn't even deserve a dog's life. His expectancy is roughly one-seventh that of a mayfly. (*He suddenly looks at the audience and smiles.*) Look at us——

FIRST SOLDIER } (*challenging the audience as they see it for the*
SECOND SOLDIER } *first time*): Halt! Who goes there?

GENERAL: Put your rifles away.

SECOND SOLDIER: It may be wiser. We're outnumbered.

FIRST SOLDIER: Are those people out there in the shadows?

GENERAL: Yes, and we must be very polite to them; we're entirely dependent on our tourist trade. (*He addresses the audience.*) Good evening. You will find us only on the very best atlases, because we are the smallest country left in Europe—and when I say country, I don't mean principality or grand duchy. I don't mean a haven for gambling or income tax evasion—I mean self-respecting country which deserves, and sometimes achieves, a colour of its own on the map—usually a dyspeptic mint green, which misses the outline of the frontier by a fraction of an inch, so that one can almost hear the printer saying damn. Our population is so small, that it's not worth counting. We have no cannons, we need no fodder. (*To* SECOND SOLDIER.) Don't fiddle with your rifle, there's a sport. It's dangerous.

SECOND SOLDIER: They're only blanks.

GENERAL (*shocked*): I should hope so!

[18]

SECOND SOLDIER: Well, I believe in armed force.

GENERAL: Oh, on statues, symbolized by a cluster of angels striding upwards into nowhere, there's nothing like it.

SECOND SOLDIER: Do you mean that, as a General, you're not the tiniest bit ambitious for our military future?

GENERAL: I prefer our military past. The harm's done and there it is. As for being a General, well at the age of four with paper hats and wooden swords we're all Generals. Only some of us never grow out of it.

SECOND SOLDIER: But—aren't you proud of the fact that we won the last war?

FIRST SOLDIER: No one won the last war.

GENERAL: We tactfully declared war on Germany several hours before her surrender. As a consequence we were offered six acres of land which didn't belong to us by the grateful Allies. This we cleverly refused. And now we are on good terms with everyone.

FIRST SOLDIER: You live in the past, General. Our future lies in the abolition of frontiers. The day will dawn when the workers will tear down the Customs sheds, demolish the road blocks, and extend the hand of friendship across the artificial gulfs imposed by nationalists and capitalist warmongers.

GENERAL (*sadly*): You read a great deal, don't you?

SECOND SOLDIER: Our future lies in our discipline and in the cultivation of heroism in the very young. To my mind, every mother who has successfully borne five children should be given a free issue of toy bayonets by a grateful nation.

GENERAL: And yet, my dear friends, our love for what is ours is far subtler, far deeper than all your silly foreign ideas. And I'll prove it to you. I only have to start singing a folk-song for you two to join in, despite your better judgement.

FIRST SOLDIER
SECOND SOLDIER } (*derisively*): Folk-song!

GENERAL (*singing softly, and with love*):

> An angel weary of Paradise
> Came down to visit the Earth.
> She floated over hill and dale
> Till she heard laughter and mirth.
>
> What is that ripple of happiness
> That wafts through the trees like a song?
> What is that shout of banners
> Which crowns the distant throng?

It's our army of rocking horses
Off to a bloodless war.
It's our princes and captains
On their way to the sandy shore.

Our swords are made of good white wood.
Our castles are made of sand,
Our lances are made of plasticine;
We're off to defend our land!

The angel returned to Paradise
A younger, wiser girl,
And swore she'd never journey again
Her head was in a whirl.

For as the sky has its paradise
So the Earth has its pearl;
Our country! Our country!
The Earth has its pearl!

Gradually the other two have joined in, at first humming the melody, then singing elaborately and fluently in parts. They finish. A silence.

SECOND SOLDIER: Well, we did it.

FIRST SOLDIER (*disgusted*): And to think the words are meaningless. They're nursery rhyme stuff, devoid of a social message.

GENERAL (*serenely*): Social messages change according to social conditions, while nursery rhyme nonsense is eternal. It has set many a wise foot tapping, and has cradled the great men and the idiots of tomorrow in a lilting sleep.

A window of the building on the audience's right opens with a clatter. An angry man in pyjamas, and wearing rimless glasses, looks out.

ANGRY MAN: Can't a guy get a decent night's rest round here? If it is not the cathedral clock, it's drunks.

GENERAL: Drunks? I beg your pardon, Ambassador.

ANGRY MAN: Who's that? Oh, Mr. President—please forgive my outburst. It was a great party last night. Or should I say this morning.

GENERAL: Thank you.

ANGRY MAN: The idea of wearing masks was just great.

GENERAL (*modest*): It's traditional.

ANGRY MAN: Hey! I still have mine on! What do you know? The damndest thing! (*And indeed, a black mask adorns his forehead like the goggles of a motor-cyclist.*) Well, sure makes me wish you had Independence Day every day.

GENERAL: We do, but we can't afford to celebrate it more than ten or fifteen times a year.

ANGRY MAN: Is that so?

GENERAL: We have gained our independence at least four hundred times, which makes us cumulatively the most independent people in Europe.

ANGRY MAN: Is that so? Well, that's certainly worth knowing.

GENERAL: Unfortunately, we have lost our independence even more frequently.

ANGRY MAN: Is that a fact? You sure live and learn.

WOMAN (*voice, hooting*): Hooper!

ANGRY MAN: Coming, sugar.

WOMAN (*voice*): Are you crazy, standing in that window with your arthritis?

ANGRY MAN (*sheepish*): Well, I guess you fellers heard. See you. (*He disappears*).

FIRST SOLDIER (*sour*): Warmonger!

   The opposite window opens, and another angry man looks out.

SECOND ANGRY MAN: Ppsst!

GENERAL: Ambassador! Good morning.

SECOND ANGRY MAN: He said something?

GENERAL: Who?

SECOND ANGRY MAN: Him. He——

GENERAL: Not much, no.

SECOND ANGRY MAN: I can hear him speak if I put my ear to the window, but I can only catch the sounds, not the words.

GENERAL: We woke him up with our singing. I hope we didn't do the same to you.

SECOND ANGRY MAN: I don't sleep.

GENERAL: Never?

SECOND ANGRY MAN: Never.

GENERAL: Insomnia?

SECOND ANGRY MAN: Policy.

GENERAL: Gracious.

SECOND ANGRY MAN: May I congratulate you, Mr. President, on the reception last night, which perceptibly increased our solidarity?

GENERAL: I enjoyed it. I was the last to leave, and got rather drunk.

SECOND ANGRY MAN (*without humour*): Drunkenness in pursuit of solidarity is not a sin.

WOMAN (*voice, strident*): Vadim!

SECOND ANGRY MAN: Da, golubchik.

WOMAN (*voice*): Paidi Suda!

SECOND ANGRY MAN (*conciliatory*): Sichas . . .

GENERAL: You'd better go.

SECOND ANGRY MAN (*suspicious*): You understand our language?

GENERAL: I understand . . . the situation.

Abruptly the SECOND ANGRY MAN *disappears. A decrepit saint strikes the bell.*

St Simon Stylites . . . I make it seven sixteen.

FIRST SOLDIER: Seven four.

SECOND SOLDIER: A quarter to eight.

They put their watches away.

GENERAL: Oh, well, St Simon never had much use for time, up there on his giddy column.

FIRST SOLDIER: That clock's a national disgrace.

SECOND SOLDIER: For once I agree with you.

GENERAL: Why? The only one who's always punctual is Death . . . whatever the time, he always strikes his knell at the first streak of dawn . . . and believe me, he knows what he's doing. How I hate the dawn! It's the hour of the firing squad. The last glass of brandy. The ultimate cigarette. The final wish. All the hideously calculated hypocrisy of men when they commit a murder in the name of justice. Then it's the time of Death on a grander scale, the hour of the great offensives . . . fix your bayonets, boys. . . . Gentlemen, synchronize your watches . . . in ten seconds' time the barrage starts . . . a thousand men are destined to die in order to capture a farmhouse no one has lived in for years. . . . And finally, dawn is the herald of the day, our twelve hours of unimportance, when we have to cede to the pressures of the powers, smile at people we have every reason but expediency to detest. . . . A diplomat these days is nothing but a head-waiter who's allowed to sit down occasionally. . . . (*Playing to the house on audience's left.*) Yes, sir, and how do you want your imports, in oil? In petrol! Underdone? Overdone. If I may say so, sir, your taste is impeccable. May I say so, sir? Thank you very much. (*Playing to the house on audience's right.*) Yes, sir, of course, I guarantee not to serve the other customer any secrets. . . . I'll tell him secrets are off the menu—although you and I know, don't we, sir, that—? Ha, ha, ha—(*Surprised*). Sir, service is included. . . . Oh, well . . . if you insist . . . (*With elaborate gratitude.*) Thank *you very* much . . . (*He comes up from his deep reverence and looks searchingly at the soldiers.*) You

[22]

hate the night because you find it boring. . . . I hate the day because it's an insult to my intelligence, a slur on my honour, and a worm in the heart of my integrity, whereas the night . . . (*He basks in his thought*.) . . . That night is marvellous . . . because it is the time when the great powers are asleep, recovering their energies for the horrors of the ensuing day . . . and in that time of magic and of mystery, our horizons are infinite . . . they stretch not only to the north, south, east, and west, but up towards the moon, down towards the centre of the earth. In peace, and in harmony with nature, we send out our vast battalions to colonize the imagination . . . When others sleep, our Empire knows no bounds.

> *A cock crows. The street lamps go out.*

(*Heavily.*) There. Our daily winter has begun.

SECOND SOLDIER (*softly*): Look.

GENERAL: Oh, look.

> *A pair of lovers wander into the square, too involved in each other to know where they are. They wear evening dress, and masks dangle round their necks.*

(*Softly, heartfelt.*) Oh, I hope they found each other very early in the night, for now he may notice a wrinkle under the weary, longing eye, while she may spy a trace of cruel satisfaction around his mouth. (*Sadly.*) Ah, the morning after! Ah, dawn! Let us be tactful.

FIRST SOLDIER: My turn to give the order.

GENERAL: Sh! Dismiss, but for goodness sake don't do it as you were taught.

FIRST SOLDIER (*whispering*): Regiment. Salute the flag! Dismiss!

> *They march off on tiptoe with a last sentimental look at the lovers. The lovers break from a long, long kiss and look at each other in adoration.*

HE: Are there words which have not been used before?

SHE: There are silences which have not been shared before. Why do you look at me so critically?

HE: Critically?

SHE: Are there bags under my eyes?

HE: I would be lying if I told you you weren't tired.

SHE (*hiding her face*): Then don't look at me.

HE (*lifting her face again*): I want to guess what you will look like at seventy.

[23]

SHE: It's late. We're getting silly. It's the sunlight and the weariness and the sad farewell of old champagne on the tongue. There was no edge to our thoughts when the candles and the cut-glass ornaments sent shivering milky-ways up to the ceiling, and when your eyes sparkled like mineral wealth from the rock of your face.

HE (*sadly*): You can't recapture it by language.

SHE: I know.

HE: Enchantment fades so quickly that after five minutes you doubt if it was ever there.

SHE: Do you doubt it?

HE: No. I remember it.

SHE (*desperate*): But I am still here!

HE (*holding her*): Yes, a warm, a living thing, which I desire. Last night we were as one, creatures in a dream, selflessly united in an endless waltz. From now on we are opposed, a man and a woman in love—the greatest, most exhausting struggle in the world—two moths racing for the flame, two cannibals devouring each other.

SHE: Have you known many women?

HE: I am a sailor by profession.

SHE: Thank you for your honesty.

HE (*smiles*): You're afraid that I will compare you to the others?

SHE: Inevitably.

HE: And what if I say that you are better?

SHE: That's not enough. I want to be alone.

HE: You have never kissed a man?

SHE: Only four. And Freddie.

HE: Do you mean only four, and Freddie? Or do you mean five?

SHE (*surprised, she turns it over in her mind*): Five? No, I mean four, and Freddie.

HE: Who's Freddie?

SHE (*enraptured*): You're jealous!

HE: I'm waiting for an answer.

SHE: Freddie? He's my fiancé.

HE: I see.

SHE (*a little foolishly*): He's in refrigerators.

HE: I don't understand.

SHE: He makes refrigerators. His father made refrigerators before him.

HE: A hereditary gift.

SHE: Freddie believes he has a mission in refrigeration. He told me once when he was drunk that in the event of war, he has a device which can freeze the Gulf Stream, and make everyone but us very uncomfortable. Oh, Lord, I shouldn't be telling you this, should I?

HE: No.

SHE: You have no accent, darling. I keep forgetting who you are.

HE (*with pomp*): I serve aboard the icebreaker *Red October*. Ironic, isn't it, that it may one day be my duty to crash through Freddie's most cherished daydream.

SHE: Oh, how awful. Now everything's spoiled.

HE (*kindly*): Why? Surely love recognizes no didactic frontiers?

SHE (*desperate*): But Igor! Creatures in a dream, selflessly united in an endless waltz——

HE: I said that, didn't I?

SHE: Yes.

HE: Curious how romance tricks the otherwise logical mind into inaccuracies. Naturally, the waltz could not have been endless, otherwise it would still be going on—(*As he sees her incredulous face*)—and that is impossible since we are now here.

SHE (*in real agony*): Oh, no!

HE (*suddenly*): Does what I say sound very humourless and . . . and un-Western when I talk like that? (*Silence.*) I must apologize. I can never regret a phenomenon as beautiful or as powerful as our love, but I must admit that it has created within me the most reprehensible ideological confusion. I must consult my textbooks before I can hope to interpret to you in scientific terms the exact extent of my spiritual deviation.

SHE (*hopeful*): You mean you love me more than Marx?

HE (*sharply*): Please do not speak sarcastically. It doesn't suit you.

SHE: I'm sorry, but I'm jealous of the man.

HE: I do not make light of your beliefs.

SHE (*tenderly*): I can't make you out.

HE (*running his hands through his hair in agony*): I can't make myself out. It's all so simple in the Arctic.

SHE: Do you blame the climate, my darling?

HE: No. No, it's relatively simple in the Black Sea also.

SHE: You blame dry land then?

HE: Yes. It must be that. Although a great deal of good solid work has been accomplished on dry land. That is undeniable. In fact, a considerable amount of Das Kapital was conceived in the British Museum, which makes it all the more remarkable.

SHE: Women? In general. Do they confuse you, dearest?

HE: Women? I've seen women before. I served on a ship under a woman captain, although in fairness to her, you wouldn't have guessed that she was a woman. *She* did not disturb me in the least. (*Slowly, and with considerable difficulty.*) The fact is, I love you.

SHE (*ecstatic*): Oh . . .

HE (*severe*): Please don't interrupt me. For my own good, for our future, I must analyse my reasons for loving you in spite of vast and irreconcilable spiritual and political divergencies. First of all, we were wearing masks. Your mask could have hidden the eager face of a freckled collective-farm girl. When we tore them off at midnight, it was already too late. I was in love.

SHE: Oh, Igor, that's not true. No collective-farm girl has an American accent.

HE: Yes, I was cheating. Forgive me. (*Fierce.*) I must be honest with myself. I think I know what drew me irresistibly towards you.

SHE (*coquettish*): What is it?

HE (*very serious*): You couldn't possibly be the captain of a ship. You're one of the only women I've ever met who couldn't possibly be the captain of a ship.

SHE: Dad bought me a dinghy last fall. It's moored near Cape Cod. I love the sea, angel, just the way you do.

HE (*gentle*): Could you bring a six-thousand-ton cargo ship into Murmansk harbour . . . without a pilot . . . backwards . . . in a snow-storm?

SHE: I've never tried.

HE: No, you couldn't. And nor could I. Glory to our women trawler-captains.

SHE: Glory to them indeed. Kiss me.

HE: Not yet. I must first reach certain ethical conclusions.

SHE: Igor, there's so little time! (*To break his mood.*) I know what I like about you.

HE: What?

SHE: Your profile.

HE: The façade.

SHE: I never read a book unless I like the title. Igor, I like the title. I want to read the book.

HE: I fail to understand.

SHE: I like that, too. You could never understand. Kiss me.

HE: I forbid——

SHE: You want to.

HE: No.

SHE: Please!

HE: Thank you.

They embrace, and lose themselves in the silent game of love, oblivious to all around them. The TWO SOLDIERS *reappear, one from either side, now dressed as peasants, in rags. Both carry various merchandise. They see each other with some annoyance.*

FIRST SOLDIER: Aren't you resting?

SECOND SOLDIER: It's too hot to sleep.

FIRST SOLDIER: It didn't take you long to change into your street clothes.

SECOND SOLDIER: The same might be said of you. I believe you tried to cash in on the market before I was properly up and about. Not a very socialistic impulse, if I may say so. (*Suddenly, cooing to the lovers.*) Keepsakes, bangles, prehistoric coins, religious postcards beautifully picked out in silk and sequins.

FIRST SOLDIER (*angry*): You jumped the gun! (*Glutinous.*) Peanuts, traditional salted marzipan, raffia table-runners, English collar studs, back numbers of *True Detective Magazine.*

SECOND SOLDIER: There's nothing more suitable to announce your engagement to your friends than a nice religious postcard. It takes away all frivolous aspects from the negotiation, and has a spontaneous dignity which no amount of subsequent teasing can ever dispel. On the other hand, if the minor prophets picked out in petit-point seem too formal for the younger approach, shall we say, I have a large selection of cards which fall into the profane to saucy category—milady surprised in her bath, in art colours that will not run—Cupid's indiscretions, a lovely series in a new Japanese polychrome process, smuggled into the country only last Wednesday——

FIRST SOLDIER: No table is complete without raffia table-runners and, incidentally, I can supply the table as well. The clash of raffia and mahogany may seem abrupt, and even startling, to the eye as yet unattuned to artistic adventure——

HE: Yes, but——

[27]

FIRST SOLDIER: —Yet I am assured that even Paris, that mecca of the beau-monde, is following, albeit timidly, the trail we so boldly blazed. No? Now, my friends, let us not be blind idealists—love's first impulse quickly deepens into habit—a habit which is termed a "mature understanding between two people". It is at this second, and far more important, stage of marriage that these complete back numbers of *True Detective* will come in more than handy. Husband back home late, madam? Baby crying, sir? Here is a nerve-steadying remedy—tales of horror and revenge, at a quarter of their original price!

SHE (*desperate*): Oh, do please leave us alone!

SECOND SOLDIER: This is a free country, madam. We have a right to share your privacy in a public place.

The lovers resume their interrupted kiss. The GENERAL *enters in a morning suit.*

GENERAL: What? Still at it? This must be what they call the real thing.

FIRST SOLDIER: It must be. Death to commerce.

GENERAL: The real thing! And I don't even know the false thing! You live, and learn that you know nothing.

SHE (*spinning round, furious*): Oh, please——!

GENERAL (*amazed; adjusting his pince-nez*): Miss Moulsworth!

SHE: Sh! Don't tell Dad, please!

GENERAL: I envied your idyll without ever realizing it involved the much-admired Miss Juliet. Merciful heavens, Lieutenant Romanoff!

HE: Silence! (*He looks round nervously.*) I implore you not to say a word of this to anyone. If you do, my career is finished.

The GENERAL *laughs.*

HE: Why do you laugh?

GENERAL: I began life as a ne'er-do-well, but was discovered cheating at cards, and so my career was finished. Look at me now.

HE: You are confusing me.

SHE: Oh, please, don't confuse him!

GENERAL: Are you really in love? I ask as an innocent, not as a technician.

SHE: Yes, only he won't let himself go. It's psychological. He's gotten to the stage of sorting out his emotions, and kind of freeing them from all those men, you know, Marx, Lenin, Trotsky.

HE (*rising, violent*): Trotsky! I can never forgive you for that!

GENERAL (*hastily*): She meant Engels. The names are somewhat similar. You need my help.

HE: No.

GENERAL: Yes, I can see from your utter misery, from your eagerness to misunderstand each other, and from your thoroughly bad temper, that this is the real thing. You wish to meet again to-night?

HE ⎱
SHE ⎰ No.

GENERAL: Yes, very well, I'll see what I can do. To-night is the thousandth anniversary of our liberation from the Lithuanians.

FIRST SOLDIER: Is it really? I thought——

GENERAL: Who cares for accuracy? It may not have been a thousand years ago, and it almost certainly wasn't the Lithuanians, but we celebrate whatever it was to-night, and that's an order.

SECOND SOLDIER: With fireworks?

GENERAL: Naturally. With whatever we can afford. (*The* SECOND SOLDIER *produces a couple of rockets from his pocket to the disgust of the* FIRST SOLDIER.) Two fireworks. Well done. It will be dark at eight o'clock.

GENERAL: Leave it to me.

HE ⎱
SHE ⎰ No!

GENERAL: Does eight o'clock seem very long to wait? I understand: Try not to be impatient.

HE (*abruptly*): Goodbye.

GENERAL: That's right. This is no time for emotion. Bear your separation with fortitude.

SHE: I'm going.

GENERAL: That's it. Bite your lip, like a heroine.

> Without looking round, the lovers go to their respective Embassies. They are tempted to look back at the door.

No, no, resist temptation! Orpheus, don't look back at Eurydice! There are only twelve hours of Hades. Earn your joy to-night!

> Precipitately, the lovers disappear. The GENERAL sighs romantically; the SOLDIERS dry their eyes.

We're a sentimental people . . .

FIRST SOLDIER: I'm glad I didn't sell any of those stinking table-runners . . . they deserve better . . .

SECOND SOLDIER: And my postcards are in such bad taste . . .

GENERAL: Oh, my God! (*With sudden anguish.*) I thought of it as a love story, beautiful, pure, simple. Simple? . . . it's a diplomatic earthquake!

> As he freezes, a MAN *dressed as a spy enters, looking too anonymous to be possible. He goes quickly and silently to the* SECOND SOLDIER.

SPY: Have they arrived?

SECOND SOLDIER: Eh?

SPY: What I ordered.

SECOND SOLDIER: Oh, it's you . . . yes . . . (*He produces a small packet or two surreptitiously.*)

SPY: Is this all?

SECOND SOLDIER: For the moment.

SPY: How much?

SECOND SOLDIER: Eight hundred.

SPY: Too much.

SECOND SOLDIER: They cost me almost that.

SPY (*takes them*): Put them on my account.

SECOND SOLDIER: But when——?

SPY: You will be paid. And—you have seen nothing. I never talked to you. I don't exist.

> The SPY *vanishes into the Embassy, audience's right.*

FIRST SOLDIER: What's all that? Since when have you had commercial relations with the Russians?

SECOND SOLDIER: Even a fascist must live. I supply him with postcards.

FIRST SOLDIER: Who is he?

SECOND SOLDIER: Isn't it obvious?

GENERAL (*suddenly*): Men, I need your help.

FIRST SOLDIER: We're off duty.

GENERAL: We are all in the service of the god of love.

SECOND SOLDIER: But we can't live on our military pay alone.

GENERAL: Well, claim at the Ministry. Do as I do. (*Suddenly.*) What kind of mercenary prattle is this? Just now you shed a tear for them. Is it in the traditions of our country to confuse love with high finance?

SECOND SOLDIER: No, it isn't. That's what's wrong with us.

GENERAL: What did you say? Lef . . . wait for it, left turn. In step this time. This is war. Left-right-left.

They go, as though on parade, at the double. As another saint comes out to hit the clock, the face of the American Embassy is flown to reveal JULIET *sitting in an attitude of deep dejection in the small section of the drawing-room shown. The door opens, and* MR AMBASSADOR MOULSWORTH *enters.*

MOULSWORTH: Well, and how's my girl? Tired, heh? Don't I get my kiss? Hey, I got news to put the sparkle back in your eye.

JULIET (*fiercely*): Dad, I've got to tell you.

MOULSWORTH (*good-humoured*): O.K., and I won't tell Freddie.

JULIET (*amazed*): You know, then?

MOULSWORTH: Sure, I saw you . . . and let me tell you, you looked just great . . . standing there in the moonlight in that Paris-type exclusive dress . . . and let me tell you something, the guy you were with . . . well, he was a tribute to your taste, and there's no reason on God's earth why Freddie should ever know . . .

JULIET (*pale*): You liked Igor?

MOULSWORTH: Who's that?

JULIET: The boy I was with.

MOULSWORTH: Yeah. Swell physique. Great golfer, I bet. What was his name again?

JULIET: Igor.

MOULSWORTH: Well, what's in a name? I had a classmate called Epiphany. Anyway, that's all over now. (*He beams.*) Now, listen to this, baby. Are you ready?

JULIET (*emotional*): Pop, if you've got good news, give. Right now I need to hear it, but bad.

BEULAH MOULSWORTH *enters.*

BEULAH: Have you told her, Hooper?

MOULSWORTH (*tetchy*): I'm on the point of doing so, Beulah. Give a guy a break. (*Beaming.*) Great news, Julie——

BEULAH: And how's my daughter this morning? (*Smothers* JULIET *with kisses.*)

JULIET: Hi, Mom.

BEULAH: What have you said to her?

MOULSWORTH (*pointed*): Nothing, yet. (*Beaming.*) Great news, Julie——

BEULAH: Great news indeed. You're a big girl now——

MOULSWORTH (*with terrible patience*): Let me handle this, Beulah. Julie——

JULIET: Yes?

[31]

MOULSWORTH: Freddie.

JULIET: What about him?

MOULSWORTH: He's flying in on the midday clipper!

JULIET (*pale*): Oh, no . . . (*She faints.*)

BEULAH (*sarcastic*): You'll handle it, Beulah.

MOULSWORTH: What's the matter with her?

BEULAH: Get some water, Hooper. She's fainted.

MOULSWORTH: Fainted—that's impossible.

BEULAH: Get some water. There, there, mother's here, mother's here.

BEULAH *cradles* JULIET *in her arms.*

(*Loud.*) You're just the most tactful man I've ever met, that's all.

MOULSWORTH *returns with a glass of water.*

MOULSWORTH: I am forthright. In Washington they call me Forthright Hoop Moulsworth. I've heard them.

BEULAH: Julie's a girl, Hooper. A girl. Girls don't go for forthrightness.

MOULSWORTH: How was I to know that?

BEULAH (*with an embarrassing sweetness*): Girls thrive on a lingering uncertainty . . . on a tremulous half-doubt . . . I know. I was a girl myself.

MOULSWORTH: Beulah . . . if I ran my business the way you think. . . . How is she?

BEULAH: Coming round, oh so slowly. She's sensitive.

MOULSWORTH: We're all sensitive. (*Beaming.*) How's my honey?

JULIET (*softly*): Dad . . .

MOULSWORTH: Yeah, here I am, right here.

JULIET: I've got to tell you . . . I am not in love with Freddie.

MOULSWORTH: Not in——? Now, wait a minute.

BEULAH: She must have calm, Hooper.

MOULSWORTH: So must I have calm.

BEULAH: Up to bed, my only sweet one.

JULIET (*rising*): I'm going . . . but first I got to tell you . . . I'm in love with Igor.

BEULAH (*a girl again*): There's someone else. . . . What's he like?

JULIET: Dad saw him.

MOULSWORTH: Beulah, this is far too serious to accept as a matter of course. Remember, Freddie's flying out here at his own expense. Who is this other guy?

[32]

JULIET: Igor Vadimovitch Romanoff, the son of their Ambassador.

MOULSWORTH (*a great shout*): What?

JULIET (*quiet*): I'll go lie down now—get some rest, if I can.

She goes out. Long pause.

BEULAH (*very quiet*): Maybe we didn't treat her right when she was a baby . . . maybe it's our fault——

MOULSWORTH (*rising, pale*): I guess there comes a time in the life of every parent——

BEULAH (*suddenly violent*): Oh, Hooper, this isn't a board meeting!

MOULSWORTH (*shouting back*): She must know what she's doing to me . . . her father? Why, if this ever gets out! It's impossible. I don't believe it ever happened. And you can sit there and tell me——

BEULAH: The fault, dear Brutus——

MOULSWORTH: Don't quote at me! (*Pause.*) Beulah. We summon all our resources of tact and understanding.

BEULAH: I was never sold on Freddie being right for her.

MOULSWORTH: That is neither here nor there. Freddie's father rowed in my boat at Princeton, but I'm deliberately forgetting all that—all my personal loyalties. The fact is that our only daughter has fallen for a Commie—a Communist, Beulah—and when I say Communist, Beulah, I don't mean a guy who sent a food package to the wrong side in Spain—I mean the son of a high-ranking Soviet executive!

BEULAH: You always show everything up in its worse possible light.

MOULSWORTH: Good God, Beulah, don't be such a damned fool.

BEULAH: Oh, that wicked temper of yours! First degree mental cruelty!

Pause. MOULSWORTH *walks about.*

BEULAH: It may just be a girlish crush—a teenage urge.

MOULSWORTH: Julie's twenty.

BEULAH: Oh, Hooper, don't be so hideously unimaginative! She never had any of the usual teenage urges. She may be starting late.

MOULSWORTH: Yeah, that's it, a juvenile infatuation. Of course. Why didn't we think of that before?

BEULAH: And then again—it may be love.

MOULSWORTH: I don't want that word mentioned again. Come, my dear, let us, you and I, go talk to her, calmly and with a modicum of dignity. What we cannot achieve by our persuasiveness, let us achieve by our example. After all, we are her parents, and the scriptures declare in no uncertain terms that we command her honour and her obedience. One thing only I wish you to promise me before we go up to our daughter.

BEULAH: And what is that?

MOULSWORTH: That you keep your mouth shut and let me do the talking.

> *They go.* JULIET, *who appeared in the upstairs room soon after she left her parents, is laid on her bed in an attitude of tragic resignation. The façade of the Embassy falls as the façade of the other Embassy rises.* IGOR *stands. The* SPY *sits at a table, a few pieces of paper stretched before him.*

SPY: And?

IGOR: And . . . ? More I can't remember.

SPY: A confession of only eight pages? It appears as though you were still attempting to conceal something. (*Pause.*) Comrade Kotkov's recent confession ran to two hundred and fourteen typewritten pages, and was written in a clear, concise, functional style. At the end, the reader had a vivid impression of the author's inner rottenness. It was a model of how such documents should be prepared. (*Pause.*) You have nothing to add? (*He sighs.*) Very well, let me help you. There are some comrades who can do nothing for themselves. Page eight, line twenty-three. You claim that love guided your deviation. (*He laughs.*) I had over-estimated your intelligence, Lieutenant.

IGOR: Because I speak the truth, no doubt.

SPY: Love recognizes frontiers, just as do armies.

IGOR: Only cynicism has no bounds.

SPY: Explain yourself.

IGOR: If my thoughts are simplified even further to suit your intellect, I shall soon be reciting the alphabet.

SPY (*deeply suspicious*): Which alphabet—ours or theirs?

IGOR (*exasperated*): Oh, my God!

SPY: What name did you mention?

IGOR: When?

SPY: God, did I hear?

IGOR: Why not?

SPY: Are you a believer?

IGOR: I have a perfect right to believe if I wish.

SPY: I did not ask you whether you had a right to believe. I asked you whether you do believe.

IGOR: I don't see the difference.

SPY: All the difference in the world. In the old days it was criminal to believe. With the advent of democracy, we are now given the choice of belief or disbelief, but naturally, we are put on our honour to make the right choice. Otherwise, democracy would have no meaning.

IGOR: Oh, the devil take you.

The SPY *immediately crosses himself.*
What are you doing?

SPY (*pleasantly, in spite of his nervousness*): Belief in the devil has never been forbidden by any regime.

The SOVIET AMBASSADOR *and* MRS ROMANOFF *enter.*

ROMANOFF: Good morning.

EVDOKIA: Good morning.

ROMANOFF: What is there for breakfast?

EVDOKIA: Caviar.

ROMANOFF: Caviar, caviar, caviar. Is there no end to this monotony? (*Hastily.*) I say this with all deference to our splendid sturgeon fisheries and our modern canneries.

SPY: One moment. Another subject has priority. Your Excellency. I must denounce your son.

ROMANOFF: Again?

EVDOKIA: Just a minute. Women have equality. I demand to speak first.

SPY: The fact that women have equality gives them no special privileges, as they have in the West. You cannot expect to enjoy both equality and the bourgeois myth of "ladies first".

EVDOKIA: I am the wife of an Ambassador. I have the right to speak first.

SPY: Only outside the Embassy. Within these walls the fact that I am your chauffeur is forgotten, and I revert to being a high ranking officer of the police.

ROMANOFF: Let him speak, Evdokia. It is more prudent. Let him denounce Igor before you denounce me.

EVDOKIA: How did you know I was going to denounce you?

ROMANOFF: No breakfast is complete without it.

SPY: Now——

IGOR: No! Let me denounce myself!

[35]

ROMANOFF (*warmly*): That's the spirit. That's my son.

IGOR: I am in love!

EVDOKIA (*scandalized*): A fine time you choose. I must say, with Junior Captain Marfa Vassilievna Zlotochienko arriving to-day.

IGOR: With who arriving?

EVDOKIA: Your betrothed. The heroic commander of the sloop *Dostoievsky*.

IGOR: My betrothed? But I've never even heard of her.

ROMANOFF: We intended to introduce her to you before the marriage.

IGOR: I should hope so.

ROMANOFF: Don't be ridiculous, and start behaving like a spoiled child. I met your mother for the first time at our wedding. There was no time for surprise. We were both spared the degradation of emotional behaviour.

IGOR: I refuse to marry this female!

EVDOKIA: You will do as you're told! We have noted with considerable regret that you are prone to unstable and introspective behaviour, and that at times you are as self-pitying as a fascist.

ROMANOFF: Evdokia, you are going too far!

EVDOKIA: Yes, and I know where he gets it from. Talking in your sleep about imperial occasions in St. Petersburg. St. Petersburg, if you please, not even Petrograd.

SPY: Most interesting.

ROMANOFF (*a pathetic figure*): I don't believe you.

EVDOKIA: You even sang a snatch of the Imperial Anthem, and lay to attention in bed. Your abrupt movement made the eiderdown slide to the floor, and I had to get out of bed to pick it up.

ROMANOFF (*roused*): And what about you? Yesterday, when I took you shopping, you lingered a full quarter of an hour outside a shop displaying French hats!

SPY: Oh—ho!

EVDOKIA (*uncertain*): I did it to pour my scorn on them.

ROMANOFF: Yes, but while your mouth was muttering malice, your eye was roving avariciously over those odious shreds of tinsel. Deny it if you can—you were dying to try them on!

EVDOKIA (*after a terrible pause—a hunted woman*): Have I not suffered enough in my life without this? I was strong when I defied the Cossacks and carried vital messages under an arcade of knouts to the red sailors of the Baltic Fleet. I was strong when I distributed

potato-soup to our troops through three days and three nights without
sleep. I have survived revolution, war, pestilence and famine. Have I
now surrendered my dignity—to a hat?

SPY (*sly*): Well—have you?

EVDOKIA (*emotionally*): Yes, I have. I have! I admit it. I—I confess!
It is a tiny confection made up of three black feathers, with a coronet
of cheeky silver lace. (*Defiant.*) I love that hat! Last week they removed it from the window, and I was nearly ill. I retired to my bed
and wept. I thought they had sold it. Yesterday, I passed the shop—
and there it was again! My life suddenly held a new meaning for me.
All unpleasantness was forgotten. I kissed my husband in the street.

ROMANOFF: Evdokia! That is how you gave yourself away. (*He
kisses her on the forehead with emotion.*)

SPY: A most interesting revelation.

ROMANOFF: You underestimate us, my friend. Do you think that
we are the only fallible beings here? What about this, which I discovered among your personal belongings? (*He produces an American
magazine from his pocket.*)

SPY (*trembling*): You have been through my suitcase?

ROMANOFF: You go through my desk every evening. I only returned
the compliment. And what do I find? Decadent American magazines!
Stories of drug addiction in Cincinnati! The adventures of lascivious
space-men! And as if that were not sufficient—postcards of an in-
disputably suggestive nature, depicting the ruins of Pompeii in a
most unscholarly light, and dwelling with shocking emphasis on the
murky corridors of the Follies. Explain yourself, comrade.

SPY (*uncertain*): I collected this material in order to furnish the
Party with proof of Western decadence.

ROMANOFF: The decadence of the West is well enough known by
the Party not to need proof. Can you deny that these items constitute
part of a vast and well-documented private collection?

SPY: I . . .

ROMANOFF (*ferocious*): Confess!

SPY (*with a cry*): Ah, that terrible word! (*Slowly—on his knees.*)
I confess . . . but you cannot know the loneliness of a spy's life . . .
everyone is frightened of me . . . women are only good and kind to
me if they want me to overlook some indiscretion, and it's a calculated,
a charmless, and a frightened love they give me . . . (*He weeps.*) To
me, women surrender everything but their secrets, and their company
makes me feel more lonely than I feel alone.

ROMANOFF (*embarrassed*): Come, come, not before breakfast.
Here's my handkerchief.

[37]

SPY: A handkerchief! When I could flood the Volga with my tears!

ROMANOFF (*with some pride*): There is no doubt about it. No nation can confess as magnificently or as completely as we.

SPY: Ah, the relief . . . the relief!

ROMANOFF: Now, now, you are a most distinguished secret agent. We will forget your little lapse.

SPY: No, no! Never forget it! Ah, my soul. How good it is to suffer so remorselessly.

ROMANOFF (*with some impatience*): What kind of architecture is this? One brick is displaced, and the entire edifice collapses.

IGOR: You have more experience than we have, father. You are older. I fall in love. The chauffeur gives in to his loneliness. Mother surrenders herself to a hat——

EVDOKIA (*burying her head in her hands*): My hat! What a disgrace. (*Sudden horrified realization.*) And it isn't even my hat!

IGOR: You, father, you only let yourself go at night, when you dream of Leningrad.

ROMANOFF: Leningrad? St. Petersburg. That is an historical fact, and not subversion. (*Dreamily.*) I remember the city in nineteen thirteen. The light streaming through the windows of the Winter Palace into the snow.

IGOR (*romantic*): You were outside, in the cold with the peasants.

ROMANOFF: I was inside, in the warmth, with the court—planning the revolution. I was the Party's inside man. My duties were to dance with the wives of army commanders, and surreptitiously find out the dispositions of their husband's units. It was delicious . . .

IGOR: Then surely, father, with your experience, you can understand me when I tell you that I am in love—desperately, wholeheartedly, in love.

SPY: I understand you, brother.

EVDOKIA: Who is she? Some penniless local girl?

IGOR: Does it matter?

ROMANOFF: We—that is, your mother and I—wish you to marry well, my son, high up in the hierarchy.

IGOR: But that is snobbism!

EVDOKIA: Don't be ridiculous. Snobbism was abolished in nineteen seventeen.

IGOR: I am in love with the daughter of an Ambassador!

EVDOKIA (*ogling*): Just a moment. Which Ambassador?

IGOR: The Ambassador of the United States of America.

A terrible pause.

ROMANOFF (*his voice breaking with emotion*): Are you aware of the words you have just uttered?

IGOR (*standing stiffly to attention*): Yes, father. Otherwise I could not have uttered them.

ROMANOFF (*suddenly losing all control, screams*): Swine! (*Pause.*) Saboteur! (*Pause.*) Interventionist! (*Pause.*) Anarchist! (*Pause.*) Trotskyist! (*Pause—with a sob.*) My son!

> *During each of these accusations, it seems as though tears are being scattered round the room like grain. The* AMBASSADOR, *scarlet with passion, shouts each word like a military order.*

SPY (*in ecstasy*): This surpasses all other confessions!

ROMANOFF (*contorted with fury and yet with traces of compassion and contrition, almost hopefully*): Can you change your mind?

IGOR (*stiff*): No, father.

ROMANOFF (*with ill-concealed pride in his son*): You will go up to your room.

IGOR: Yes, father.

ROMANOFF: Why do you smile?

IGOR: I will not be alone. (*He goes, stiffly.*)

ROMANOFF: You!

SPY: Me?

ROMANOFF: Breakfast is laid for three. You will join us.

EVDOKIA: A spy at the dining table?

ROMANOFF: Evdokia, we have lost our son.

EVDOKIA (*with a shriek*): Vadim!

ROMANOFF (*calm as ice*): Caviar, you said? Let us enjoy it . . .

> *As* IGOR *appears upstairs, the façade falls. Two people enter the square, one a huge and cheerful* AMERICAN, *the other a pretty but grim* RUSSIAN *girl. They are followed by the* TWO SOLDIERS.

RUSSIAN GIRL: Thank you for allowing me to share your taxi.

AMERICAN (*gay*): That's O.K. Anything else I can do for you?

RUSSIAN GIRL (*cold*): No.

FIRST SOLDIER: Peanuts, traditional salted marzipan, raffia table-runners, English collar-studs, back numbers of *True Detective Magazine*?

SECOND SOLDIER: Keepsakes, bangles, prehistoric coins, religious postcards, beautifully picked out in silk and sequins?

RUSSIAN GIRL: You have no sociological novels?

FIRST SOLDIER: No.

AMERICAN: And no flowers?

SECOND SOLDIER: No.

AMERICAN (*gay*): Well, that's it. No flowers. (*Takes out a note.*) Give me something for that. Oh, anything. Bangles. Sure. That's fine. Just great. Do I get any change? O.K., I know the answer to that one. Americans. No change.

RUSSIAN GIRL (*studying him keenly*): You are not thrifty.

AMERICAN: I'm in love.

RUSSIAN GIRL: All the more reason for thrift.

AMERICAN: See you, beautiful.

RUSSIAN GIRL: Goodbye, sir.

> *They go to their respective Embassies, and enter. The* GENERAL *tiptoes quickly on to the stage.*

GENERAL: Who were they?

FIRST SOLDIER: Search me.

SECOND SOLDIER: The plot thickens.

> *Vaguely, like a chant, the words* "Romanoff" *and* "Juliet" *can be heard, very softly.*

JULIET: Romanoff.

IGOR: Juliet.

GENERAL: Sh! What's that?

FIRST SOLDIER: I can't hear——

GENERAL: Listen.

JULIET: Romanoff.

IGOR: Juliet.

FIRST SOLDIER: Ho—yes.

JULIET: Romanoff.

IGOR: Juliet.

SECOND SOLDIER: It sounds like . . . Romanoff . . .

FIRST SOLDIER: And . . . Juliet?

GENERAL (*very softly*): Where's it coming from?

FIRST SOLDIER (*near one Embassy*): Up here.

GENERAL: Balconies . . . ? Then there's hope . . .

> *The figure of Death the Reaper wobbles out and strikes the bell.*

FIRST SOLDIER: It's Death!

GENERAL: Death again? Death at a quarter to nine?

FIRST SOLDIER: . . . Eight thirty-three?

SECOND SOLDIER: . . . Nine fourteen?

GENERAL: It's the first time I've ever known Death make a mistake.

CURTAIN

ACT II

Noon to afternoon.

It is later in the day. The light is no longer the pale silver of early morning, but has the deep orange glow which makes the sky intensely blue and the walls the colour of peaches. As the curtain rises the clock strikes three. The Embassy walls rise slowly. Both lower rooms are empty, but the upper rooms are occupied by JULIET *and* IGOR. *They are both in positions of romantic dejection. The* TWO SOLDIERS *lie lazily in the street. It is siesta time. One is asleep, the other strums lazily on a guitar. Their merchandise lies by their side.*

JULIET *is the first to come slowly to life.*

JULIET: Oh, why must the mind hover, a blind bee, over dead flowers? And yet, maybe I like my flowers dead . . . maybe I'm not the happy, open-minded daughter parents dream about . . . maybe I'm not the normal, healthy modern girl who makes a sane selection of a mate after mature consideration in a night club . . . Do I betray my age group by thinking? Am I old fashioned . . . and just meant for tragedy? (*With profound self-pity, and a sudden interest.*) . . . Oh, perhaps tragedy. (*She looks at photo of Freddie.*) To look at a man . . . to visualize children with his eyes and my nose . . . Oh, Freddie, if only I hated you . . . but no, I like you . . . quite . . . in your silly, keen, determined way . . . I never quite know what you're being determined about, but that look makes older men call you promising. Freddie, you're a skyscraper of a guy. You'll hold our babies in all the right positions . . . You'll teach them baseball before they can walk and you'll teach them to count before they can read . . . only Freddie . . . I won't be those babies' mother . . . why? Because I like you, dear . . . and because I don't love you . . . (*She drops the photo, and takes up an empty frame.*) Igor, I love you . . . but I don't really like you much . . . maybe the two don't go together . . . when I was small, I always swore I'd marry a man with blue eyes . . . your eyes are brown . . . brown like damp patches on the wall, like school-book covers . . . and yet, when I look into them, I lose my way . . . I forget my discretion, my education, my table-manners . . . (*She holds the empty frame close to her face and shuts her eyes.*) Oh Igor, the way the warmth creeps into those eyes against your better judgement . . . like a slow wave of sunshine washing up a pasture late on a winter afternoon . . . made more welcome by surprise . . .

[42]

She is lost in her reverie, and cries quietly. IGOR *stirs and leaps to his feet with the violence of a romantic.*

IGOR: Theory is a corset. I can no longer breathe. Was Karl Marx ever in love? Are there frontiers which even the greatest of teachers have never crossed? Would the barricades have attracted so many martyrs if love had been as easy to find as death? I wonder. . . . For the first time in my life, I feel a coward. I love the sea, but I love a woman more. A woman? If I could take her home—if it were possible —they would criticize her frivolous and untheoretical mind. How I hate it myself at times. They would even criticize her looks—that vapidly romantic expression—those great grey eyes which ask endless questions, and which make me smile as I think of them—that concern with dress, with personal appearance—so unfeminine . . . and yet . . . as one who has been nurtured on the truth, the accurate, didactic truth, I must shout for the good of my Slavonic soul, "I am in love!" If I have to die for it, if I have to kiss the soil with frozen lips, I shall have known this exultation . . . and Juliet, the silences . . .! Stretching so intimately into infinity, silences which seem to wander among the stars and among stray thoughts, reducing all mysteries to the shape of a sweet and knowing smile, exalting each tremulous flicker of an eyelash to a vast, unfathomable mystery. Juliet . . . the tender gravity of our silences! (*He turns his head away violently.*) Oh, how un-dignified to feel the hot tears rolling down where rain and sleet hammer so ineffectually! Remember, in your lucid moments, Igor Vadimovitch Romanoff, that you are second-in-command of a warship. . . .

He stands stiffly to attention—his back to the audience—then breaks his stance, and says brokenly.

No, Igor Vadimovitch Romanoff . . . there are no lucid moments left . . . you are a man in love. . . . (*He sits heavily.*)

JULIET (*with sudden anger*): Oh, drink your vodka with your buddies. What do you care if I'm on the verge of suicide? You probably chalk up the number of your conquests on the hull of your ice-breaker. I can see you now, joking with your awful poppa about how you insinuated your way into a reactionary's heart. I hate you! (*She picks up Freddie's photograph.*) Poor Freddie . . . I said such heartless things about you. . . . (*She studies the photograph with compassion and tenderness.*) Oh, Freddie, you're dreadful. . . . (*She drops the photograph again.*) Forgive me . . . Igor, Freddie . . . both of you . . . I'm not . . . myself. . . . (*She relapses again.*)

IGOR (*he rises angrily*): And yet I doubt whether you have the capacity to suffer as I can suffer . . . you come from a new and super-ficial race . . . we have suffered from time immemorial, and when

[43]

necessary, we fall into the bitter practice gracefully and unnoticeably . . . no doubt you are seeking consolation with your father, who is successfully cheering you up by recounting his exploits on the Stock Exchange . . . it is your education I must blame, not you . . . I know my duty . . . I will suffer for us both. . . . (*He sits and suffers.*)

JULIET (*a murmur*): Oh Igor . . . Igor . . . Igor.

IGOR (*a murmur*): Juliet . . . Juliet . . . Juliet.

> *They are lost in darkness as* HOOPER, BEULAH *and* FREDDIE *enter the downstairs room.*

FREDDIE: Well, when's the next plane back?

MOULSWORTH: You seem to take the whole ghastly situation very lightly, if you don't mind my saying so.

FREDDIE: I take it easy, sir. I've never forced anyone to do anything they didn't want to do. Hell, a girl can change her mind about a guy. I've changed my mind about a good number of girls.

BEULAH: Oh, it's all too dreadful . . . and to think that Freddie has flown . . . How many miles is it, Freddie?

FREDDIE: Four thousand.

BEULAH: Four thousand miles!

MOULSWORTH: That figure is beginning to annoy me, Beulah. We've had it several times already. You've even consulted an atlas.

FREDDIE: I made it four thousand two hundred and seventeen miles, counting the trips to the airport. But what the hell. I like flying.

MOULSWORTH: Exactly. He likes flying, Beulah. Now. I knew your father, son.

FREDDIE: I know you did, sir . . . and he knew you.

MOULSWORTH: He did indeed . . . and what's more . . . I liked him.

FREDDIE: I never talked about it with him, sir . . . But I'm pretty certain he liked you.

MOULSWORTH (*a little irritated*): *I* talked to him about it. He did like me. He liked me a lot. He was a fine, upstanding man, and the best Number Three ever to row for Princeton. Now, young man, let me tell you right here from the shoulder what your father would have done under those circumstances. He'd have gone up those stairs and he'd have shouted his way into the girl's heart.

FREDDIE: I beg to differ with you, sir. Dad was a gentleman. He'd never have raised his voice against a lady.

BEULAH (*in triumph*): There!

MOULSWORTH (*to his wife*): What are you so happy about? Just stabbing me in the back all the way down the line.

[44]

FREDDIE: Dad would have gone right out there and clobbered that Russian.

BEULAH: Ho, how romantic!

FREDDIE: Yes, ma'am, he was of the "let-the-best-man-win" school. He always won. He weighed 'most three hundred pounds.

BEULAH: Maybe that's the solution. Women just adore brave men. Look at the bullfighters.

MOULSWORTH: What the hell have bullfighters got to do with it? D'you think I want an international incident on my hands?

FREDDIE: No, and then I'm not a scrapper. I studied law for half a year. I'm a firm believer in negotiation.

MOULSWORTH: Good God, man. The days of negotiation for a wife are over. Nowadays marriage like everything else is strictly business, and business is pressure. Go up there, son, and fight for your wife. Start shouting, or you'll lose her to the next customer.

FREDDIE: Mrs Moulsworth.

BEULAH: Yes, dear?

FREDDIE: I'll do anything you think wise within reason. I'm deeply attached to your daughter, but I think it only fair to tell you that when I asked her to marry me she never said more in reply than that she'd think it over.

MOULSWORTH: In business that's tantamount to an acceptance. She may argue the terms of the contract, but she's initialled the rough draft, that's how I see it. Son, go up there and clinch that deal.

BEULAH: Oh, Hooper, do stop seeing everything in terms of business. When he proposed to me, he slapped me on the back, and said, "Beulah, how about going into partnership?" Then when Juliet came, I woke up to find him standing at the foot of the bed with some flowers. The first words I heard him utter as I came out of the haze and the agony were "Well, first one off the production line".

MOULSWORTH: Well, I got you, didn't I? That just proves my point.

BEULAH (*her eyes shut in exquisite suffering*): There is such a thing in life as beauty, Hooper. It's a very wonderful thing. And your life has been the poorer for the lack of it.

MOULSWORTH (*loud*): I like beauty when it's practical, Beulah. I like a beautiful swimming pool, but only if it's got water in it. I like a beautiful marriage, but I'll still breathe a whale of a sigh of relief when both parties have said "I do". Now, son, are you going to let me down?

[45]

FREDDIE (*good-naturedly*): I hate to say this to you, sir, but it's my marriage, not yours.

MOULSWORTH: No, sir. The blue chips are down. I'm talking to you and appealing to you as one good American to another. Julie's a girl we both love and cherish, I as a father, you as a man who found it in himself to propose marriage to her. Son, she's drifting out of our life. She's in love with a Communist. If this thing goes through, it may mean that she could be guilty of attempting to destroy the government of the United States by force.

FREDDIE: Oh, that's ridiculous.

MOULSWORTH: It may sound ridiculous to you and to me, but it won't sound so ridiculous before a Federal Investigating Committee; and that's what we'd have to face, all of us . . . indictments, suspicions . . . ruin . . . and all because of her stubbornness. . . .

FREDDIE: Well, what d'you want me to do, sir? Talk to her? Or marry her?

MOULSWORTH (*after a short pause*): Whatever you think best, son. You're right. I was kind of hasty and . . . well, I'm a little sore about what has happened. . . . It all seemed so great before breakfast. . . .

FREDDIE (*with a grave, deep sigh*): I guess that's . . . life.

MOULSWORTH (*with a reciprocal sigh*): Never said a truer word, son. That's what it is. Life. The mighty Unpredictable.

FREDDIE: Just at the start of the home run, why, you have to break your ankle.

MOULSWORTH: Precisely right.

FREDDIE (*rising*): Well, I'll go up there. Talk to her.

MOULSWORTH (*extending his hand, moved*): That's my boy. Put it there.

BEULAH (*who has been lost in a profound reverie*): One small question, Freddie. If she changes her mind and wants to have you, what will you do?

FREDDIE: Oh, I'll marry her. I believe in marriage, Mrs Moulsworth.

BEULAH: And do you believe in love?

FREDDIE (*as though it were unimportant*): Sure, sure.

BEULAH: Then go up there, and our blessings go with you. Freddie, be gentle.

MOULSWORTH: Yeah, be gentle, but don't forget to be real tough.

FREDDIE *goes.*

MOULSWORTH: Goddam gutless generation. If it wasn't for the fact that I'm a diplomat, I'd have shot my mouth off. His girl going to

[46]

marry a Red, and he talks about negotiation where possible, all six foot six of him sits there looking solemn and pious, talking of negotiation where possible.

BEULAH: He's very sensitive.

MOULSWORTH: You always say that. A little mousy guy I can understand being sensitive, but a guy his size just hasn't the right.

BEULAH: Sh!

They both look at the ceiling. FREDDIE *has knocked at Juliet's door.* JULIET *stirs.*

FREDDIE: Julie . . . it's me . . . Freddie.

JULIET: Go away, Freddie . . . I'm not in a state to see anybody.

FREDDIE: I only wanted to say goodbye, kid. . . . I've come four thousand miles to say it.

JULIET: D'you mean that?

FREDDIE: Sure. I understand.

JULIET: Are you alone?

FREDDIE: I swear it.

JULIET: I'll let you in for a moment, Freddie, if you promise not to look at me.

FREDDIE: That's a tough assignment but . . . I promise.

She unlocks the door. FREDDIE *enters.*

Julie!

JULIET (*her back to him*): You promised!

FREDDIE: Sure. Well I—well, there's really not much to say.

JULIET: How's business?

FREDDIE: How the hell do I know. Dad bought up 'most all his competitors before he died, There's nothing left for me to do.

JULIET: You mean you've gone sour on refrigerators?

FREDDIE: I guess I'm just . . . mature. (*Sees his photograph.*) Hey, where d'you get that awful photograph?

JULIET: I don't know . . . I had it.

FREDDIE: No wonder you fell out of love.

JULIET (*pained and weary*): Is Dad very upset?

FREDDIE: Yes . . . I guess he is . . . (*Without much enthusiasm.*) He's a great guy.

JULIET (*dull*): The greatest. What can I do?

FREDDIE (*he smiles*): I know what I'd do, but then I'm not you, and I don't think any advice of mine would be much value to you.

JULIET (*to him for the first time, with a kind of interest*): Freddie, you've changed.

FREDDIE (*with charm*): Have I? (*Not looking at her.*) Hey, Julie, what's it like being in love? Really in love?

JULIET: Hell.

FREDDIE: Is that so? Gee, I'm sorry.

JULIET: What are you going to do now?

FREDDIE: Oh, I don't know. Marry. Settle down.

JULIET: Anyone in mind?

FREDDIE (*smiling*): Never less than six. Put it down to my business training.

JULIET: I envy all six.

FREDDIE: That's sweet of you.

    Pause. But during this pause:

BEULAH: They're talking. I can hear the voices.

MOULSWORTH: That's not talk, that's mumbling. He'll never get to first base that way.

FREDDIE: D'you want me to go?

JULIET: Not particularly.

FREDDIE: I think maybe I ought to anyway.

JULIET: Aren't you going to tell me I'm crazy and unpatriotic to fall for a Commie?

FREDDIE: No, I'm not going to tell you that. You're the only person can convince yourself of that.

JULIET: God knows I've tried, Freddie.

FREDDIE: Yeah, I think you have.

JULIET: These barriers ought not to exist.

FREDDIE: Sure, there ought to be no more wars, no religious intolerance, no race discrimination, no bombs—everyone in his right mind thinks that, and yet somehow, when we all get together, we find all these things are still there, and just a bit worse than before.

JULIET (*with a trace of humour*): You're not very helpful.

FREDDIE: I know it.

JULIET: I don't know what's happened to you, Freddie. You've started to think.

FREDDIE: Sure. It was tough, but I made it.

JULIET: And you're a bit of a pessimist.

FREDDIE (*with a vast smile*): Me, a pessimist? Not while there's baseball. Don't matter where I am, Paris, France, or this place, I have the scores phoned through to me every day.

[48]

JULIET (*affectionately*): There's my boy.

FREDDIE: Yeah. One thing about baseball. It never lets you down.

JULIET: I'm sorry, dear.

FREDDIE (*lightly*): That's O.K.

JULIET (*after a pause*): D'you want to kiss me?

FREDDIE: No. I know when I'm licked.

JULIET (*very upset*): Freddie!

FREDDIE: It wouldn't have worked, kid. You feel too strongly for me, know what I mean? I could never get as upset as you do, and that'd only upset me. I don't talk good, but you know what I mean. There'd be days with my great corny smile and the way I talk, well, it'd only irritate you. I really need a girl who doesn't want much out of life but what she sees . . . a girl who likes luxury but doesn't show it all the time . . . you see, I've got my problems too. Money's a hell of a thing to inherit. (*He rises.*) See you, Julie. Oh, I bought you some bangles off a guy in the street. I don't suppose you want them though.

JULIET: No, I don't . . . yes, give me them . . . they'll remind me of the dearest, sweetest guy I ever went with.

FREDDIE: I came out here with a brand-new custom-made morning suit for my wedding . . . I'll go home alone, but remembered by a bangle . . . well, like I always say, that's life . . . I'll see you some place sometime . . . maybe you'll bring your husband over to see us . . . the kids can play in the pool. . . .

JULIET (*crying*): Don't, Freddie . . .

FREDDIE: God bless you, baby. Keep pitching.

He leaves her. She just stands, immobile.

BEULAH: That was the door, Hooper. Listen! They're both coming down the stairs. I can hear four feet.

MOULSWORTH: You'd better be right.

BEULAH (*gentle*): Well, take that pioneering look off your face.

MOULSWORTH *smiles with some difficulty. His smile vanishes much more easily as* FREDDIE *re-enters alone.*

MOULSWORTH: Well?

FREDDIE: Well, I talked to her . . . (*He lights a cigarette.*)

MOULSWORTH: We are waiting to hear what you said.

BEULAH: Freddie, what did *she* say?

FREDDIE: I don't know that we have a right to judge her.

MOULSWORTH (*incredulous*): What was that?

FREDDIE: You see, sir . . . Mrs Moulsworth . . . I don't think I've ever seen anyone in love before . . .

[49]

BEULAH: Then it's . . . real?

FREDDIE: Oh sure. Talking to her is about as hard as talking in church. Everything you say, why, you get a feeling you're interrupting even when you're not. When I knew her, she was pretty. Now, she's beautiful. I can't explain it better'n that.

BEULAH (*her handkerchief to her cheek*): I know what you want to say, Freddie. I am a woman . . . and a mother. (*Suddenly surprised by the silence of her husband.*) Hooper?

MOULSWORTH (*who has sat down heavily*): All the values of human conduct which I have learned to respect lie scattered around me. I just don't recognize anybody or anything any more. I'm just not fit to continue, that's all. I'm an old timer, a has-been.

FREDDIE: Once again, sir . . . I guess that's life.

MOULSWORTH (*snarling*): It's nothing of the sort, it's a goddam disaster. Young man, there's no plane back to Miami until to-morrow morning. You're welcome to stay here, only keep out of my sight.

BEULAH (*conciliatory*): Hooper . . .

MOULSWORTH (*violent*): You too.

> The façade falls as the other rises. The other FAMILY is in session.
>
> MARFA ZLOTOCHIENKO is holding forth, and appears to be in full control.

MARFA (*blonde and ferocious*): I shall be forced to report un-favourably on the state of this Embassy when I return. Your Secret Service man is in tears. No man who is in the habit of clouding his vision with tears can be consistently vigilant.

SPY (*elated*): On the contrary, I am only just beginning to see! How can one understand our great and tortured history except through the magnifying glass of tears?

MARFA: Disgraceful. You, Comrade Ambassador, are guilty of indisputable apathy, and you, Comrade, who should be a mirror in which your husband can see his errors are but the distorting glass of the fun fair. As for your son—marriage is, of course, out of the question. It is totally unrealistic to embark on marriage with widow-hood as imminent.

ROMANOFF (*rising*): You can't mean what you are saying!

MARFA: What is the fate of the sleeping sentry? You are all asleep at your posts!

ROMANOFF: Evdokia! What has happened to you since we left Moscow?

EVDOKIA: We are traitors.

[50]

ROMANOFF: But why? Why? My son, you, me—is the rottenness in ourselves?

SPY (*with staring, happy eyes*): I shall become a monk, that's what I will do—and place my tremendous capacity for patience at the disposal of meditation and the illumination of manuscripts.

ROMANOFF: There you are, it is contagious. Why?

EVDOKIA: If this means Siberia or death—I shall go out and buy that hat to-day—I have already telephoned the shop and asked them to reserve it for me—I must have a few hours of pleasure.

ROMANOFF: It must be this confounded country which is subversive —the climate—the atmosphere—(*To* MARFA.) Why do you look so sarcastic? You can know nothing about this country, you have only just arrived here.

MARFA: On the contrary, I am extremely well informed about it. Conditions are chaotic, owing to a moribund economy. The atmosphere is one of sleepy indolence, and the climate is torrid in winter and more torrid in summer.

ROMANOFF: But . . . you have not lived through these summer nights.

MARFA: Summer nights? Of course I have, in the Black Sea. My eye never left the compass.

ROMANOFF (*exasperated*): All your life you have seen nothing except that which met your eye, and you have noticed nothing except that which has been brought to your attention.

MARFA: Your insults do not affect me, Comrade. I am sure that I know more about this country than you do, in spite of your ambassadorial pretensions. What is the annual rainfall of the capital?

ROMANOFF: I haven't any idea, nor do I think that it affects the political situation.

MARFA: Three millimetres.

ROMANOFF: Thank you very much. I'm sure that the information will prove most valuable.

MARFA: And how many kilometres of narrow-gauge railroads are there?

ROMANOFF: I don't know. We walk.

MARFA: Six point seven, with another five which has been under construction since nineteen twelve. And how many secondary schools are there?

ROMANOFF: One.

MARFA: None.

ROMANOFF: Near enough.

MARFA: On the contrary. A hundred per cent error. So don't tell me that I notice nothing but that which has been brought to my attention. I inform myself about everything, and as a consequence I am able to speak with authority. As for you, your Excellency, you are precisely the type of old-style foreign representative which Honoured Artist K. K. Bolshikov attacked so brilliantly in his five-act drama, "Kill the Swine".

ROMANOFF: A subtle title.

MARFA: You speak of subtlety as though it were a virtue.

ROMANOFF: It is a mark of intelligence. (*He studies her.*) Strange to have such a beautiful face, disfigured from inside.

MARFA: Are you criticizing me?

ROMANOFF: We have a perfect right to criticize each other. It is a pastime encouraged by the Party. You have been criticizing me since your arrival. Now it's my turn. My criticism will take the form of a history lesson. Don't interrupt me—I am sure you know many more dates than I do, but I know more about our revolution than you do, because I was there! I remember the first glimmer of hope on a horizon which had been dead for years, no larger than a feather floating on the sea, but it was enough. I am not a religious man, but I used to go to church to hear the voices. There is no people which can sing as we can, and when the liberated passion of a thousand hearts streams into the golden dome, clashing, weaving, murmuring, roaring, then a man can believe in anything, for our battle cry is ecstasy. Some nations surpass themselves out of love, others out of hatred, others by contemplating the still waters of reason. We immortalize ourselves by ecstasy—and when the people saw that flicker of hope, they sang, millions of them, and made the sky more resonant than the cathedral roof. I saw expressions in the crowd which I shall never forget, the upturned eyes of dirty Byzantine angels, the smiles of women who believe in a truth so simple it defies description. The machine guns chattered in the cold, laughing victims fell painlessly to their death, the snow was stained with blood. Other voices took up the song, other feet stepped forward, other hands grasped home-made weapons. In the morning, victory was ours, and many of the dead were smiling still. Those were the days of our enthusiasm. And what has happened since? Our land has become a huge laboratory, a place of human test-tubes. Our language, so rich, so masculine, so muscular, is but a pale shadow of its possibilities. Our literature, which ravished the dark soul of man with such pity, is now mobilized to serve an empty optimism. Our music, divorced from sadness and the twilight, has lost its anchor in an ocean of dreariness. You, my dear child, were born into this monotonous nursery, and you have never played with other toys than boredom, pride and smugness. I blame you for nothing. You know nothing. You are nothing. And worse, you are no one. Do with us what you will. I have rediscovered my enthusiasm, and I will know how to laugh, even in death.

EVDOKIA (*emotional*): Vadim! We have a fine son!

> *Before the pale* MARFA *can say anything,* EVDOKIA *and* VADIM *embrace with passion.* MARFA *goes out.*

SPY (*with eyes sparkling*): Love must spread like a plague. . . . Oh God, save those who have been immunized against emotion . . . help those who marvel at figures of wheat production, but who do not pause to marvel at an ear of corn.

> MARFA *reappears above.*

MARFA: Lieutenant Romanoff!

IGOR (*waking from his gloom*): Who are you?

MARFA: Junior Commander Marfa Vassilievna Zlotochienko.

IGOR (*with a wan smile*): Oh, my wife. Are you blonde or brunette, thin or immensely fat?

MARFA: It is my duty to inform you that owing to the scandalous and anti-democratic attitude of your entire family, I will be forced to return by the first aeroplane to-morrow morning, and will further be forced to denounce the staff of this Embassy for anarchistic and fascist tendencies in surrendering to emotionalism of the most dangerous and subversive variety.

> IGOR *starts laughing happily, almost hysterically.* MARFA *is taken aback, as though slapped in the face. The* PARENTS *break from their embrace, the* SPY *from his prayer.*

EVDOKIA (*gaily*): It's him laughing . . . Igor . . .

ROMANOFF (*delighted*): Yes . . .

> *They laugh. The* GENERAL *has reappeared in the street, and listens, surprised, as the front of the Embassy descends. The* SOLDIERS *stir. The light begins to lose its lustre. The* GENERAL *is dressed formally with top hat, gloves, a walking stick and a portfolio.*

GENERAL: What a curious noise.

SECOND SOLDIER (*yawning*): It's the Russians laughing.

GENERAL (*surprised*): Yes. Have you noticed anything? Has anyone entered or come out of the Embassies?

FIRST SOLDIER: No. There's a seasonal slackness of business which lasts all the year round.

SECOND SOLDIER: You're pretty warmly dressed for this weather, General.

GENERAL (*weary*): It's not without reason that diplomats wear this kind of costume. Gloves, walking stick, portfolio, three articles to leave behind, if necessary.

FIRST SOLDIER: Are you going in there?

GENERAL: I have been summoned to both Embassies at the same hour, and accepted both engagements in a fit of absentmindedness. What is the time?

SECOND SOLDIER: What's the use of asking us? There hasn't been a saint in sight for the past couple of hours. (*He looks at the clock.*) They must be having an argument in there.

FIRST SOLDIER: Listen!

> *There is a hiss of machinery.* THREE SAINTS *appear very quickly, strike each other in the confusion, and disappear at high speed.*

That's called making up for lost time.

GENERAL: I came here with plenty of time in hand. Now I suddenly find myself in a desperate hurry. Men, I've had an idea. You remember this morning when Death made a mistake?

FIRST SOLDIER } Yes.
SECOND SOLDIER }

GENERAL: Why shouldn't Death really make a mistake? Couldn't it be that our old friend up there was just dropping us a gentle hint? And isn't it possible that our Fatherland not only corrupts the living by making them oblivious of time, place, even of hatred—but that it makes even Death lazy and forgetful of his solemn duties? You don't follow. Human nature being what it is, legend and literature are full to overflowing with tragic lovers—there's hardly a couple who don't end up horizontal, bloody and fruitless. Why should that be? What is the point of suffering if you can't survive afterwards to enjoy the relief?

SECOND SOLDIER: I told you, if we weren't so weak, we could threaten the two Governments responsible for their unhappiness.

GENERAL: Don't make light of our weaknesses. These days you have to be very, very strong to allow yourself the luxury of being weak.

FIRST SOLDIER: What do you suggest?

GENERAL: A trick! The prerogative of the weak. To-night we celebrate the Royal Marriage of our Boy King Theodore the Uncanny to the Infanta of Old Castile in thirteen eleven, which led to the coalition of Saragossa, and the eventual expulsion of the Albanians from our soil.

SECOND SOLDIER: Steady, sir, that's not till next Friday—and you said this morning that it was the Lithuanians who were driven out a thousand years ago to-night.

GENERAL: Did I?

SECOND SOLDIER: Yes.

GENERAL: Well, the great virtue of history is that it is adaptable. I have a very definite reason for wishing to-night to be the celebration of a wedding, with the symbolic blessing of two papier-mâché dummies by the Archbishop. So shall we say that with the help of the Spaniards we drove the Lithuanians out?

FIRST SOLDIER: Doesn't sound very probable.

GENERAL: The pretext hardly matters. It's the celebration which people enjoy. Unfortunately even Easter has become largely a matter of eggs. Now kindly serenade the young lady with an apt folk-song . . . a melancholy one. Don't overdo it . . . not tragic . . . just melancholy.

FIRST SOLDIER   ⎱ (*sing softly with guitar accompaniment.*)
SECOND SOLDIER ⎰

> Oh, won't someone open the door of the cage
> And set the bluebird free?
> Set it free. Set it free.
> It was caught in the spring, at a tender age
> It languished in summer, forgot how to sing
> In the autumn it lost the use of one wing
> Before winter comes and wild winds sting
> Set it free. Set it free.
> Set the bluebird free.

JULIET *appears sadly and inquisitively on her balcony.*

JULIET (*drab, with a little smile*): Oh, it's you.

GENERAL: Miss Moulsworth. Greetings. Listen to me. It is extremely urgent. I need your help.

JULIET: You need *my* help?

GENERAL: Yes. If you wish to see the Lieutenant again, you must do as I tell you.

JULIET: What do you want me to do?

GENERAL: Sh! Not so loud. I want you to knot the sheets of your bed, and to hang them from your balcony.

JULIET (*with some enthusiasm*): Like I did when I ran away from school?

GENERAL (*with excessive delight*): Did you? Yes. (*Conspiratorial again.*) Then I want you to write a farewell letter to your parents.

[55]

JULIET: What? Oh, I couldn't. As though I was going to—no. Dad's got a weak heart.

GENERAL: You surprise me. Couch the letter in somewhat ambiguous terms. There's no need to mention the possibility of any rash act—just thank them for all they've done for you and say that you have run away to join the man you love.

JULIET: Even that might kill Dad.

GENERAL: The fact that you're happy?

JULIET: The fact that I didn't consult him first.

GENERAL: Really, I am running a little short of sympathy for him, Miss Moulsworth.

JULIET: He's a darling, really . . . at heart.

GENERAL: Must I doubt that you are really in love?

JULIET (*hotly*): You've no right to doubt that, after what I've been through.

GENERAL: Then do as I tell you, and you will spread happiness round you like a cloak. You must trust me.

FIRST SOLDIER: You must trust him!

SECOND SOLDIER: Be a sport!

JULIET (*doubtful*): Well . . .

GENERAL: It is a matter of life and death . . . for several people . . . don't let your parents go into old age with you on their conscience. It isn't fair. It isn't Christian.

JULIET: Yes, that's a thought. O.K., I'll do it.

GENERAL: You won't regret it.

JULIET *goes in.*

FIRST SOLDIER: What now?

GENERAL: Another folk-song . . . something maritime . . . something about a sailor.

FIRST SOLDIER)
SECOND SOLDIER)

> Sailor where are you? are you?
> Is the storm on the sea, is the storm in your heart?
> Which of these storms keeps us apart?
> Sailor where are you? are you?
> Are you faithless or dead
> Are the clouds in the sky, are the clouds in your head?
> Sailor, my sailor, we'll never be wed.
> Sailor where are you . . .

IGOR *appears on his balcony, a haggard figure, holding a revolver.*

[56]

IGOR: Why do you interrupt me?

GENERAL: Great heavens, Lieutenant Romanoff, what is that in your hand?

IGOR: A revolver. The classic solution to misery.

GENERAL: Are you aware that they are forbidden by law?

IGOR: How do you commit suicide then?

GENERAL: There are many other, less dangerous, methods.

IGOR (*lifting it*): You are too late.

GENERAL: Lieutenant, you will see Juliet to-night.

IGOR (*with a bitter laugh*): Really? Do you believe in the hereafter?

GENERAL: I believe in the herein.

IGOR: What's that?

GENERAL: Life as it is lived, with all its little annoyances.

IGOR: Little annoyances? You have never suffered.

GENERAL: No, and I don't intend to. Lieutenant, do something for me before you die.

IGOR: What?

GENERAL: Write a farewell letter to your parents.

IGOR: I have already done so. It covers seventeen pages. Then I ran out of ink.

GENERAL: And, Lieutenant, will you tie the sheets of your bed together, and then fix them to the balcony?

IGOR: As though I were running away?

GENERAL: Yes—No! As though you were advancing to happiness.

IGOR: I am an officer, sir. I am incapable of cowardice.

GENERAL: I understand your prejudice, sir, since, believe it or not, I am an officer myself. I am incapable of almost everything, but at the moment I do happen to know what I am talking about. If you wish to see Juliet again, alive, well, happy, do as I tell you. Give me a startling demonstration of seaman's knots.

IGOR: I cannot. My mind is made up.

> The SPY *sidles out of the Embassy, then rushes up to the General.*

GENERAL (*horrified*): What do you want?

SPY (*desperate*): I am on your side. Help me, and I will help you.

GENERAL: What do you want?

SPY: Asylum.

GENERAL: Granted.

SPY: And——

GENERAL: What?

SPY: A letter of introduction to the most austere, the most rigid and terrible monastery in your country.

GENERAL: We will send you to the Mauve Friars. They never sit or stand. They walk about on their knees.

SPY (*grasping the General's hand and kissing it rapturously*): Oh, exquisite. My eternal gratitude.

IGOR *is about to shoot. The* GENERAL *sees this.*

GENERAL: Quick!

SPY: "Last night we were as one, creatures in a dream, selflessly united in an endless waltz. From now on we are opposed, a man and a woman in love, the greatest, most exhausting struggle in the world, two moths racing for the flame, two cannibals devouring each other."

IGOR (*limp, he lets the revolver drop with a clatter*): Farewell, resolution. How did you remember that?

SPY: I listened in the shadows, and took it down in shorthand. Then as I read it in my room at night, I began to feel lonely again, and jealous that such phrases should not have been addressed to me.

IGOR: Jealous? Am I capable of inspiring jealousy? Even in my present condition?

SPY: Oh yes, brother . . . yes . . . your life is still before you, even if it only lasts ten minutes . . . while I must expiate my sins in endless penances and terrifying disciplines.

IGOR (*with a little sigh of relief*): What a fool I am . . . we must rely on one another to understand ourselves. What did you want? Ah yes. Sheets. Is it for some joke?

GENERAL: Yes, yes, a joke.

IGOR: I like jokes. (*He goes.*)

SPY: Now—your part of the bargain.

GENERAL: Boys, take this gentleman to my office. I'll be along presently.

SPY: I'd rather wait in church if I may.

FIRST SOLDIER (*in disgust*): Church?

GENERAL: Well, I'll find out in which establishment the bread is hardest, the water dirtiest, and liqueur least potent.

SPY: Thank you, thank you.

As the TWO SOLDIERS go, both façades rise. HOOPER MOULSWORTH is alone and consults his watch. In the other Embassy, VADIM ROMANOFF is also alone, and also consults his watch. Both seem exasperated. Upstairs, JULIET is writing a letter, and choosing

[58]

her words carefully, while IGOR *is tying his sheets in complicated knots. The* GENERAL *enters the American Embassy.*

GENERAL (*beaming*): Not too early, I trust?

MOULSWORTH: I make you just on two hours late, but then I don't know the time around here any more than anyone else does. As it happens, it's not important as my Washington call seems to be delayed. Cigar?

GENERAL: Thank you.

MOULSWORTH: Now, let's come straight to the point. I talk blunt. When I want to know something, I just ask. That's the way I operate.

GENERAL: I appreciate that. In my position, I have to appreciate almost everything.

MOULSWORTH: Are you or are you not going to come into the Western community? I've got to know right now?

GENERAL: And how is your charming daughter?

MOULSWORTH: What's that? She's just fine, thanks. Just fine. Now if you're not going to play ball with us, just who are you going to play ball with, and why?

GENERAL: Yes. She looked exquisite last night, I thought.

MOULSWORTH: Who?

GENERAL: Your daughter.

MOULSWORTH: Didn't she though? Now lookit, no nation can afford to remain neutral these days, not with the bomb and economic pressures.

GENERAL: Who was that attractive young man she was with?

MOULSWORTH (*livid*): Leave him out of this.

GENERAL: Her fiancé perhaps? Will we soon hear the bells?

MOULSWORTH: No!

The telephone rings.

Oh, damn it! Excuse me. I thought I told you I didn't want to be interrupted . . . Who? (*Different voice.*) Washington? (*Ingratiating.*) Mr President . . .? Oh, just fine thanks . . . sure, she's fine too . . . Sure, and she's fine too . . . Just fine, all of us . . . I'm doing my damndest, sir . . . I hope to have them wrapped up and in the Western community by nightfall. . . . Oh, sure, I've pointed that out . . . They've got a lot of pretty old-fashioned ideas . . . No, sir, I can't talk too freely right now . . . That's it, sir, that's the situation . . . Right here with me . . . Yeah, I'll do that, he'll appreciate it. . . .

The SOVIET AMBASSADOR *manifests considerable impatience in his room.*

[59]

Yeah . . . No, I don't need anything, sir . . . I'd be grateful if you could tell me the time though, sir. Then I'd add six hours and fifty minutes, and know what time it is here . . . Is that right? Why, thank you, sir . . . (*He adjusts his watch while talking.*) O.K., sir, yes . . . And our fondest personal regards to Mrs President . . . Goodbye . . . (*With a sudden burst of laughter.*) Sure I remember the time . . . When I fell in the swimming pool with all my clothes on? . . . Sure, sure . . . had a hell of a lot of laughs . . . Goodbye . . . (*He hangs up.*) Great guy. Hey, you know something . . . you were two hours and forty-six minutes late.

GENERAL: And I thought I was ten minutes early.

MOULSWORTH: What were we talking about? Oh, before I forget it, Mr President sends his warmest good wishes for the financial prosperity of your nation.

GENERAL: Thank you, sir. And when you next telephone him, would you express to him my warmest good wishes for the financial prosperity of your nation.

MOULSWORTH (*no longer interested*): Sure. Thanks. Now—

GENERAL: We were talking about your daughter.

MOULSWORTH: We were? Hey, you noticed nothing . . . nothing strange last night, did you?

GENERAL: With your daughter?

MOULSWORTH: Yes. Nothing . . . visibly . . . untoward?

GENERAL: No, except that she seemed radiantly happy.

MOULSWORTH (*weary*): Don't tell me, don't tell me. Those facts I don't retain. It's certainly a pretty exhausting life you lead us diplomats. Always celebrating, never an evening at home. (*Suddenly firm.*) We were going to discuss the Western community, weren't we, before you side-tracked me?

GENERAL: Not now, Your Excellency. You have pointed out yourself that it's very much later than we thought. I have to open a bridge half an hour ago.

MOULSWORTH (*very energetic*): I must have your answer tonight.

GENERAL (*elegant*): Perhaps we could find a moment to talk during the celebration?

MOULSWORTH: Celebration?

GENERAL: Yes, the Russians will accept, I feel sure.

MOULSWORTH: Another Independence Day?

GENERAL: Yes. Two as it happens. (*Awkward pause. Suddenly—*) Goodbye.

*He goes, leaving his portfolio and his gloves, and crosses swiftly
to the Russian Embassy. The* U.S. AMBASSADOR *finds the articles,
makes to follow, then throws them down, and pours himself a
whisky. The* GENERAL *enters the Russian Embassy.*)

Not too early, I trust?

ROMANOFF: Only if I misunderstood the appointment, and it was
for to-morrow.

GENERAL (*laughing*): I apologize.

   MARFA *enters.*

ROMANOFF: What is it?

MARFA: Good afternoon.

GENERAL (*surveying her*): Good afternoon.

MARFA: Because of the defection of your habitual cipher-clerk,
I have intercepted the message.

ROMANOFF (*takes a typewritten document*): Thank you.

   MARFA *goes.*

Please excuse me.

GENERAL: Yes, of course.

ROMANOFF (*he reads quickly*): Now, I am directed to enquire of
you whether or not you have finally decided to adhere to the Eastern
Bloc.

GENERAL: How is your charming son?

ROMANOFF (*abrupt*): Not well. He will be leaving soon. It is imperative that we know by to-night.

GENERAL: He seemed to be throwing himself into the spirit of our
national carnival.

ROMANOFF: It is a temptation which all of us must resist.

GENERAL: Otherwise you might become like us?

ROMANOFF: A sense of humour sabotages industrial development.

GENERAL (*laughs—then realizes that a joke was not intended*): He
was with a very beautiful girl last night.

ROMANOFF: Please stick to the point. (*He consults the document*).
I see that the President himself has asked for your co-operation. I
quote "At any price" unquote.

GENERAL (*incredulous*): You know more than I do.

ROMANOFF: You must know that we tap your wires.

GENERAL: I know you do, but we don't. I always find a keyhole
an unsatisfactory frame.

ROMANOFF: It depends on your possibilities. Once we have taken

[61]

the trouble to penetrate their codes, it is a pity not to benefit from the results.

GENERAL: Quite. It's like acquiring a degree, and then not practising. (*He rises.*) I hope to see you at our little celebration to-night.

ROMANOFF: My wife is very tired . . . so am I . . .

GENERAL: The Americans have accepted.

ROMANOFF (*with a deep sigh*): We will be there.

GENERAL: Goodbye, sir.

ROMANOFF: Goodbye.

> *He leaves—without his walking stick. He crosses to the American Embassy. The* SOVIET AMBASSADOR *finds the stick, puts it down absently, and pours himself a vodka. The* GENERAL *appears in the American Embassy.*

GENERAL (*genial*): I find I left my portfolio.

MOULSWORTH: And your gloves.

GENERAL: Those are not my gloves.

MOULSWORTH: No?

GENERAL: No.

MOULSWORTH: Oh. Drink?

GENERAL: No, thank you.

MOULSWORTH: Cigar?

GENERAL: Thank you. Incidentally, they know your code.

MOULSWORTH (*beaming*): We know they know our code.

GENERAL: Oh, really.

MOULSWORTH: Sure. We only give them things we want them to know.

GENERAL (*after a very long pause in which the* GENERAL *tries to make head or tail of this intelligence*): Goodbye.

MOULSWORTH: See you. *And make up your mind!*

> *The* GENERAL *leaves as the* U.S. AMBASSADOR *chuckles with pleasure. The* GENERAL *crosses to the Russian Embassy.*

GENERAL: I think I forgot my walking stick.

ROMANOFF: Here it is.

GENERAL: Incidentally, they know you know their code.

ROMANOFF (*laughing*): That does not surprise me in the least. We have known for some time that they knew we knew their code. We have acted accordingly—by pretending to be duped.

GENERAL (*after another incredulous pause*): I never realized before how simple my life was.

ROMANOFF: Remember. To-night is the deadline.

GENERAL: Goodbye. (*He leaves and crosses to the American Embassy.*

>ROMANOFF *sits sadly. Pause. The* GENERAL *enters the American Embassy.*

MOULSWORTH: Oh. Come right in. So you've come to sign, heh?

GENERAL: Not yet. I find on investigation that those gloves were mine after all.

MOULSWORTH: I thought they were. This life seems to be getting you down. Cigar?

GENERAL: Thank you. Incidentally, they know you know they know you know the code.

MOULSWORTH (*genuinely alarmed*): What? Are you sure?

GENERAL: I'm positive.

MOULSWORTH (*hearty*): Thanks. I shan't forget this.

GENERAL (*amazed*): You mean you didn't know?

MOULSWORTH: No!

GENERAL (*his majesty restored*): Goodbye.

MOULSWORTH: You haven't left anything?

GENERAL: No. Goodbye.

>*He goes and meets the* TWO SOLDIERS.

FIRST SOLDIER: We had to leave him in the church. We go on guard in half an hour.

GENERAL: I could do with a quick prayer myself. Cigar?

>*He puts one in his own mouth. All three light up and tiptoe out as the* TWO LOVERS *begin to let their sheets over the balcony. They see each other.*

JULIET: Igor!

IGOR: Juliet!

>*As their hands reach ineffectually for each other:*

THE CURTAIN FALLS

ACT III

Evening to night.

It is evening, and the stage presents a scene of imminent enchantment. The street lamps are lit, and an elaborate gilt altar-piece has been erected in the available space between the two Embassies. It is evidently of considerable age, and its spiral columns of tawny gold are lit by a host of candles. There are flags here and there. In the distance, music, music for the open air, brass instruments and the murmur of people.

The TWO SOLDIERS *enter, in their uniforms, now more formal in appearance. They carry two life-size papier-mâché figures of the type used in religious celebrations. They have doll-like faces, staring eyes, and are evidently either of great antiquity or else made by most spontaneous and artistic peasant craftsmen. The front views of these figures, one male, one female, have a weather-beaten beauty, and are picked out in drab and subtle colours. On their backs, however, are attached priceless robes of a former age, their magnificence enhanced by their oldness. The* GENERAL *follows the soldiers on. He is dressed in a uniform which hovers between the exquisite and the ludicrous. Plumes, swords, spurs, the rest.*

FIRST SOLDIER: Where d'you want them?

GENERAL: Here will do. (*He mops his brow.*) Everything in place? The sheets? Yes. The letters? Attached to the sheets. Splendid. There's so much to think about.

SECOND SOLDIER: The Archbishop didn't seem very pleased at your suggestion, General.

GENERAL: A deaf Archbishop can be a nuisance, but to-night he may have his advantages. Of course, he only became Archbishop because he is entirely closed to the world of sound. It gave him an austerity which visibly enhanced his capacity for meditation.

FIRST SOLDIER: Look out. Here he is.

GENERAL (*irritated*): He mustn't come here! We don't want to have to start shouting under the very walls of the Embassies.

But the ARCHBISHOP, *who is at least 100 years old and very small, approaches with a royal and terrible step. His train, which is of extreme length, and his mitre, which is of extreme weight, are being supported by our friend the* SPY, *now dressed in mauve rags, his head practically entirely occupied by an enormous tonsure, his eye brilliant with ecstasy.*

(*Ingratiating.*) My Lord Archbishop.

ARCHBISHOP (*who has a querulous but frightening voice*): General, this is an outrage! I have consulted many Holy books, and I find what I had indeed suspected, that the celebration of that most Royal Marriage between the Boy King Theodore the Uncanny and the Infanta of Old Castile does not fall until next Friday, and that to-night we celebrate our heroic participation in the Children's Crusade—so kindly have these invaluable symbols transported back to the National Museum with all dispatch.

GENERAL (*very loud*): To-day is Friday.

ARCHBISHOP: Kindly stop mumbling.

GENERAL (*shouting*): To-day is Friday.

ARCHBISHOP: You must speak up more.

GENERAL (*softly, to the audience*): I surrender. I tell him to-day is Friday, and——

ARCHBISHOP: To-day Friday? Nonsense. To-day is Wednesday the fourteenth. It has been since midnight.

GENERAL (*recovering from the shock—very, very softly*): Can you hear me now?

ARCHBISHOP (*irritated*): Of course I can hear you. If people wouldn't mumble so, I could hear everything.

GENERAL (*soft*): It's all the fault of the clock of St Ambrose.

ARCHBISHOP: What's wrong with the clock of St Ambrose?

GENERAL: Since it was built it has been losing time.

ARCHBISHOP: Losing time?

GENERAL (*normal*): Yes.

ARCHBISHOP: Mumbling again!

GENERAL (*very soft*): I beg your pardon. Yes. It has been computed by our Academy of Sciences that since thirteen eleven it has lost precisely two days.

ARCHBISHOP: The clock was not built in thirteen eleven.

GENERAL: It would have lost two days had it been built in thirteen eleven.

ARCHBISHOP: Gracious. Then it's Friday to-day.

GENERAL: Exactly.

ARCHBISHOP: Then we are not celebrating our contribution to the Children's Crusade at all.

GENERAL: No, we aren't.

ARCHBISHOP: What are we celebrating then?

[65]

GENERAL: The marriage between the Boy King Theodore the Uncanny and the Infanta of Old Castile.

ARCHBISHOP (*joining in*): Infanta of Old Castile. We shall then need the traditional altar of St Boleslav and the religious figures of the young couple for the symbolic wedding.

GENERAL: They are already in place. Now, if I may refresh your memory, Your Altitude . . .

> GENERAL *redirects Archbishop's attention to Altar and the two figures.*

ARCHBISHOP (*sees them*): My, my, how thoughtful of you. Verily, we have an efficient President at last.

GENERAL (*with some amusement*): I see, my Lord Archbishop, that you are well satisfied with the new convert I sent you.

ARCHBISHOP: To whom are you referring?

GENERAL: The Mauve Friar at your heels.

> *The* ARCHBISHOP *extends his hands with a smile. The* SPY *comes forward on his knees and is patted on his bald head, which he finds an elevating experience.*

ARCHBISHOP: He was admitted into the Holy Unorthodox Church an hour ago, and was the only one to volunteer to carry my mitre, which is of crushing weight, and my train, which is of transcendent volume, on this great occasion. It is disgraceful how lazy we are as a nation. Mark my words, he will go a long way. Maybe, when I am gone—

SPY: No, no, no . . .

ARCHBISHOP: He has been absolved for one day from his vow of silence, as he will help me with the ritual. Owing to my extreme age, my memory has failed me, thank God, before my heart or mind. I will prepare for the solemnities.

> *The* GENERAL *and the* TWO SOLDIERS *bow as the* ARCHBISHOP *leaves with the overburdened* SPY.

SECOND SOLDIER: Even if one doesn't approve of your politics one has to admire you.

FIRST SOLDIER: I suppose so. (*He spits.*)

GENERAL: Boiled sweet would you care for?

> *The façades of both Embassies rise. The* U.S. AMBASSADOR, *in full tenue, enters. He is having difficulty with his tie.* BEULAH *follows in a violet evening dress. The upstairs rooms are empty.*

BEULAH: I can't help you with your tie, Hooper, if you won't stay still.

MOULSWORTH: I'm nervous. I've taken twelve vitamin pills and I'm still nervous. How do you like that?

BEULAH (*working on his tie*): I wish we didn't have to go.

MOULSWORTH: For the thousandth time, Beulah, we just have to go. A doctor is always on call. So's a diplomat. That pact has just got to be signed to-night.

BEULAH: I never realized this country was so important.

MOULSWORTH: A casting vote is the important vote in any board meeting. Where's Freddie?

BEULAH: He went out a lot earlier.

MOULSWORTH: What to do?

BEULAH (*blank*): Have some fun, he said.

MOULSWORTH: Fun. I'm glad he's not marrying Julie. Positively glad. Have you finished?

BEULAH: Stand still.

MOULSWORTH: Has Julie eaten?

BEULAH: I put a tray by her door, but she just didn't answer.

MOULSWORTH: Goddam it, Beulah, you're heavy-handed.

   The RUSSIAN COUPLE *enter.*

ROMANOFF: Evdokia, I asked you to help me with my tie.

EVDOKIA: Come here, into the light.

ROMANOFF: Where is that odious Comrade Zlotochienko? Every room I go into I expect to find her there, tapping wires, or thumbing her way through my papers.

EVDOKIA: She went out to do a social survey of living conditions here. She wants to lecture her crew when she gets home.

ROMANOFF: I don't envy them. And Igor? Has he eaten?

EVDOKIA: The loaf of bread I left by his door has not been touched. I knocked, but he was sulking.

ROMANOFF: Ow!

EVDOKIA: I'm sorry. I'm tired. I wish we didn't have to go.

ROMANOFF: It's my last manoeuvre for Moscow. I might as well do it properly. Why do you look so sad?

EVDOKIA: I shall never be a grandmother.

BEULAH: There.

MOULSWORTH: Yeah. Feels good. Well. Time for a drink?

BEULAH: Hooper, you'd better not. Not after all those pills. Not if you have to sign a treaty.

MOULSWORTH: Guess you're right. Well. Got everything?

[67]

EVDOKIA: Finished.

ROMANOFF: Thank you. Now, shut your eyes.

EVDOKIA: What?

ROMANOFF: Shut your eyes, and don't turn round.

EVDOKIA (*resigned*): Are you going to shoot me?

ROMANOFF: We'll think of that to-morrow. (*He produces her beloved hat from a small box, and puts it gently on her head.*) You may open your eyes.

EVDOKIA (*whose fingers are feeling her head; with a shriek of joy*): Vadim! The hat!

> *They embrace.*

How could you?

ROMANOFF: I left and came back by the tradesmen's entrance.

EVDOKIA: Oh, Vadim.

ROMANOFF: There. Let us go.

EVDOKIA: One more kiss.

MOULSWORTH (*about to exit*): I've been thinking, Beulah.

BEULAH: Yes, Hooper?

MOULSWORTH: How about a real good holiday soon? Just the two of us, like it was our honeymoon.

BEULAH: Hooper, d'you mean that?

MOULSWORTH: Never meant anything more sincerely in my life.

> *They kiss, too.*
>
> *The Embassies close. The* GENERAL *marches up and takes his position centre stage. The doors of both Embassies open, and both couples emerge at the same time. They bow coldly.*

GENERAL: Ah! How nice to see you here. The formal part of the celebrations are about to begin. Then afterwards we abandon ourselves to more profane pleasures.

FIRST SOLDIER: Regiment. Present—arms!

GENERAL (*sotto-voce*): Quite smart, but a little late. Try to remember next year . . . (*Loud again.*) Now, maybe a short historical résumé of the character of this Thanksgiving will not be entirely out of place. If you can find us on the map, and there are many, alas, who cannot, you will see at once that our position, geographically, militarily, financially, politically, administratively, economically, agriculturally, horticulturally, is quite hopeless. Consequently we have acted as a magnet to the invader throughout our long and troubled history. The English have been here on several occasions on the pretext that we were unfit to govern ourselves. They were invariably followed by the French on the pretext that we were unfit to be governed by the English. The Dutch made us Protestants for a while, the Turks made us Mahommedans, the Italians made us . . . sing quite beautifully . . . and these many centuries in close proximity to homesick and miserable soldiers has brought quick maturity to our men and babies of all colours to our women. . . . The year 1311 was not a particularly eventful one in our history . . . apart from the fact that the Albanians and the Lithuanians were both casting envious eyes on our territory at the same time, which rendered our traditional policy of balance of feebleness impractical. There was in fact an unwritten treaty between these two powers to split our land between them. The treaty was unwritten because at that period in history neither the Albanians nor the Lithuanians could write. The situation was further aggravated by the assassination of our Emperor, Thomas the Impossible, by an Albanian desperado disguised as a bunch of flowers. However, our Boy King came to our rescue and contracted a rapid Spanish marriage which brought Spanish troops to our assistance on condition we became Catholic. We did for a while until the Albanians and Lithuanians decimated each other when we reverted yet again to the Holy Unorthodox Religion of our fore-fathers. It is this subtle trick which we celebrate to-day with much pomp and majesty. These are the symbolic figures, this of Theodore 1310-1311, Boy King. And this of Inez, the Infanta of Old Castile.

BEULAH: Isn't that interesting! I just adore history. It's so old.

MOULSWORTH: I wish there was some place to sit.

GENERAL: Ah! Silence please. The gentlemen will remove their hats.

The ARCHBISHOP *enters and stands before the Altar. The* SPY *follows on his knees, and squats by his side.*

EVDOKIA: By all that's holy! Do you see what I see, Vadim?

ROMANOFF (*unsurprised*): With him you can never tell if he's not still engaged in his old profession.

MOULSWORTH: Sh!

ARCHBISHOP: We are gathered here to observe in great solemnity the matrimony which saved our land on one of, alas, numerous occasions, from the savage heel of the invader. People of our country! Great powers to the east and to the west gird up their loins for war. Their regiments abound with Goliaths. We have only one David with which to oppose them—the Boy King Theodore the Eighth. He, in his wisdom and uncanniness, begs for the hand of Inez, the Infanta of . . . (*He dries up.*)

SPY (*softly*): Old Castile.

ARCHBISHOP: Old Castile. She accepts. The marriage which saved our fatherland is celebrated again. The tapestry of history unfurls. Let us . . . (*He dries up.*)

SPY (*consulting a document, softly*): Remember . . .

ARCHBISHOP: Remember the days of our distress. The bells are silent, the soil untilled, the fields barren . . . (*He dries up.*) What now?

SPY (*softly*): Come forth . . .

ARCHBISHOP: Oh, yes. Come forth, Theodore Alaric Demetrius Pompey, by the Will of the People Most Divine Protector of the Unwilling, Mentor of the Undecided, Emperor Absolute and Undisputed. Come forth, Inez Dolores Chiquita Amparo Conchita Concepcion Maria, Infanta Extraordinary of Old Castile, Hereditary Inheritor of Splendour, Purveyor of Wisdom, Holder of the Keys of Pamplona.

> The SOLDIERS *carry forward the figures and place them before the Archbishop, with their backs to the audience. Their absence from their original positions now reveals the sheets hanging from the balconies.*

BEULAH (*with a shriek*): Hooper! Julie's window! It's open.

MOULSWORTH: She's gone!

EVDOKIA: Vadim, the balcony!

ROMANOFF: He has escaped!

EVDOKIA: He's left a message!

BEULAH: She's left a message!

GENERAL: A little quiet, please. This is the most solemn part of the ceremony.

MOULSWORTH (*furious*): You must have known about this—why didn't you tell us?

GENERAL (*pointedly*): We never interfere with the internal affairs of other nations.

ROMANOFF: You mean you left these sheets dangling from our balconies for everyone to see?

GENERAL: Very few people pass by here. Now, silence, please!

ARCHBISHOP: The marriage will now be solemnized.

BEULAH (*who has read the message howling*): Julie! She's gone, Hooper! Gone to find her happiness with . . . with *him.*

MOULSWORTH (*furious, to* ROMANOFF): You had a hand in this. (*To the* GENERAL.) I'll get you for this. I'll declare war. My only daughter.

EVDOKIA (*a scream*): Vadim . . . he speaks of suicide . . . life no longer holds anything without love or dialectic . . . wishes to die.

ROMANOFF (*frantic, to* MOULSWORTH): It's all the fault of your confounded daughter. My son, my son.

> *He kneels and weeps.* EVDOKIA *throws herself on him. During this the* ARCHBISHOP *has been muttering.*

MOULSWORTH: I . . . I . . .

BEULAH (*screeching*): Hooper. *Do* something!

MOULSWORTH: Stop that man from talking first.

GENERAL (*loud*): The Archbishop is stone deaf.

ARCHBISHOP: Do you, Theodore Alaric——

MOULSWORTH: I'll get my car——

ARCHBISHOP: Demetrius Pompey——

MOULSWORTH: Search every—have the frontier sealed.

GENERAL (*indulgent*): Quiet, please!

ARCHBISHOP: By the Will of the People——

MOULSWORTH: Let me see that note.

BEULAH (*desperate*): It has no forwarding address.

ARCHBISHOP: Most Divine Protector of the Unwilling——

MOULSWORTH: I'll call Washington.

ARCHBISHOP: Mentor of the Undecided.

MOULSWORTH (*to* GENERAL, *fuming*): Call out the police!

ARCHBISHOP: Emperor Absolute and Undisputed . . . (*He dries up.*) Yes?

SPY: Alias Igor Vadimovitch Romanoff.

MOULSWORTH: Hey, those figures have shrunk!

ARCHBISHOP: Alias Igor Vadimovitch Romanoff.

ROMANOFF: Igor!

ARCHBISHOP: Take this woman to be your lawfully wedded wife?

IGOR (*dressed in robes*): I do.

ARCHBISHOP: Do you, Inez Dolores—

MOULSWORTH: Stop the ceremony! It's a trick!

> *The* SOLDIERS *bar the passage with their rifles.*

ARCHBISHOP: Chiquita Amparo——

ROMANOFF: Stop! Stop! Stop!

EVDOKIA: Vadim, why?

ARCHBISHOP: Conchita Concepcion——

MOULSWORTH (*to the* GENERAL): I'll have you bombed. . . . I'll summon the United Nations.

ARCHBISHOP: Maria, Infanta of Old Castile——

[71]

BEULAH: My girl, my girl.

ROMANOFF: We are impotent.

ARCHBISHOP: Hereditary Inheritor of Splendour.

MOULSWORTH: This calls for concerted action.

ROMANOFF: We have not the habit of collaboration.

ARCHBISHOP: Purveyor of Wisdom.

MOULSWORTH (*to* GENERAL): You have threatened the United States Ambassador——

ARCHBISHOP: Holder of the Keys of Pamplona—— (*He dries up.*) Yes?

SPY: Alias Juliet Alison Murphy Vanderwelde Moulsworth.

ARCHBISHOP: Alias Juliet Alison Murphy Vanderwelde Moulsworth . . . I don't remember that in the ritual.

MOULSWORTH (*shouting*): Sure you don't! I said, sure you don't!

SPY: It is here, in illuminated letters of the fourteenth century.

ARCHBISHOP: Then it must be my memory again. Do you take this man as your lawfully wedded husband?

MOULSWORTH: No!

JULIET: Yes.

> BEULAH *needs comforting—so does* EVDOKIA.

ARCHBISHOP: I hereby pronounce you man and wife. Kiss your wife.
> IGOR *does so.*

ARCHBISHOP: He is surprisingly mobile for a papier-mâché figure. Place the ring on her finger. Now go out there, my son, and beat the Albanians. Let the bells be rung.

> *The bells ring. A great shout of triumph rises from the populace. Fireworks begin to crackle. The married couple, who had substituted themselves for the wax figures during the discovery of the sheets, turn towards us, radiantly happy.*

A miracle! Oh, well. That's quite usual here.

> *The* ARCHBISHOP *and the* SPY *leave, the* SPY *triumphant and laughing.*

MOULSWORTH: It's not valid under American law.

ROMANOFF: It will not be recognized in the Soviet Union.

EVDOKIA: But Vadim—to see our son so happy!

IGOR: Father. Mother. May I present——?

JULIET: Dad. Mom. I want you to know——

> *The* U.S. AMBASSADOR *and* SOVIET AMBASSADOR *turn their backs. Shyly,* BEULAH *and* EVDOKIA *look at each other.*

[72]

BEULAH: Why, Mrs Romanoff . . .

EVDOKIA (*emotional*): Comrade Moulsworth. . . . What are we to do? Isn't it always left to the women to make peace?

BEULAH: Why, yes, to see our children so happy . . .

MOULSWORTH (*sharply*): Beulah, I refuse to let you listen to that woman's peace feelers.

ROMANOFF (*sharply*): Evdokia, whatever you may have said and felt, we are Russian. You are walking into a capitalist trap.

A pause of indecision.

BEULAH (*precipitately*): Julie.

JULIET: Mother.

They embrace.

BEULAH: May I kiss Igor, and welcome him into our family?

IGOR: My second mother.

They kiss.

EVDOKIA: Igor!

IGOR: Mamasha!

EVDOKIA: And now let me welcome my new daughter.

JULIET: Oh, Mrs Romanoff . . .

They kiss.

MOULSWORTH (*who is dying to turn round*): Beulah, I shall not forget this. Your foolishness has cost me my job, my dignity, and my self-respect.

BEULAH: Hooper, darling, don't be so silly.

MOULSWORTH: You are condoning the actions of a government which has threatened your husband with loaded rifles.

GENERAL: Loaded? Only with blanks.

ROMANOFF: What?

GENERAL: Regiment. Into the air. Fire!

Two mild little shots, like caps.

GENERAL: Good.

MOULSWORTH: D'you mean to tell me . . . ?

GENERAL (*smiling*): We could only have acquired live ammunition by joining either the Western Community or the Eastern Bloc. We manufacture none ourselves.

JULIET (*appealing*): Pop.

IGOR (*appealing*): Pappa.

Pause. In a rush, the fathers embrace their children.

[73]

GENERAL (*triumphant*): From now on, we will no longer celebrate the marriage of our Boy King . . . let the effigies rest in peace in the museum . . . the Lithuanians and Albanians no longer threaten anyone . . . like us, they cling to existence with the claws of hope . . . from now on and into the future, we will celebrate this, our greatest victory . . . every year . . . on the right day . . . at the right hour . . .

ROMANOFF (*suddenly*): Tell me . . . why am I not unhappy? By the rules of prejudice, I should be overwhelmed with bitterness.

IGOR: You are not unhappy because I am happy, father . . . and because we're in a happy country . . .

ROMANOFF: I need proof of that. Happy? It can't be happy without a single factory, without a collective farm, without a communal centre.

FIRST SOLDIER: I thought that, too, Your Excellency—but tonight. I wonder . . .

MOULSWORTH: I don't get it, either, now we're talking about it. I ought to be just thunderstruck, just right in the throes of a breakdown, and yet I feel as though . . . as though I'd just had a shower in champagne. (*He kisses his daughter.*) What's your subsoil like?

GENERAL (*pleasantly*): I haven't the slightest idea.

MOULSWORTH (*investigating the ground*): I bet it's lousy with oil.

GENERAL (*violently*): Then kindly leave it where it is. We only need to strike oil in order to be invaded to-morrow.

MOULSWORTH: Hey, some philosophy. Will you get that? A guy who doesn't want to own a Cadillac, on account of it's bound to be stolen.

JULIET: It makes sense to me, Pop.

MOULSWORTH (*laughing*): Already? You've been here too long.

BEULAH: May I compliment you on your hat, madame?

EVDOKIA (*blushing*): Thank you.

BEULAH: It's just darling.

ROMANOFF: I still need proof that I am legitimately happy—

IGOR (*amused*): Father, you're so didactic.

ROMANOFF (*severely*): So were you, yesterday. If we are to stay here—and obviously we cannot return to Moscow with any degree of safety—then I must know why I am so happy. Is it owing to a deeply frivolous nature, or is there something strangely, yet pleasantly, subversive in the very atmosphere of this place?

GENERAL: Ah, he's getting warmer. Isn't he, men?

SECOND SOLDIER (*with a sigh*): Yes, he is. It's in the air . . .

MOULSWORTH: Yeah. We can't return home either, Beulah. What can we tell the neighbours? So, we'll have to stay here for a while. But somehow—can't put my finger on the reason—but right now, I don't care. I don't care who signs which treaty with who. It's all way behind me—or maybe, it's way below me.

ROMANOFF: Yes—but speaking personally, I must know the cause. I must have proof.

The SPY *runs conspiratorially round the corner.*

SPY: Proof?

ROMANOFF: Have you been listening?

SPY: That is one habit I can never lose. If you want proof, hide— hide, quickly.

BEULAH: Where?

MOULSWORTH: Why?

SPY: Don't ask questions, and you will see. Hide, anywhere in the shadows.

He hides, too. The stage is peopled, but seems empty. Pause. The orchestra begins a waltz.

FREDDIE *and* MARFA *enter, obviously deeply in love. Gasps and whispers. A pause while they kiss.*

FREDDIE: Are there words which have not been used before?

MARFA: There are silences which have not been shared before . . .

They embrace.

IGOR (*hotly*): They're using our words.

JULIET (*pained*): They've stolen our dialogue!

GENERAL (*gently*): It is our country which is talking through their hearts, as before it talked through yours.

JULIET: You mean we invented nothing of our own?

GENERAL: You invented everything—even the country which is yours.

MARFA: Why do you look at me so critically?

FREDDIE: Me? I never criticize anything, on account of I have no opinions.

JULIET (*affectionate*): Trust Freddie to break the spell.

MARFA (*coquettish*): No opinions at all . . . then how do you know that you love me?

ROMANOFF: A logical question.

FREDDIE: I don't know, but I do.

MOULSWORTH: That's a pretty good blocking reply.

[75]

FREDDIE: Why do you love me?

BEULAH: Freddie's going right in there like a bulldozer.

MARFA (*a little sigh*): I don't know, either. I haven't any reason. I have every reason not to love you. You are a capitalist. (*Amorously.*) What do you manufacture?

FREDDIE: Refrigerators, washing machines, vacuum cleaners.

MARFA: What volume of laundry can you wash at one time with your largest model?

FREDDIE: I don't know.

MARFA: And how much dirt is needed to fill the bag of your lightest vacuum cleaner?

FREDDIE: I don't know.

JULIET (*irritated*): Oh, Freddie, try.

MARFA: You don't know . . . perhaps . . . perhaps I love you because you don't know . . . it's such a relief . . .

EVDOKIA (*delighted*): Ah, the disease is taking root.

FREDDIE: You're a ship's captain, aren't you?

MARFA (*with a sigh*): Yes . . .

FREDDIE: Gee, that's great . . .

MARFA: I'm captain of a sloop.

FREDDIE: Sloop. Sloop. That's a nice word. What's the tonnage?

MARFA: Why do you ask? You're not interested.

FREDDIE: No, that's right. I'm not. (*With a little laugh.*) I know what I like about you.

MARFA: What is it—(*Recklessly.*)—my love?

FREDDIE: Let me finish what I got to say, and then I'll kiss you. Of all the girls I've ever known you're the only one who could possibly be captain of a ship.

MARFA: The only one?

FREDDIE: My mother, she could have been an admiral—but you, you're the only one who could have been captain of a ship.

MARFA (*her eyes shut*): I'm waiting.

FREDDIE: One other thing. How about you and me getting married?

MARFA: You're practical. I like that.

FREDDIE: I'm a capitalist.

MARFA: I hardly know you.

FREDDIE: That's why I ask you so soon.

MARFA: What would you do if I accept?

FREDDIE: I'd be very surprised.

[76]

MARFA: I accept.

FREDDIE: I'm very surprised.

They kiss with increasing passion.

SPY: Proof enough?

In silence, HOOPER *kisses* BEULAH, VADIM *kisses* EVDOKIA.

JULIET: I'm jealous of them already. I want it all to begin again.

IGOR: With all our agony?

JULIET: Oh, that was nothing . . .

They kiss, too.

GENERAL (*to the audience*): It is the night. Our victory is won. Do visit our country, if you can. The fare is as cheap as walking to the corner of the street to post a letter; accommodation is magnificent. All you need do is to shut your eyes, and in the night, with tranquil minds and softly beating hearts, you will find us here . . . the realm of sense, of gentleness, of love . . . the dream which every tortured modern man may carry in his sleep . . . our landscape is your pillow, our heavy industry—your snores . . .

He retires in the darkness, and blows out the candles on the Altar.

The music is a lullaby. The four love scenes continue in silence.

FIRST SOLDIER: D.

SECOND SOLDIER: R.

FIRST SOLDIER: D.R.E.

SECOND SOLDIER: A.

FIRST SOLDIER: D.R.E.A. . . . Oh . . .

SECOND SOLDIER: Ah . . .

FIRST SOLDIER: M.

SECOND SOLDIER: One—love.

CURTAIN

THE MOMENT OF TRUTH

A Play in Four Acts

THE MOMENT OF TRUTH was presented by Linnit & Dunfee Ltd. at the Adelphi Theatre, London, on 21 November 1951, with the following cast:—

THE PRIME MINISTER	Charles Goldner
THE FOREIGN MINISTER	Donald Eccles
THE GENERAL	Anthony Marlowe
THE GIRL	Josephine Griffin
THE MARSHAL	Eric Portman
THE NURSE	Noelle Hood
THE PHOTOGRAPHER	Brian Wilde
THE VICTOR	Cyril Luckham
THE STRANGER	Harry Gwyn-Davies

The play directed by
JOHN FERNALD
With Settings and Costumes by
FANNY TAYLOR

———

SYNOPSIS OF SCENES

ACT I: *The Nation Appeals.*

ACT III: *The Nation Occupied.*

ACT III: *The Nation Liberated.*

ACT IV: *The Nation Shows its Gratitude.*

ACT I

The Council Chamber of a Democratic Republic. It is in this room that a Cabinet sits, ever changing in accordance with the wishes of an educated, and therefore fickle, population. Formal. Portraits of National Heroes. Arms of the Republic. Flags gathered into bouquets. Long table, and chairs. Atmosphere of a board room in a company more respectable than successful. Door right.

At the curtain-rise, it is late at night. The PRIME MINISTER *is about to take an injection. He is small and dapper. The* FOREIGN MINISTER *is weeping unashamedly. He is large and bald. The* GENERAL, *a tall, cold, youthful man, manifests impatience, although his face is deathly pale. Terrible tension under the sombre green lights.*

Pause.

GENERAL (*strident*): This hysterical behaviour will get us nowhere!

FOREIGN MINISTER: Ssh!

    Pause.

GENERAL: What's the matter?

FOREIGN MINISTER: I thought I heard gunfire.

GENERAL: Nonsense. They're miles away.

FOREIGN MINISTER: There it is again! Not the deep rumble of our artillery. Theirs has a higher, sharper note.

PRIME MINISTER: May I just crave a moment of silence while I actually take my injection? I am not yet quite used to the idea of it, and it needs a little courage.

GENERAL: Courage! Outside people are losing arms and legs, and you can talk of courage when you prick yourself with a hypodermic!

PRIME MINISTER (*smiling*): You forgot to mention that some of them are also losing their lives.

FOREIGN MINISTER (*shocked*): Really, sometimes I think you have no heart.

PRIME MINISTER: A Prime Minister with a heart would cut a pretty figure—for twenty-four hours. And then he'd be out. The people mistrust politicians with hearts.

FOREIGN MINISTER: Have they ever mistrusted me?

PRIME MINISTER: Yes.

    Pause, while the FOREIGN MINISTER *weeps afresh.*

GENERAL (*icy*): I deplore your attitude, sir.

[83]

PRIME MINISTER: Why? Because I said people were losing their lives, General? Courage is not a requisite for the loss of life. While it is for an injection, if you're not used to it. (*Laughs.*) There's irony for you.

GENERAL: More like blasphemy.

PRIME MINISTER (*quiet*): You are a sentimental ass, my friend. And you exaggerate horribly as a consequence. People die every day crossing the road, and they are doubtless just as patriotic as those poor unwilling wretches who perish at the hands of the enemy.

GENERAL (*twitching, after a pause*): You revolt me, sir.

PRIME MINISTER (*injecting himself*): Sssh! There. Why do I revolt you? What does death mean to you? You, a General? It means figures on a sheet of paper. Exactly what it means to me. A division was wiped out this morning. What does that mean? It means ten thousand vacancies to fill, urgently. The loss of the equipment is more important, because equipment is more expensive, and the creation of a rifle involves technical skill, while the creation of a man only involves instinct.

GENERAL: That is not all death means to me!

PRIME MINISTER: No, no, it also means a stiff and sanctimonious expression on the face, a capacity to display false emotion under the impact of second-rate oratory over the tomb, an ability to place wreaths tidily on monuments so that they don't topple over in the wind, a gift for standing rigid for seeming eternities of tear-laden time, a penchant for conventional consolation. And that is all.

FOREIGN MINISTER: You can say that so soon after the Minister of Education's death?

PRIME MINISTER: The idiot committed suicide this morning, thereby creating a vacancy. The space he left behind him is more eloquent than he ever was.

FOREIGN MINISTER (*weeping*): What are we to do?

PRIME MINISTER: Now that the army has failed?

GENERAL (*bursting out*): You make it sound deliberately as though the collapse was the army's fault!

PRIME MINISTER (*smiling*): Isn't it?

GENERAL: It is the fault of politicians! Why have we outmoded tanks, ill-equipped infantry, fortifications which crumble under enemy gunfire?

PRIME MINISTER: Because you, the Generals, are congenitally unable to assimilate innovations.

GENERAL: That is a lie!

PRIME MINISTER: What do you know about it? You have only been a General for five days—and you would never have been a General at all if I hadn't made you one, over-riding your superiors.

GENERAL: Do you expect me to thank you?

PRIME MINISTER: I am a politician, and I never expect thanks from anyone. I expect a stab in the back from you all, and the only occasions on which I am ever surprised are when a stab is not forthcoming. Our General Staff is a pack of bigoted and ridiculous idiots, and I promoted you in order to try and infuse a little new blood into our supreme command.

GENERAL (*calmer*): You left it too late.

PRIME MINISTER: That was my only fault. It is fashionable to blame politicians for military follies. General, I brought a design for a heavy tank to the Staff, a tank capable of fifteen miles an hour over rough country. It was refused on the grounds that this device—"device", I use the exact words of the Commander-in-Chief—could do nothing that a horse couldn't do.

GENERAL: The design was unsatisfactory.

PRIME MINISTER: It was better than nothing.

GENERAL: Yes . . . it was.

PRIME MINISTER: I brought a— (*To the* FOREIGN MINISTER.) Can you possibly stop making that noise?

FOREIGN MINISTER: It's all so terrible, so terrible. My poor country!

PRIME MINISTER: This is no time for demonstrative patriotism. Save yourself for the last act of the tragedy.

GENERAL: Go on—

PRIME MINISTER: I brought a new asphyxiating gas to their notice—

GENERAL: I agree with them for having refused it.

PRIME MINISTER: Why? What on earth has war to do with gentlemen? The days of heraldry are over. The professional military have unfortunately overstepped the confines of their calling, and have involved the so-called man in the street, and the man in the street, cowering in his shelter, has no patience with the elegance of war. If gas will end this unfortunate interruption of his little commercial existence, he is for it. And, after all, I am only his servant. I must obey his wishes.

GENERAL: What if the enemy uses gas on him?

PRIME MINISTER: Too bad. The idea is to be first, though. Surprise, General, is very important, you will agree, and I'd rather win a war in an ungentlemanly fashion than lose it as we are doing, filled with a

[85]

feeling of righteous indignation because we have done nothing that is remotely unfair. Wars were invented so that they could be won, not lost.

FOREIGN MINISTER (*wailing*): Why were wars ever invented at all?

PRIME MINISTER: Without them we would have no Empire to lose.

GENERAL: We will not lose our Empire. We will continue to fight there even when the Fatherland is lost.

PRIME MINISTER: No, General, we will surrender in a dignified manner, and cut our losses.

GENERAL: I will never surrender.

PRIME MINISTER: That is entirely your affair. What I am saying is that the rest of us, the Government, will surrender.

FOREIGN MINISTER (*suddenly emotional*): The rest of us? No! I shall not surrender either.

PRIME MINISTER: Don't be ridiculous. You will do as I tell you.

FOREIGN MINISTER: No. I resign my portfolio.

PRIME MINISTER: What a highly-developed sense of farce you have. What am I supposed to do? Accept your resignation? Accept the resignation of a Foreign Minister now that we are impotent to negotiate treaties with anyone? Weaken the Government by agreeing to let you go, now that the two of us are the only ones left at the helm? No, that is too easy a way out. The Minister of Education shot himself in order to efface from his conscience any association with this imminent defeat. Our colleagues of the Health, Public Works, Transport and War Ministries, of all things, have run away. The Ministers of Marine and Pensions have taken refuge in a neutral Embassy. The Minister of Air has stayed at his home, complaining of a bad cold. The Minister of the Interior left for the front, to set an example. The Minister Without Portfolio tried to resign his portfolio, and I told him not to be an ass. He has now had a nervous breakdown, because he had never realized, apparently, that he had no portfolio to resign.

GENERAL (*violent*): This is not the moment for jokes!

PRIME MINISTER (*equally violent*): It is the exact moment for jokes! (*Bitterly.*) Don't you think it a splendid joke for my last colleague to hand in his resignation from a Cabinet consisting of two members? He doesn't want his name to go down in history as one associated with surrender. He wants someone else to do the dirty work for him.

GENERAL: There is no need for anyone to surrender.

PRIME MINISTER. Really? What do you suggest then? You, who hold such a deep reverence for life that you grew righteously angry when I passed a few innocuous quips on the commonplace subject of death? D'you want the butchery to continue? Do you want the end of our nation on your conscience? Personally, I prefer surrender.

GENERAL: We have allies.

PRIME MINISTER: To whom we shall have to be fawningly grateful for the rest of our existence as a nation if they succeed, and if they fail we will pay the price of our stupidity.

GENERAL (*shouting*): There is such a thing as integrity.

PRIME MINISTER (*angry*): And, although it is hard to believe, there is still such a thing as common sense. It is my intention to surrender, in order to stop useless bloodshed. If you wish to continue the fight elsewhere, you will have to disobey my orders, and suffer the consequences.

FOREIGN MINISTER (*an outburst*): You have lost all honour!

PRIME MINISTER: Honour? What's that? A word. A word like wit. The people who use it most are those who have the least knowledge of what it means.

GENERAL: It is honourable to keep your word.

PRIME MINISTER: Even when such an act means bringing dishonour to your name for ever by killing thousands of intellects, thousands of personalities, thousands of educations, unnecessarily?

FOREIGN MINISTER: Is our independence unnecessary?

PRIME MINISTER: It is pleasant, but it is already lost.

FOREIGN MINISTER (*sweating*): No!

PRIME MINISTER: Ask your friend, the General. Have we a chance of saving the nation?

FOREIGN MINISTER: Yes!

GENERAL (*calm*): No. We must rely on our allies.

PRIME MINISTER: Exactly. An honourable occupation for us. Poor relatives. Junior partners.

FOREIGN MINISTER: There must be a way!

PRIME MINISTER: There is . . .

GENERAL: We have already over-ruled your solution.

PRIME MINISTER: I will tolerate your natural pomposity, General, but I find your impertinence a little irritating.

GENERAL: Your criticism is ill-timed.

PRIME MINISTER: So is your defeat.

FOREIGN MINISTER (*rising precipitately*): When they come, I shall be there to meet them.

[87]

PRIME MINISTER: What do you mean?

FOREIGN MINISTER: Wrapped in the National Flag, I shall fall under their bullets.

PRIME MINISTER (*smiling and pointing to the flags*): You have a splendid selection of flags to choose from. There is not much time left. I should try them for comfort.

FOREIGN MINISTER (*hysterical*): How dare you insult the flag?

PRIME MINISTER: I apologize. It was nostalgia that got the better of me. In peacetime there was nothing I liked better than mannequin parades.

   The FOREIGN MINISTER *collapses in tears.*

GENERAL (*stiff*): I must ask you to stop this cynical behaviour.

PRIME MINISTER: Why? Listen to him. He, whose whole political life has been a dictionary of empty phrases, is now thinking of a last line that will go down in history.

   He rises.

You both see yourselves in terms of posterity, and leave me to face the dirty, the vile, salacious realities of to-day. He indulges in an hysterical orgy of patriotism, and will, if he finds the physical courage, die gloriously at the moment when he knows that most people are looking in his direction. Trust him, whatever he does, he will not die unobserved. You, because your profession has traditions, will know how to end your life on the altar of honour which decorates the extremity of a soldier's imagination. But, but, but . . . you hope it will not come to that. You told me that I had promoted you General too late. You deeply resent the fact that destiny seems to have cheated you of a magnificent personal victory before the time that the age-limit plunges you into the bitter and distinguished obscurity you so deeply dread. You wish to escape to our allies, beg them for an army—a so-called army, it will be a battalion or two—and then return to the capital as a liberator, a Narcissus ripe for the rewards of self-adulation. Statues and postage-stamps, General. Those are your hopes. Statues and postage-stamps. All this while I must stand naked and unsung before an onslaught of facts, a true servant of my people. I stay at the helm, while you take to the boats. You called my behaviour cynical. No, sir. My language is cynical because I am surrounded by the cynical behaviour of others, and because I am unfortunately endowed by nature with a superior intelligence, but my behaviour is forcibly devoid of cynicism. Forcibly. It is hard, because of my intelligence, not to fall into the bad habits which even you, in your considerable stupidity, contrive to exploit. Your behaviour is cynical, both yours and the Foreign Minister's. Mine is not.

[88]

GENERAL (*cold*): That is what you like to imagine. I can forgive your insults, because, under your mocking mask, you are quite as perturbed by events as we are.

PRIME MINISTER: Quite as perturbed? I am far more perturbed than you!

GENERAL: That is the vision *you* have of yourself. Naked and unsung, indeed. You are the victim of self-pity, my friend.

PRIME MINISTER: Not at all. I have a solution to the situation. I don't want to die. I don't particularly want you to die.

GENERAL: There are times when death is preferable to life.

PRIME MINISTER: No. That is a military platitude. It is untrue. The propaganda of fanaticism.

GENERAL: What do you know about death?

PRIME MINISTER: Enough to be allergic to it.

GENERAL: And do you know how hard life can be in servitude?

PRIME MINISTER: I can guess. I am intelligent.

GENERAL: Were you ever a prisoner of war, as I was, in the last war?

PRIME MINISTER: No. I had a staff appointment.

GENERAL: Exactly. Well then, how can you conceive of the agony of men when their self-respect is denied them? As you said, you are at the helm. The nation is captained by a man who does not know the realities of captivity, who is not competent to judge. Its choice is being arbitrarily made for it by a leader whose experience is confined to the comfort of an untroubled, a luxurious civilian existence.

PRIME MINISTER: Does it need so very much more than a vivid imagination to understand the misery and humiliation of captivity?

GENERAL: Yes.

PRIME MINISTER: How can you gauge my imagination? How do you know that your imagination would not be more faithful if it had not been shackled by the experience of a single, terrible event? Who are you to know that I do not understand the choice we must make even better than you do?

GENERAL: We have no time to engage in a metaphysical discussion.

PRIME MINISTER: And no qualifications either.

GENERAL: —But you will surely understand that a man who has been a prisoner for four years has an authority to talk about these things which is denied to a man who has enjoyed—well——

PRIME MINISTER: Go on, go on. Enjoyed what? His life? Women?

Pause.

Women?

[89]

GENERAL: I did not bring the subject up.

PRIME MINISTER: The soft life of society? Women?

GENERAL: You know your reputation as well as I do.

PRIME MINISTER: Yes. The press call me a dandy. My interest in perfume and pomade has always been used as a weapon by my political opponents. So have women. That is the penalty for being in the public eye. They laugh all the more because a man with a heavy provincial accent like mine has no right to enjoy the life of the capital. But let me tell you something. I have loved and been loved, hopefully, hopelessly, grimly, capriciously, daintily, brutally, boringly, enchantingly, in all manner of ways. I know what men and women can feel about each other, and I know that in all its phases, from the sentimental to the passionate, love is the element in life which, more than any other, makes it worth living. You are a bachelor. Have you ever loved a woman?

GENERAL: Please don't be frivolous.

PRIME MINISTER (*thunderous*): Frivolous! (*Calm.*) Can you understand what our soldiers feel as they are subjected to a slaughter which is, by now, not only hopeless, but stupid. They are the youth of our nation, selected with subtle discrimination for their physical fitness. Many of them are in love, or live in hopes. Think of the little armoury of treasured photographs which each soldier carries with him in his breast-pocket. Think of the terrible, furtive farewells in the dim light of railway stations. Think of the letters, conceived in the agony of a crowded solitude, with the dispassionate eye of the military censor for ever peering over the shoulder. Think of the lonely colloquy to imaginary darlings, or to smiling pictures in silver frames. Think of the trembling hands opening the uneloquent envelopes to reach either a symbol of adoration or a rigid note of condolence. Think of the great cloud of apprehension and suffering which hangs over our land, and ask yourself, is this colossal sacrifice justified? General, it is time to put an end to it.

GENERAL: You are just being sentimental.

PRIME MINISTER: Don't you sometimes wish you could be?

GENERAL: No.

PRIME MINISTER: Then you have no right to hold views on the future of our people.

GENERAL: Why not?

PRIME MINISTER: Because the people are sentimental. Deeply sentimental. Wedding rings mean more to them than weddings. Uniforms mean more to them than war.

GENERAL: I deplore your patronizing attitude towards a virile and warlike nation.

FOREIGN MINISTER (*slightly recovered*): So do I. I deplore it.

PRIME MINISTER (*smiling*): I seem to be outvoted. But wait a moment. A fourth voice has entered into our argument.

GENERAL: What do you mean?

PRIME MINISTER: Listen!

The roll of distant gunfire.

FOREIGN MINISTER: What is that?

GENERAL (*expressionless*): Gunfire.

FOREIGN MINISTER (*terrified*): Ours?

GENERAL: Theirs.

FOREIGN MINISTER: What about ours?

PRIME MINISTER (*quiet*): It is silent.

FOREIGN MINISTER: Oh, God!

GENERAL: That means that our front has given way.

PRIME MINISTER: Has disappeared. (*He looks at his watch and frowns.*) Now, let us continue our conversation. Where were we?

GENERAL: I am leaving.

PRIME MINISTER (*pleasant*): Goodbye.

GENERAL: I give you one more chance.

PRIME MINISTER: And I return the compliment.

GENERAL: You refuse to join me?

PRIME MINISTER: I shall stay here, at my post . . . under the guidance of the Marshal.

GENERAL
FOREIGN MINISTER } The Marshal?

PRIME MINISTER: Yes. He has accepted my offer to come out of retirement, and lead his people in their hour of trial.

FOREIGN MINISTER (*a ray of hope*): The Marshal? Who led us to victory the last time? Why didn't we think of it before?

PRIME MINISTER: Because it would have been ridiculous. Now that the situation is ridiculous, it makes sense.

GENERAL (*angry*): Is it your intention to make a mockery of our army?

PRIME MINISTER (*cold*): I shall be less successful than you.

FOREIGN MINISTER: He should have taken over at the outset.

GENERAL: He's mad!

PRIME MINISTER: That, General, is insubordination.

GENERAL: I revere the Marshal. I was his favourite pupil. But now— you know very well . . .

PRIME MINISTER: I know he has in his possession something none of us have. A reputation.

GENERAL: Alexander the Great has a reputation.

FOREIGN MINISTER: He's dead.

GENERAL: Unfortunately the Marshal is still alive.

FOREIGN MINISTER: Sacrilege!

GENERAL: He saved the country once. He should be left where he is, in history.

FOREIGN MINISTER: He is the greatest military genius this country has had since the seventeenth century.

GENERAL: Nonsense. He was a cavalry man. His knowledge of infantry and artillery was practically non-existent.

PRIME MINISTER: It is very short-sighted of you to use the past tense. He can still render his country his greatest service.

FOREIGN MINISTER (*reproaching himself*): Why did we not think of this before?

GENERAL: Because it is preposterous.

PRIME MINISTER: No. I am not seeking his military advice.

GENERAL: What?

PRIME MINISTER: To talk a language you understand, General, I will say that he is the most valuable postage-stamp in our national collection. His head only goes on to very heavy parcels. Yours, at the climax of your career, would only go on to postcards.

GENERAL: Talk sense.

PRIME MINISTER: I am talking sense! What has happened at the end of every major war? Generals from the opposing sides hasten to visit each other, and compare notes about the slaughter they have conducted. They commiserate with each other's misfortunes and miscalculations; they pin medals on each other's breasts and exchange souvenirs, because secretly they were on the same side against their peoples.

FOREIGN MINISTER (*furious*): You have gone too far!

GENERAL: Civilians have no self-control and no clarity of vision. It is not I who wish to compromise with the enemy. I have no intention of hobnobbing with their generals, or of accepting souvenirs from them. It is you——

FOREIGN MINISTER: Yes, it is you——

PRIME MINISTER (*in irritation, to the* FOREIGN MINISTER): Kindly acquire a viewpoint of your own, and stick to it. General, you are certainly a man superficially endowed with a sterling integrity, which means that you have a deficiency of political sense. I am not inviting you to exchange souvenirs with your enemies. I am inviting them to exchange souvenirs with the Marshal. Now do you understand?

GENERAL: I cannot understand the advantages to be gained.

PRIME MINISTER (*patient*): I wish to play upon the soldierly senti-mentality of our victors, who will certainly be more lenient towards a venerable figure like the Marshal than they will to a greenhorn General like you or a verminous politician like myself. He defeated them twenty-five years ago——

GENERAL: When he was a younger man.

PRIME MINISTER: His age is on our side.

GENERAL: But he is incapable of coherent reasoning.

PRIME MINISTER: Which makes him all the more touching.

GENERAL (*after a brief pause*): This is a dastardly idea.

PRIME MINISTER (*with icy accuracy*): It is a patriotic idea.

FOREIGN MINISTER: I believe he could save the military situation.

GENERAL: Nonsense.

FOREIGN MINISTER: His reputation will strike dismay into the enemy.

GENERAL: You can't strike dismay into a wall of metal.

FOREIGN MINISTER: He will revive our faith in our arms!

PRIME MINISTER: No, he will melt the enemy's heart. That is our only way.

GENERAL: I tell you he is ill, and incapable of decision.

PRIME MINISTER (*brutal*): I don't care. The sillier he is, the better.

GENERAL: I want no part in this.

PRIME MINISTER (*robust*): Then go. Get out. Leave us.

GENERAL: I will.

FOREIGN MINISTER: Where are you going?

GENERAL: Away. To carry on the struggle. I have my personal aeroplane in readiness. Are you coming?

FOREIGN MINISTER: No. Not if the Marshal is going to take over. And, in the light of our decision, I consider it your duty to stay also.

GENERAL: On the contrary. I have made my position clear. I am more resolved than ever.

FOREIGN MINISTER (*furious*): In other words, you are placing your selfish interests above those of your mother country?

GENERAL: No, sir. I feel sure we will meet again. Goodbye.

He is about to leave, when a GIRL *rushes into the room. She is blonde, young, and in a high state of nerves. She wears a wet raincoat. Artillery louder . . .*

FOREIGN MINISTER: Who are you? What do you want?

GIRL: You mustn't do it!

PRIME MINISTER: What? Wait a minute. I remember you.

GIRL: I am the Marshal's daughter. You are the Prime Minister.

PRIME MINISTER: Yes. We are expecting your father. Do sit down.

GIRL (*standing*): I have come to appeal to you.

FOREIGN MINISTER: Eh? How did you get in here?

GIRL: Does that matter?

PRIME MINISTER: The halls are empty. The civil service has fled.

GIRL: The streets are deserted. Shells are falling in the suburbs.

A red flicker far away.

PRIME MINISTER (*at the window*): Hullo. Look at that. That's towards the river.

GENERAL: It seems to be raining.

GIRL: It's pouring . . .

GENERAL: I'm glad. It will help our fire-fighters.

GIRL (*blurting out*): Please don't bring my father here!

PRIME MINISTER: Hm? Why not? You should be proud.

GIRL: Proud? Why? Which of us can be proud at this moment?

PRIME MINISTER: The General. He's very proud. Very proud indeed. His hour of escape has arrived. He will live in a comfortable hotel in our allies' capital, and spin savage yarns about us. Do you expect us to do the same?

GENERAL (*hoarse*): Don't try my patience too far!

GIRL: I don't care what any of you do. I'm only a student, and a woman. It's none of my business. My only duty is to look after my father, and I implore you not to send for him.

FOREIGN MINISTER (*epic*): Why not? The hero of the last time . . .

GIRL: He's ill.

PRIME MINISTER: The General even said at one point that he's mad.

GIRL (*recoiling*): Don't say that——

GENERAL: I was overwrought. I apologize.

GIRL: He's old. Very old.

[94]

PRIME MINISTER: Eighty-eight. Titian was still painting pictures at his age, and Sophocles was at the height of his powers. The country needs him.

GENERAL: You don't need him. You need his name.

PRIME MINISTER (*sweet, but firm*): The two are inseparable.

GIRL: I refuse to let you use him.

PRIME MINISTER (*laughing quietly*): You show some of the old man's spirit.

GIRL: I'm not ashamed of that.

PRIME MINISTER: Nor should you be. But you are contradicted in your demand by the voices of the entire nation.

GIRL: That is a silly parliamentary remark.

FOREIGN MINISTER: It's the truth.

GIRL: I'm not interested in the nation.

FOREIGN MINISTER (*aghast*): What!

GIRL: There's no room in my heart for more than my poor helpless father, and . . .

PRIME MINISTER: And?

GIRL: My father.

PRIME MINISTER (*fierce*): And?

GIRL (*quiet*): My fiancé . . .

PRIME MINISTER: Where is he?

GIRL: I don't know.

PRIME MINISTER: In the army?

GIRL: Yes . . .

PRIME MINISTER: Rank?

GIRL: Major.

PRIME MINISTER (*relaxing*): And presumably you wish to see him again . . . if he is still alive.

GIRL (*as firm as she can be*): If he is still alive.

PRIME MINISTER: You see, General, it is only the unattached, the lonely like you who can think of that vast romantic abstraction, the nation. There comes a time when we, who are in love, or have private responsibilities, only think of our private tragedies.

GENERAL: You are wrong!

PRIME MINISTER: No doubt, but we are in the vast majority, thank God.

GIRL: I refuse to allow my father to accept office.

PRIME MINISTER: Wait a minute, wait a minute.

GIRL: There is no time. I can only think of one thing. I must force you to understand me.

FOREIGN MINISTER: What are your objections?

GIRL: My father . . . is no longer responsible for his actions . . .

FOREIGN MINISTER (*horrified*): Surely you don't mean his mind is affected?

GIRL: No! He is just removed from reality. He lives in past campaigns . . . talks to friends long dead . . . rebukes old enemies for forgotten offences . . .

FOREIGN MINISTER (*overawed and reverent*): He is living in the time of his greatest glory . . .

PRIME MINISTER (*quiet*): But don't you think, my dear, that he may even now serve, not the arms, but the dignity of our cause?

GIRL (*heartcry*): How? How can he?

PRIME MINISTER: By inculcating in the tender-hearted enemy generals a taste of that mystery he commands . . .

GIRL: I don't understand.

PRIME MINISTER: He will elevate reality to a level of poetry. His mumblings will touch their hearts, and purge them of their savagery.

GIRL: You talk of him as though he were a secret weapon.

PRIME MINISTER: He is! The last card we have to play.

GIRL (*flashing*): He is my father. Not a Marshal, not a Hero. My father. A poor defenceless, affectionate old man.

PRIME MINISTER: I feel bound to point out that he has accepted my invitation as though he expected nothing else. He was even somewhat irritated that he had not been summoned before.

GIRL: Of course. He would.

PRIME MINISTER: Do you really think you are qualified to go against his wishes?

GIRL: I am appealing to you as a man in full possession of his senses, and as a man with a heart.

GENERAL: You will have far to look.

GIRL: You will be sacrificing his life and his reputation on a speculative gamble.

PRIME MINISTER (*quiet*): Don't imagine that I can't understand your feelings.

GIRL: That's not enough!

PRIME MINISTER (*firm*): It's as far as I am prepared to go under the circumstances. The acme of a politician's generosity is reached when he is sympathetic.

GIRL (*desperate*): I shall no longer appeal to you then. I shall demand you to release him.

PRIME MINISTER (*smiling*): I cannot prevent you from beating your head against a rock, I can only dissuade you.

GIRL (*furious*): Will you do as I say?

PRIME MINISTER: You must try to be practical, and appear the nice, pleasant, attractive young lady you are instead of borrowing disagreeable words from the jargon of the Trades' Union leader. Demand, indeed.

GIRL: I'm not interested in your verbal embroidery. I want an answer of a single word. Otherwise . . .

PRIME MINISTER: Otherwise what?

GIRL (*losing her nerve, bitterly*): I don't know . . .

PRIME MINISTER: Exactly. Now sit down in a comfortable chair, and greet your father when he arrives without tears on your face. . . .

GIRL: If only I were a man . . .

PRIME MINISTER: If you were a man you wouldn't be here, and even if you were, I wouldn't treat you so leniently.

The door opens and a homely NURSE *looks in.*

NURSE: Oh, I'm sorry . . .

PRIME MINISTER: Come in, come in.

NURSE: Is this the right room? I'm afraid I'm rather lost. There's no one about.

AN ANGRY OLD VOICE IN THE CORRIDOR: Nurse! You've left me freezing. There's a headwind in the corridor. Lead me to the battle-field.

PRIME MINISTER (*hushed*): Is it him?

FOREIGN MINISTER (*springing to attention*): The Marshal?

NURSE (*sympathetic*): Yes, the poor dear.

GIRL (*near collapse*): I don't want to see this!

PRIME MINISTER: Bring him in.

NURSE: Yes, sir.

THE OLD VOICE: Nurse! Dammit! I'm growing icicles!

NURSE (*cooing as she goes*): I'm coming, my old dear. Here I am.

THE OLD VOICE: Old dear is for peacetime. You'll call me by my proper title from now on . . .

The MARSHAL *appears in a wheel-chair, huddled and heart-breaking. He wears full uniform. The* NURSE *pushes him.*

FOREIGN MINISTER (*foolishly*): Marshal!

[97]

MARSHAL: Who are you? A soldier? You stand like one. Artillery legs. Not used to marching. Where's your uniform?

FOREIGN MINISTER: I am the Foreign Minister, Your Excellency. At your orders.

MARSHAL: A civilian? But you served in the Artillery?

FOREIGN MINISTER: No, sir. Pay Corps.

MARSHAL: Same thing. You can't cheat me. Nobody ever succeeds.

He sees the GENERAL.

Lieutenant!

GENERAL (*unenthusiastic*): Sir.

MARSHAL: What are you doing in that uniform? Gold stars. Oak leaves. Laurel clusters. Victory Cross. Order of St Matthew and St. Mark. Foreign decorations. What's the meaning of this masquerade?

GENERAL: I am a General, sir.

MARSHAL: Nonsense, you're a Lieutenant. I never forget a face.

GENERAL: Time has passed, sir.

MARSHAL: What has passed? Speak up.

GENERAL: Time, sir.

MARSHAL: That's no reason for dressing up like a play-actor. Get your Lieutenant's uniform, and put yourself under arrest. (*To the* PRIME MINISTER.) Who are you?

PRIME MINISTER: The Prime Minister, Your Excellency.

MARSHAL: I see. Is it you who called me to lead the nation?

PRIME MINISTER: Yes, Your Excellency.

MARSHAL: You are a criminal, sir, for leaving it so late. How many Army Corps do we dispose?

GENERAL: None!

MARSHAL: Silence!

PRIME MINISTER: Fifty-three.

GENERAL: On paper!

MARSHAL: Very well. Paper's as good as anything else. Call on my old colleague, General Pansetti. He will command the central armies.

PRIME MINISTER: That will be difficult . . .

MARSHAL: Why?

GENERAL: He died six years ago.

MARSHAL: What? Why did nobody tell me? What is our Intelligence doing?

NURSE: Don't strain him, please . . .

MARSHAL (*seeing the* GIRL): Who's that? Women on the Staff?

The GIRL *looks up sorrowfully.*

MARSHAL: Lieutenant, bring that woman here. Who is it? A spy? I had eight shot the last time.

The NURSE *goes up to the* GIRL.

NURSE: Please come forward, Miss.

MARSHAL: Eh? Why didn't you obey me, Lieutenant?

GIRL: Father . . .

MARSHAL: Oh, it's you? I ordered you away to the country. Why are you here?

GIRL: Because . . . I . . .

GENERAL: Because there is no country left to go to!

PRIME MINISTER: General, you had better leave.

MARSHAL: What did you call the fellow?

PRIME MINISTER: Lieutenant, you are dismissed.

MARSHAL: That's better. Now. (*To the* GENERAL.) Are you going?

GENERAL: Yes. In order to carry on the war.

PRIME MINISTER (*loud*): You think we are wrong. Very well, leave us in our folly. Don't try to put us right.

GENERAL: You are murdering the Marshal.

FOREIGN MINISTER: How dare you?

GENERAL: The victory will be ours, and we will be compelled, by the pressure of public opinion, to make an example of him.

PRIME MINISTER (*mocking*): And of us too?

GENERAL (*fiercely*): I am not concerned with you! I am concerned with my old chief, a soldier of value, a piece of our history.

MARSHAL (*irritated*): I really cannot reach any momentous decisions with this intolerable noise going on.

NURSE: Please don't excite him.

MARSHAL: Nurse, shut up! And you, Lieutenant, clear out before I am reduced to other arguments. In my youth, death was the penalty for insubordination.

GENERAL: Remember what I have——

MARSHAL: Hup! Hup, sir! Not another word.

Moment of tension. In answer to an appealing gesture of the GIRL, *the* GENERAL *breaks away, and goes out. The* PRIME MINISTER *is visibly relieved.*

Now, give me a graphic outline of the military situation.

PRIME MINISTER: It is, Your Excellency, fraught with difficulties,

MARSHAL: As you know, I thrive on difficulties.

The FOREIGN MINISTER *breaks into a sycophantic smile.*

PRIME MINISTER: Our allies—

MARSHAL: Have let us down!

PRIME MINISTER (*eagerly seizing on the opportunity*): Exactly. That is exactly what has happened. What incredible insight!

MARSHAL (*flushed*): It is a military maxim that allies always let you down. It is invariably safer to trust your opponents. At least you know where you stand.

FOREIGN MINISTER: If only we had had the benefit of your advice before, Your Excellency.

MARSHAL: You have only yourselves to blame. Bring me a map of the front . . . large scale . . . compass and calipers . . . two pencils, sharpened . . . india-rubbers . . . full reports of our intelligence . . . complete communiqués of both sides since the commencement of hostilities . . . and a list of available General Officers . . .

FOREIGN MINISTER (*soft, awed*): What wonderful decision!

PRIME MINISTER (*aside, disinterested*): Yes, yes, very wonderful indeed . . . now go and get what he asked for . . .

FOREIGN MINISTER (*dismayed*): Where from?

PRIME MINISTER (*furtive*): Never mind. Improvise. Invent.

MARSHAL: Hup! Hup! Do I have to wait all night?

PRIME MINISTER: Go to every office till you find what he wants.

  Artillery.

MARSHAL: What is that noise?

PRIME MINISTER: Artillery.

The FOREIGN MINISTER *goes out.*

MARSHAL: Ours?

PRIME MINISTER: Theirs.

MARSHAL: Fifty-four millimetres?

PRIME MINISTER: A hundred and twenty millimetres.

MARSHAL: Technically inadvisable. The heat will melt the barrels.

PRIME MINISTER: Yes.

MARSHAL: How has their advance been conducted? And who is to blame for our difficulties?

The NURSE *approaches him.*

What do you want?

NURSE (*with a handkerchief*): Your nose is running, dear.

MARSHAL: Let it run! And it isn't running anyway . . .

[100]

NURSE: You don't want to look dirty, do you?

MARSHAL: I don't look dirty.

NURSE: You do at the moment.

MARSHAL: I don't.

NURSE: You can't see yourself.

MARSHAL: Call me "sir".

NURSE: Sir.

MARSHAL: Very well then.

The NURSE *blows the* MARSHAL'S *nose for him.*

There. Now, where were we?

Suddenly he sees the GIRL, *who is huddled up, her head in her hands.*

What is that person doing here?

The PRIME MINISTER *registers impatience.*

NURSE: It's your daughter, dear.

MARSHAL: Nurse!

NURSE: It's your daughter, sir.

MARSHAL: My daughter? Impossible. I sent her to the country.

PRIME MINISTER: I thought we had decided——

The NURSE *beckons him to be silent. He walks impatiently to the window to watch the distant bombardment.*

MARSHAL: What is the meaning of this insubordination?

Slowly the GIRL *looks up at her father with a tear-drenched face.*

GIRL: I came back because I love you, father.

MARSHAL: That is no valid reason. You have always loved me, yet you have always obeyed me. Where is your fiancé? I never can remember his name. Only his rank. He's a Major, isn't he? Acting Major?

GIRL (*toneless*): Yes. Acting Major . . .

MARSHAL: Where is he?

GIRL: Somewhere. At the front.

MARSHAL: You're lying to me.

GIRL: What?

MARSHAL: I always know where you're lying.

GIRL (*quiet. Ashamed*): He's gone away.

MARSHAL: Deserted!

GIRL: Gone away. By aeroplane. For . . . for patriotic reasons . . .

PRIME MINISTER: Oh, I see . . .

GIRL: By now he's gone away. With the General.

MARSHAL: With whom?

GIRL: With the . . . Lieutenant . . .

MARSHAL: Lieutenant?

GIRL: Who was here just now.

MARSHAL: And where have they gone to?

GIRL: To our allies.

MARSHAL: Which allies? (*Irritated, to the* PRIME MINISTER.) What allies have we got?

PRIME MINISTER: Those who have since become our enemies.

GIRL: That's not true.

MARSHAL: And your fiancé has gone there? Then you're not to marry him!

GIRL: I am in love with him.

MARSHAL: No longer. You will marry someone else. Someone reliable.

GIRL: I am not in love with anyone else.

MARSHAL: You will be. You will fall in love with whom I tell you. It's an absolute outrage. (*Suddenly tender.*) And you came here for consolation?

GIRL: I came here because it was my duty.

MARSHAL: A woman's duty is in the home.

GIRL: My duty is to save you.

MARSHAL: Save me?

GIRL: I could have gone with my future husband. I would have gone with him——

MARSHAL: What does that mean? If I were dead, eh? And you didn't feel the weight of my moral strength, eh? An all-pervading power, the teaching of a rigid but kindly parent.

PRIME MINISTER: May I intervene?

MARSHAL: No. In fact, you will have to leave the room if you persist in interrupting.

He sees the GIRL *struggling with her tears.*

Why are you crying? Don't try to hide your face from me. Nobody can hide anything from me. Nurse, there's a real use for your handkerchief now.

The GIRL *brushes the* NURSE *aside.*

GIRL (*fiercely*): Listen, father. My lover, the one man I will ever love, has left me. I will never see him again. I did this because he can look after himself, while you can't. Ever since I can remember I have looked after you, visited you daily, brought you your favourite plums from your orchard, brought you magazines and books of military history, kept the deaths of your old comrades from you so that you might not be upset. I have done everything I could, to the point of risking my own happiness. My fiancé bore with my daily absence, because he realized my position, he knew I had no choice. And he respected your achievements. Now I have thrown away my future, discarded my happiness, not only to look after you, but because you need me. I don't regret my choice, but I didn't make it just in order to take orders from you. I made it so that I could give you orders!

MARSHAL (*suddenly pathetic*): Don't be too hard on me, my darling.

GIRL (*tender, unsurprised*): I'm not being hard on you . . .

MARSHAL: Age is a terrible nightfall, like blindness, and my heart still has the steady beat of youth. Death has evaded me. The bullets killed my friends. They left me to breathe, and that was cruel of them. Even when the last of my comrades was passing peacefully into a new youth in some kinder world, I was left behind, fighting a lonely rear-guard action before the tomb. Daily . . . daily . . . by the minute, I await my orders. The reward of my patience has been silence. And there's not much else to lighten the burden of this ancient sentinel . . . just you, my darling . . . a little present which came to me so late in life . . . the strange surprise of your dear mother . . . a surprise and a sacrifice . . . in spite of what the doctors told her, she was determined . . . and her determination cost her her life . . . she never lived to know that you were not the boy she hoped for, for my sake . . . I never had the heart to tell her that I was praying for a girl . . . there it is . . . we humans suffer for each other more gracefully and more nobly than we suffer for ourselves . . .

GIRL (*hardly audible*): Why don't you always talk like that?

MARSHAL: I do!

The GIRL *shakes her head negatively.*

(*With a rebirth of truculence.*) I am a man with a heart. Anything I do, I do for the best.

GIRL: No . . .

MARSHAL (*annoyed*): What do you want me to do?

GIRL: Live . . . as you have lived . . . in retirement . . .

MARSHAL (*strident*): Die, that's what you really mean, don't you? Die. That is the news you're most longing to hear. "The Marshal passed away quietly in his sleep last night." Then you will wear mourning with relief, and flirt with your paramour through the mocking drapery of black veils. (*Afterthought.*) It really is scandalous how attractive women look in black.

GIRL (*expressionless*): I don't want you to die.

MARSHAL: Eh? What do you want then?

GIRL: I want you to resign.

MARSHAL: Resign? Resign what?

GIRL: Resign yourself to the nightfall . . .

MARSHAL: Die! You do mean die, damn you. You want me to stare at the ceiling in silent supplication, peopling that horrible room in the home with shadows, eating, dreaming, and sleeping memories. No! Finally and irrevocably no! I am too young for that. My whole life has been a great and splendid belligerency. I shall go in a thunder-clap, shouting an order. There will be no more breath. That's how I will go!

PRIME MINISTER (*drily*): The artillery fire is closer.

MARSHAL: Do you hear that? The menace grows. The nation has called on its greatest soldier. Dare you, a mere girl, graced by hazard with a celebrated name, ask me to defy the voice of an ancient people? What? Listen. There is the sound of your conscience, hammering on our ears! Our treacherous allies are approaching!

GIRL (*loud*): You don't know the facts!

MARSHAL (*terrible*): The facts are clear! *All* the facts!

The FOREIGN MINISTER *enters.*

FOREIGN MINISTER: There is not a single india-rubber left.

PRIME MINISTER: They have all been evacuated.

MARSHAL (*suddenly showing signs of strain*): Bring the maps here . . . now . . . I want complete silence while I study them . . .

There is a very long pause. The MARSHAL *makes notes on the maps. The* GIRL *stares at the* PRIME MINISTER, *with undisguised hatred, a fact which seems to amuse him. The* FOREIGN MINISTER *stands like a ramrod, expecting his new instructions. The* NURSE *looks at her aged charge with slight concern. The* MARSHAL *falls asleep. An elderly* MAN *in a tattered raincoat appears at the door. His coat and trilby are wringing wet. He carries a flash camera.*

PRIME MINISTER: Ah! The photographer. Marshal. (*With some alarm.*) What's the matter?

NURSE (*calm*): Nothing. The poor dear's exhausted himself. He sleeps nearly twenty hours a day, you know.

PRIME MINISTER: May I wake him up, or will you do it?

NURSE: I don't like to.

GIRL: Leave him alone.

PRIME MINISTER: It's absolutely imperative.

GIRL: Why?

PRIME MINISTER (*to the* PHOTOGRAPHER): We want a good photograph of the Marshal with a look of great determination on his face. He should be examining the maps, don't you think—or writing—or just looking in the lens. What would you say is the most effective in your experience? Remember, we want to inspire a feeling of confidence in the nation.

PHOTOGRAPHER: Well, I should think a solo portrait's the thing. I mean, we'd better not have any members of the Cabinet in the picture if we want to inspire confidence.

PRIME MINISTER: Oh, quite. I agree. (*Sharp.*) Why did you say that?

PHOTOGRAPHER: Can I have some more light?

PRIME MINISTER: Certainly.

The FOREIGN MINISTER *switches all the lights on.*

You haven't answered my question.

PHOTOGRAPHER: I don't answer questions, sir. I ask them, with my camera. The assistant editor usually answers them.

PRIME MINISTER: To your satisfaction?

PHOTOGRAPHER: We'd better have him awake now, please, sir, or we'll miss the first editions.

PRIME MINISTER: They can publish the evening papers earlier to-morrow. When can we get the picture into the afternoon press?

PHOTOGRAPHER: We go to bed at noon.

PRIME MINISTER: I'll ring the Editors. Nurse, wake the Marshal.

The NURSE *begins to shake the* MARSHAL *gently.*

(*To the* PHOTOGRAPHER.) I want to ask you a question. Perhaps you will make an exception on this exceptional occasion, and answer it.

PHOTOGRAPHER (*adjusting his camera*): I don't know, sir.

PRIME MINISTER: You are a very famous press photographer, and also a man in the street. The only man in the street left, in fact. In your opinion, will this picture, given enormous publicity and size, have the desired effect?

PHOTOGRAPHER: I don't know what effect you want, sir. Tragic, comic, a bit of both?

PRIME MINISTER: Inspirational, of course.

PHOTOGRAPHER: That's up to the assistant editor, as I said, sir. I have no mind, only eyes.

The MARSHAL *has woken noisily.*

[105]

MARSHAL: What? Leave me alone . . .

PRIME MINISTER: Wake up, sir. Wake up. It's for your photograph.

MARSHAL: Where am I? Nurse! I dreamt I was . . . no, I won't tell you. You'll scold me.

NURSE: No, I won't, dear. Not to-day.

MARSHAL: Why not?

NURSE: Because it's Tuesday.

MARSHAL (*nods in satisfaction at this observation*): I dreamt I was called upon to lead the nation in a moment of some obscure anxiety.

PHOTOGRAPHER: Look this way please, sir.

MARSHAL: Is it lentils for supper?

PRIME MINISTER: Nurse, can he look fierce?

NURSE: I'll try, but you'll have to be quick.

PHOTOGRAPHER (*resigned*): I'm ready.

He crouches professionally.

NURSE: No, no lentils, dear.

MARSHAL: Why not? I asked for them.

NURSE: I forgot.

MARSHAL: Forgot? What is there?

NURSE: Cabbage-au-gratin.

MARSHAL: Cabbage! You know I can't bear it.

NURSE: It's good for you.

MARSHAL: Good for me? How dare you! (*Banging his fist blearily on the table.*) A soldier could be shot for such disobedience!

There is a flash.

PHOTOGRAPHER: It's in the bag.

The GIRL runs precipitately out of the room. The MARSHAL falls asleep again.

PRIME MINISTER: Congratulations.

PHOTOGRAPHER: Another lie.

PRIME MINISTER (*sharply*): What did you say?

PHOTOGRAPHER (*smiles*): I told you, sir. I don't answer questions . . .

CURTAIN

[106]

ACT II

Same room. The next morning. Light streams in through the window.

The PRIME MINISTER *is in his morning suit, with a sash of office across his shirt, but is shaving in an ornamental mirror with an electric razor. The* FOREIGN MINISTER *is walking about nervously, unkempt, ill-looking.*

PRIME MINISTER: I wish you'd stop walking around. Can't you sit down somewhere?

FOREIGN MINISTER: No. Surely I'm not getting in your way.

PRIME MINISTER: I keep seeing you in the mirror, and it's distinctly annoying.

FOREIGN MINISTER: Can I borrow that razor after you?

PRIME MINISTER: I doubt whether you'll have time . . . and then, I'm a little particular about lending my personal toilet articles.

FOREIGN MINISTER: Listen . . .

There is a metallic clatter.

Their tanks are passing through the streets.

PRIME MINISTER: I don't know why you should sound surprised.

FOREIGN MINISTER: I'm just overwhelmed.

PRIME MINISTER: You knew about our retreat. Their advance was only to be expected. What is there to be overwhelmed about?

FOREIGN MINISTER: You are quite incredible. How can you be so calm?

PRIME MINISTER: A state of calm preserves your energy, and enables you to go on being calm without undue effort.

FOREIGN MINISTER: What are those injections you take?

PRIME MINISTER: A mild stimulant, to prevent the calm becoming inherent in my character.

FOREIGN MINISTER: I don't understand.

PRIME MINISTER: Well . . . women find an excess of calm disappointing.

FOREIGN MINISTER: That again . . .

PRIME MINISTER: What do you mean, "that again"? You never think ahead. You spend your private as well as your public life in a continuous state of surprise. I should really have left you at the Ministry of Justice.

[107]

FOREIGN MINISTER: What?

PRIME MINISTER: You bother to do the conventional thing, probably under the influence of a vaguely aristocratic name. You settle down. You have a wife and six children. The seed, which is not older than anybody else's, but just identifiable for a longer way back—the seed is now safely propagated into the bodies of your three sons, and also, although this is negligible and beside the point, into the bodies of your three daughters. It is like the game that children play. They stand in a circle and pass a ring round on a string. The child in the centre of the circle has to see the ring on its journey from hand to hand, and then he is liberated, and another child takes his place. The ring has passed through your hands safely. You have passed it on— but where to? Has it been seen? Has it been discovered? Will the line, the carefully recorded line, now pass into extinction?

FOREIGN MINISTER (*pale*): What do you mean?

PRIME MINISTER: Where is your family now, in this chaos? Is the seed safe? Is the aristocratic name still in being?

FOREIGN MINISTER (*shocked.*) Please!

PRIME MINISTER: Yes, but you never foresee things. I have a name which is probably the fourth or fifth most common in the country. I have no children—nothing to lose. The seed is dissipated—it is without value, intrinsic or otherwise. At my death, the name will be carried on relentlessly like a tide by butchers, bakers, tinkers and tailors. I am lucky. I am not sentimental in an impersonal way. I foresee things. I brought an electric razor, a formal suit and some sandwiches from home two days ago because I foresaw this. You left home, kissed your wife and six children goodbye, and informed the cook that you would be dining at seven-thirty.

FOREIGN MINISTER: We never dine before eight-fifteen.

PRIME MINISTER: There you are. I am a vagrant, a man unhypnotized by the false stability of a noble name and a pleasant family circle, and that is the secret of my calm. To me, this is a phase in an endless manoeuvre; to you, it is the end of a story. (*Afterthought.*) I pity you—and that is why I let you share my sandwiches.

FOREIGN MINISTER (*numb*): Thank you.

Pause.

PRIME MINISTER: I'm sorry about the razor.

FOREIGN MINISTER: That's all right.

Pause.

It's too late to die now.

PRIME MINISTER (*putting the razor away*): It's always too late or too early to die. In all my experience, I have never known anybody die at precisely the right time.

There is a clatter on the stairs.

FOREIGN MINISTER: What's that?

PRIME MINISTER: A little natural dignity now.

FOREIGN MINISTER: My hand is trembling.

PRIME MINISTER: Hold the back of the chair.

Pause. Raucous voices.

FOREIGN MINISTER: Shall I call them in?

PRIME MINISTER: You will stand absolutely still.

FOREIGN MINISTER: But they may shoot on sight.

PRIME MINISTER: In that case you will have been wrong about it being too late to die.

The door opens slowly. A grim, uniformed MAN, *armed with a revolver, looks cautiously into the room. He is covered with the dust of battle. As soon as he sees the* PRIME MINISTER, *he calls back.*

VICTOR: Two men by the door. Leave us. I have found what I wanted.

Military orders. The VICTOR *closes the door, and enters slowly.*

I seem to recognize you from the newspapers.

PRIME MINISTER: May I return the compliment, and add that your photographs hardly do you justice.

VICTOR: Thank you.

PRIME MINISTER: Won't you sit down? You must be tired.

VICTOR: Not particularly.

PRIME MINISTER: A subtle way of insulting our resistance to your troops.

VICTOR: It was, in fact, a surprisingly easy campaign.

PRIME MINISTER: For us also. The only strain imposed on us was the successful maintenance of a high average speed on our retreat.

FOREIGN MINISTER: Please!

VICTOR: From that you may imagine the strain imposed on us by the rapidity of our advance.

PRIME MINISTER: Quite. Oh, by the way, this is my ex-Minister of Foreign Affairs.

VICTOR (*bowing*): Honoured. Ex?

PRIME MINISTER (*smiling*): Yes. We are all "Ex".

VICTOR: Is there no Government left, then?

[109]

PRIME MINISTER: Why do you need a Government now?

VICTOR: To ensure internal stability behind our lines.

PRIME MINISTER: Exactly. But what are your terms?

VICTOR: Unconditional surrender.

PRIME MINISTER: Followed by unconditional subservience.

VICTOR: It depends . . .

PRIME MINISTER: On what?

VICTOR: On your acceptance of our terms.

PRIME MINISTER: And if we bargain?

VICTOR: You are in no position to bargain.

PRIME MINISTER: A nation with a large population is always in a position to bargain.

VICTOR: I don't follow you. You are defeated.

PRIME MINISTER (*smiling*): Therein lies our strength.

VICTOR: Come, come. Paradox can be pushed too far.

PRIME MINISTER: Not among the intelligent. You are still at war.

VICTOR: Of course.

PRIME MINISTER: We are not.

VICTOR: Then you do surrender unconditionally?

PRIME MINISTER: How can we if there is no responsible government with whom to sign an agreement? You hoped to inherit a disciplined community, which would run itself obediently as your lines of communication stretched across it. Instead you have inherited chaos. Forty million of unpredictable and undisciplined and embittered people without leadership. That I relegate to you with pleasure. Take it. There is no one to stop you. Make sense out of the turmoil of files, identity cards, lost army units, escaped criminals, put it in order with the handful of men at your disposal.

VICTOR: Handful? We have an army of millions.

PRIME MINISTER: For the prosecution of the war. Not for the internal administration of an occupied country. I can assure you from past experience that this nation is difficult enough to run with everything apparently in order. I wish you luck if you try to run it as it is—without a full comprehension of our foibles or traditions. Go ahead.

Pause.

VICTOR: This is an intolerable situation. It is unthinkable that a people so utterly defeated can haggle with a people so triumphantly victorious.

Slight pause.

I believe, however, that you have overlooked the possibility of sheer brutality. Cruelty is a powerful argument in the face of obstinacy.

PRIME MINISTER: Yes, admittedly. Cruelty is certainly a method of uniting a nation . . . although sometimes the results of such a unity are a little unforeseen.

VICTOR: Have you considered the effect, not of indiscriminate cruelty, but of setting an example?

PRIME MINISTER: I don't follow you.

VICTOR: If I were to have the two of you shot.

PRIME MINISTER (*smiling*): That would, admittedly, give rise to great pleasure in the nation, as we are both extremely unpopular, but it would be forgotten in five minutes. We are a people which elects governments simply in order to oppose them. You will quickly discover that.

VICTOR: If I drew my revolver now, you don't think that that might have the effect of changing your minds?

PRIME MINISTER: Do you mean, if you threatened us personally?

VICTOR: Yes.

PRIME MINISTER (*laughing*): Your precipitate entry into this room only just prevented us from committing suicide—and in any case, we are the servants of our own constitution. There are our resignations on the table. We cannot be reinstated without elections.

VICTOR: These resignations could be destroyed.

PRIME MINISTER: Yes, except for the fact that they are carried in all to-day's provincial papers.

VICTOR: I see. Well, I must congratulate you on your extreme sangfroid.

PRIME MINISTER: And impertinence?

VICTOR: And impertinence.

PRIME MINISTER (*consolingly*): I know, I know.

   Slight pause.

And now perhaps you are willing to listen to our terms.

VICTOR: What?

PRIME MINISTER: Yes, we have terms to suggest to you.

VICTOR: But . . . just a moment . . .

PRIME MINISTER: Certainly. Take a little time to recover from your surprise.

VICTOR: You have been extremely clever so far. Don't annoy me now.

PRIME MINISTER: Business men are not easily annoyed.

VICTOR: I am a soldier.

PRIME MINISTER: I am a politician, but at the moment we are both business men, buying and selling.

VICTOR: I don't understand you. I am used to plain speech. I am used to facts. You have terms to propose to me, and yet you have just told me you are not in a position to arbitrate.

PRIME MINISTER: A subtle point, but I must admit that we have not quite burned our boats. We could have a successor if you are willing to listen to reason.

VICTOR: What do you want of me?

PRIME MINISTER: Speaking on behalf of a possible authority, I demand the restitution of national authority over all national territories.

VICTOR: In other words, you want a situation exactly as it was before we—em—before you attacked us.

PRIME MINISTER: Surely you are not a victim of your own propaganda? You attacked us. Come on, you can admit it here. You are among enemies.

VICTOR: Such a demand is ridiculous.

PRIME MINISTER: There is no need to get angry. As a business man, I want the earth, but am quite satisfied with half of it.

VICTOR: It must be recognized at the outset that you are a defeated nation.

PRIME MINISTER: On paper. It cannot be denied, however, that you are not exactly victorious. Go on, prosecute your war, drive your trains and trucks and tanks through thousands of square miles of disorganized territory. Try to maintain your celebrated discipline in the face of sabotage and, well, deliberate negligence.

Pause.

VICTOR: I will not conceal the fact that we will invite your co-operation.

PRIME MINISTER: At a price.

VICTOR: What price?

PRIME MINISTER: Our sovereignty.

VICTOR: Impossible.

Pause.

PRIME MINISTER: Clever business men meet each other half way.

VICTOR: What do you suggest?

PRIME MINISTER: Give us half our country. Use the sections most useful to you. Guarantee your lines of communication.

Pause.

[112]

VICTOR: And if we ask you for troops?

PRIME MINISTER: We have fought and lost.

VICTOR: You can still win.

PRIME MINISTER: If we still wished to win, we would still be fighting.

VICTOR: Where?

PRIME MINISTER: With our allies.

VICTOR (*laughs*): To what end?

PRIME MINISTER: To satisfy our sense of morality.

VICTOR: You don't think we'll win?

PRIME MINISTER: Personally, I consider your victory likely—but I am not so convinced of the advantages of victory.

VICTOR: Why not?

PRIME MINISTER: Well, look what has happened here this morning. The victor invariably has a bad conscience, and loses his initiative. A man fights better with his back to the wall.

VICTOR: Would you refuse to furnish troops as a condition for our leniency?

PRIME MINISTER: We are not able to accept conditions. It is you who must do that. Our surrender is due to our desire for peace, and for the prevention of further bloodshed.

VICTOR: Unless we have troops from you, we will occupy the entire country by force of arms.

PRIME MINISTER: Then our discussion is at an end. Kindly arrange for a firing squad for us immediately.

> *Pause.*

VICTOR: Just a moment. I will make you a concrete offer, subject to confirmation by my government. For fifteen divisions, two of them mechanized, we will give you a free zone of one thousand square kilometres.

PRIME MINISTER: I'm sorry.

FOREIGN MINISTER: But . . .

VICTOR: Twelve divisions.

PRIME MINISTER: No.

VICTOR: Then there is no more to be said.

PRIME MINISTER: Now I have a counter-proposal.

VICTOR: Well?

PRIME MINISTER: Our zone will be neutral as far as international status is concerned.

VICTOR: Impossible. There must be a guarantee of your supporting our cause.

PRIME MINISTER: Unofficially, I agree. What I am able to offer in return for our zone is the wholehearted collaboration of our factories, of our rolling-stock, and of all branches of the civil service, including, I may add . . . police.

VICTOR: Well . . .

PRIME MINISTER: But no troops of any description. Civilian technicians, but no troops. I am sure you are intelligent enough to realize that in our present state of mind, our industry is worth ten times more than any number of divisions.

Pause.

VICTOR: But you have stated yourself that the country is hard to control. What guarantee have we that you will be able to respect any contract into which we may enter?

PRIME MINISTER: By instituting a benevolent dictatorship—not military—but pastoral, domestic, simple-minded, one which calls on the people to exercise simple virtues, naïveté, love of babies, faith in the soil and in the seasons.

VICTOR (*grunting*): You evidently know your people better than I, but it seems a vaguely preposterous programme for such a sublimely cynical and civilized race.

PRIME MINISTER (*sad*): We need a decade in a sanatorium. We need rest, and childish thoughts.

VICTOR: Can one impose such horribly virtuous things?

PRIME MINISTER (*smiling*): You seem to like us.

VICTOR: We have always admired you, and envied you. We indulge ourselves in militantly pastoral sentiments. With us such a plan would be easy. But with you——? What guarantee can you give me that such a benevolent dictatorship would work?

PRIME MINISTER (*ringing the bell*): By placing at the head of it a man the nation respects.

VICTOR: Does it respect anyone? Has it anyone worthy of respect?

PRIME MINISTER: Yes.

VICTOR: Who?

PRIME MINISTER: A ghost. A ghost living among the pages of the history book. An institution. A monument. An unfilled grave.

The door opens, and the MARSHAL *is wheeled in by the* NURSE.

VICTOR: Good God! The Marshal!

[114]

MARSHAL: Eh? I know your face. The uniform is wrong. An enemy uniform.

PRIME MINISTER: Don't you remember——?

MARSHAL: Silence. Who are you?

PRIME MINISTER (*sighing*): I was the Prime Minister.

MARSHAL: How long ago?

PRIME MINISTER: Yesterday.

MARSHAL: Oh, recently. Yes, I remember. It was you who continuously woke me up—kept me awake with your chatter. Nurse.

NURSE: Yes, dear.

MARSHAL: A peppermint.

NURSE: There you are.

MARSHAL: Now, who is this enemy?

PRIME MINISTER: Don't you remember, I told you. Our allies let us down. Went over to the enemy.

MARSHAL: No.

PRIME MINISTER: Don't say you've forgotten.

MARSHAL: I never forget. Of course I remember. Our allies went over to the enemy.

PRIME MINISTER: And the enemy came over to us.

MARSHAL: Ah. Wise of them. We are the only constant factor in the dirty game of politics.

PRIME MINISTER: Exactly. Now we must help them as we can.

MARSHAL: Help them? That's no way to talk. Let them help us, and we'll see they're rewarded.

PRIME MINISTER: The precision of your thoughts is amazing.

MARSHAL: I know.

PRIME MINISTER: Now this General has come here to collaborate with us, and to discuss the military situation with you.

MARSHAL: I am not in the habit of discussion. That suggests equality. Either my orders are obeyed, or they are disobeyed. The penalties for disobedience are severe.

VICTOR (*to the* FOREIGN MINISTER): It's a heart-breaking sight.

FOREIGN MINISTER: Heart-breaking? No. Ennobling.

VICTOR: The greatest soldier of his generation.

MARSHAL (*to the* VICTOR): Come forward, young man. When did we meet?

VICTOR: We have never met, Your Excellency.

[115]

MARSHAL: You're lying. I can always tell when a man is lying.

Pause.

Out with it. Where was it?

VICTOR (*faltering*): On the Armistice Commission, Your Excellency.

MARSHAL: When?

VICTOR: Twenty-one years ago.

MARSHAL: On a paddle-steamer?

VICTOR: Yes, the Armistice was signed on a river steamer.

MARSHAL (*piercingly*): Painted white?

VICTOR: Yes.

MARSHAL: With an oak-lounge?

VICTOR: Yes.

MARSHAL: And brass fittings?

VICTOR: Yes.

MARSHAL: And the smoke from the funnel crept under the door, until we were all coughing?

VICTOR: Yes.

MARSHAL: We defeated you then by the force of our arms, and don't ever forget it. Your deployment of cavalry was faulty. Your use of ground frequently imbecile. Your creeping barrages wasteful. Your employment of asphyxiating gas, deplorable. If, now, you wish to fight by our side, you will have to prove your worth before I place your troops in positions of responsibility. Your officers must pass our standard of Staff examinations before I even discuss strategy with them.

VICTOR (*quiet*): I don't think you fully appreciate the situation, Your Excellency.

MARSHAL: What was that? What did he say? A deliberate lie, if I remember rightly, followed by outright insurrection! Leave the room, sir.

VICTOR (*to the* PRIME MINISTER): I will communicate your proposals to my government.

PRIME MINISTER: What do you anticipate its reaction will be?

VICTOR: I cannot say.

MARSHAL: Did you hear me, young man?

VICTOR: Yes, Your Excellency. I just have a few points to discuss with the Prime Minister.

MARSHAL: Very well, if you won't leave the room, I will. Ah, if only I was the master of my own body. Nurse, wheel me out. Out of this ghastly atmosphere of insubordination.

The NURSE *looks appealingly at the* PRIME MINISTER, *who authorizes the move. The* NURSE *wheels the* MARSHAL *out.*

PRIME MINISTER (*to the* FOREIGN MINISTER): You had better accompany him. Calm him down. Flatter him.

FOREIGN MINISTER: Very well. (*Intimately, to the* PRIME MINISTER.) Congratulations. Masterly.

PRIME MINISTER (*friendly*): Thanks.

The FOREIGN MINISTER *goes.*

Pause.

Well?

VICTOR: I am a soldier, Mr Prime Minister.

PRIME MINISTER: Yes, soldiers never tire of saying that.

VICTOR: I have seen every sort of horror on the field of battle, but I can honestly say I have never seen anything more shattering than what you have shown me just now. It was, as you said, a ghost. But can a ghost hold a nation together?

PRIME MINISTER: There are two kinds of dictator, the one who goes from balcony to balcony shouting his wares, and the one who never appears at all. With all due respect, I believe the second to be the more compelling variety.

VICTOR: I must ignore the insinuation, but I see your point.

PRIME MINISTER: He must appear to the nation only in photographs. After all, he is, as you admit, a legend. Legends invariably disappoint when they become tangible and visible. He, in common with all the great figures of history, carries more conviction as a byword.

VICTOR: That is a very sweeping generalization.

PRIME MINISTER: I believe it to be quite valid. If Julius Caesar were to walk in now, we would quickly recover from our surprise, because he would begin to bore us to distraction reminiscing about the Gallic Wars.

VICTOR: I would not be bored.

PRIME MINISTER: But then you, after a successful military career, must be fairly impervious to boredom. What if Leonardo da Vinci walked in?

VICTOR: I would be bored.

PRIME MINISTER: There. I chose my examples carelessly. At all events, you know what I mean.

[117]

VICTOR: I understand. Naturally, before I can confirm even a temporary arrangement, I must consult my superiors.

PRIME MINISTER: If our telephones no longer work, it is your fault.

VICTOR: We work by radio.

> *The* GIRL *enters, calm and sad, carrying a basketful of plums and some newspapers.*

PRIME MINISTER: Good morning, my dear. I hope you managed to get some sleep in spite of everything.

GIRL: I didn't sleep. I drove to the country.

VICTOR: That was dangerous. After all, soldiers are only soldiers.

PRIME MINISTER: Oh, may I introduce? This is the Marshal's daughter.

VICTOR: Really? Delighted.

PRIME MINISTER: And this, my dear, is the Victor.

> *The* GIRL *looks at the* VICTOR *for a second, and then ostentatiously turns her back on him.*

You must wait for the treaty to be signed before you can expect a degree of civility. This is a timely indication of what you may expect if . . .

> *He shrugs his shoulders.*

VICTOR (*cold*): Such behaviour is ill-considered.

PRIME MINISTER: So, my dear fellow, was your attack on us.

VICTOR: We shall see.

> *The* VICTOR *goes to the door.*

PRIME MINISTER: May I call you back in a few minutes?

VICTOR: What for?

PRIME MINISTER: I have summoned a photographer. If all goes as we hope, it will be useful, in order to ensure the solidarity of our people, to have a picture for nationwide distribution of you shaking the Marshal by the hand.

VICTOR: And if my Government has other ideas?

PRIME MINISTER: You can still have the picture for yourself. I am sure you would treasure it. You have my word it will not be used without your permission. You may keep the negative.

VICTOR: We will see about that.

> *He goes out.*

PRIME MINISTER: Thank you . . .

> *Pause.*

[118]

You thought, no doubt, that your action would undermine my collaboration with the enemy. It so happened that it happily underlined a point I had been making.

GIRL: My actions are not as complicated as you always imagine. I turned my back on him because the sight of him made me feel sick.

PRIME MINISTER: That is quite understandable. Luckily for me, I have dealt all my life with people whose looks and actions would make any normal person sick. I'm used to them.

Pause.

Your actions are not complicated? Why did you drive to the country? It was an absurd risk.

GIRL: I went home.

PRIME MINISTER: And didn't stay there?

GIRL: I went home to fetch father some plums from the orchard.

PRIME MINISTER (*smiling*): Are his plums a matter of life and death?

GIRL: I will do everything to make him listen to me, until he stops playing his part in this horrible farce.

PRIME MINISTER: On the principle that the way to a man's heart is through his stomach?

GIRL: I have very few arguments. I must use them all.

PRIME MINISTER: You hope he will be touched by the risks you ran, and listen to you?

GIRL: There is a chance.

PRIME MINISTER: A slender one.

GIRL: Why do you say that?

PRIME MINISTER: Naturally, I can't pretend to know him as well as you do, but he seems to me the kind of man who takes personal heroism for granted. He also seems to me the kind of man who takes a regular supply of plums for granted. He would be surprised only if the daily gift-parcel was for some reason curtailed.

GIRL: The dice are loaded against me.

PRIME MINISTER: And for me. I never engage in any controversy unless I am sure that destiny is playing my game.

GIRL: Was it playing your game in the war?

PRIME MINISTER: The war was not a personal issue. I was forced into it by the public opinion of neighbouring countries. Treaties of Mutual Friendship always lead to disaster, just as Non-Aggression Pacts always lead to war.

GIRL: Where is my father?

PRIME MINISTER: He is being soothed. I should wait a little before you persuade him to retire.

GIRL: I'm a negligible opponent for you, aren't I?

PRIME MINISTER: For one reason only.

GIRL: What?

PRIME MINISTER: I can see and appreciate your point of view. You can neither see nor appreciate mine, and that puts you at a disadvantage.

GIRL: Your point of view is not my business.

PRIME MINISTER: But surely what I persuade your father to undertake is?

GIRL: I have no great logic to oppose yours. My only weapon is emotion.

PRIME MINISTER: You are a woman, after all.

GIRL: An inferior being.

PRIME MINISTER: Not at all. I envy your spontaneity and your sincerity . . . at the same time I'm quite glad I haven't got them.

GIRL: Sincerity would be difficult for a man in your position.

PRIME MINISTER: Difficult? No. Impossible.

GIRL: Yes. Yes, I suppose so.

PRIME MINISTER: But you are not entirely unsurprising.

GIRL: Why not?

PRIME MINISTER: In our extremely brief acquaintance, I have only known you as the epitome of a woman in distress. Speaking as a connoisseur, I would call you a classical example. Yesterday . . . no, a few hours ago . . . you were drenched with tears, incoherent, vulnerable . . . the sort of vision that brings out all the cruelty in a man. I thought I'd see you even more frantic to-day, if that were possible.

GIRL: You've noticed. I expected you to.

PRIME MINISTER: The initiative has passed to you. Unexpectedly. I congratulate you. What are you up to?

GIRL: I am calm.

PRIME MINISTER: I thought that was my prerogative.

GIRL: As I was driving back to the country, it suddenly occurred to me that my tears were preventing me from seeing the road properly.

PRIME MINISTER: And so?

GIRL (*forthright and deliberate*): So I stopped crying.

PRIME MINISTER (*after a momentary pause*): Now you are really beginning to worry me.

    The GIRL *smiles.*

[120]

And now you are even indulging in a smile.

GIRL: Yes. I am quite capable of smiling. I must have seemed to you one of those terrible drab creatures you get in modern literature, a colourless symbol signifying fate, or everlasting love, or just a question-mark buffeted by psychology. That is literature; I belong to life. And because I belong to life, I must obey my instincts, and fight bitterly, even hopelessly, against death.

PRIME MINISTER: I thought death would come into the argument before long.

GIRL: And you are thinking to yourself, "In spite of what she says, she has read too much. I can see traces of this book, of that film, in her attitude." And because you are unaccustomed to sincerity, because sincerity embarrasses you, you have an afterthought—"Even if she is play-acting, I must give her credit for play-acting extremely well."

PRIME MINISTER: I am glad to see that you don't suffer from modesty. It is the unhealthiest form of introspection.

GIRL: I am calm because the ship is sinking, and the cry has gone up—"Cabinet Ministers first!" I know I shall die, but it is my sacred duty to do what I can to live.

PRIME MINISTER: Deliciously complicated.

GIRL: Really? Can you doubt that we are done for?

PRIME MINISTER: Eventually we are all done for, inevitably—if by "done for" you mean death.

GIRL: Yes.

PRIME MINISTER: And that prospect makes you calm? You find a serenity in the idea of death, and ask me to believe that you consider it your sacred duty to try and live? Certainly the philosophy you have acquired in the last few hours does seem to smack of all that is best and most obscure in the modern drama.

GIRL: And it is so clear to me.

PRIME MINISTER: That is why you are so calm?

GIRL: Of course. My duty is suddenly completely simple. My man has gone away. He will never return. My place in the tragedy is assured.

PRIME MINISTER: You know the facts, and have laid aside your selfishness.

GIRL (*surprised*): Yes.

PRIME MINISTER (*reflective*): Hm. You have not only discovered your own philosophy. You have discovered mine.

GIRL: Yours?

[121]

PRIME MINISTER: Yes. I know the facts. I am not selfish. What is the point of being greedy when the future is condemned? The ship is sinking, as you say. It is a foolish man who covets his neighbour's belongings in these conditions. My intelligence prevents me from seeking my place in the sun. I have it in any case. That, like my part in the tragedy, is assured. When I die—and it will be soon—I will leave the life I know, and love—no, not love, enjoy, enjoy passionately—I will leave it in silence, unsurprised, without famous last words, without hatred or remorse, or a tedious admonition for those lucky enough to survive. I am hated alive and I will be hated dead. That is all I ask, and therefore there will be no recanting, no forgiveness will be asked, no religious comfort will be accepted. (*A sudden outburst.*) They are so selfish and so stupid, those who wish to be loved for themselves alone. You were like that yesterday, thinking only of yourself in relation to your fiancé, and, in moments of relative generosity, of him in relation to you. And the vast majority of people are like that all the time. They think of themselves, regretfully, hopefully, seriously, arrogantly—eternally. They think of their personal appearance, of the social position afforded them by their television sets, the quality of their motor cars, the type of schools they send their children to. And they fight for what they want with the desperation of hungry goldfish who can sense the shadow of the food bag thrown across the tiny world of their bowl. (*Cold again, and smiling.*) I am not like that. I am aloof and unselfish. I recognize my place in society, and I am calm. I stopped the war for their silly sakes, because you can't change human nature, and only unimaginative people like dictators try. I pander to their secret desires, and they will hate me for offering them the peace they so ardently wish for. I use the word "surrender", which is unforgivable. "Cessation of hostilities" is the fashionable phrase. The two mean the same, but I use the hated word—surrender—with relish. After all, I too have my pride.

> Pause.

Yes, I am doomed, and I know it, and my sacrifice will be commensurate with the dignity of life itself. I will enter the unknown with a private sense of nobility, for I am renouncing all that gives me pleasure . . . uncertainty, humour, wit . . .

GIRL: Cruelty. Love.

PRIME MINISTER (*surprised for a second. Then calm*): Yes, all that. I will be buried in a nameless grave, but I will not be alone. I shall have my integrity.

GIRL: Your satanic integrity . . .

PRIME MINISTER: Where would God be without the Devil? Where would the saints be without the sinners? How could morality exist

[122]

if there were no villains? Villains with integrity, not your mediocre evildoers, petty thieves, poison-pen writers, idiotic murderers, slanderers, share-pushers, the convertible, the opportunists who thrive on the street, who live on crowds—no, great proud villains in palaces. (*Smiles.*) Like me. (*Tender.*) I hope you understand. I am ambitious, because I have talent, a brain bursting with deeds and words which must be brought to life in my brief span on this earth. I would be rotten if I was virtuous. Virtue would have made of me a thoroughly disagreeable, hypocritical and untrustworthy character. It would have made me a failure, full of rancour. I prefer to be a successful villain, forthright, upright, without complexes. At the price of a superficial invention of the human race called "honour", I have saved millions of lives. They will thank me by killing me, and holding my name up in the classroom as a warning to naughty children. Those who still breathe, thanks to me, will in a few years flatter my memory by believing that I succeeded in penetrating to the farthest frontiers of perfidy. (*Pityingly.*) The fools.

GIRL: If it hadn't been for my father we would never have met. And yet you haven't mentioned his name once.

PRIME MINISTER: Why should I? He is the means to a most generous end. He is the tool, which, guided by my infinitely superior intelligence, has made our national salvation possible.

GIRL: He is still my father.

PRIME MINISTER: You cannot conserve your sentimentality if you wish to share my viewpoint.

GIRL (*quiet*): I don't.

PRIME MINISTER (*smiling*): I am not a bit surprised. My destiny allows me to brook no compromise. My fate is to be alone.

GIRL: And to be misunderstood.

PRIME MINISTER: Exactly.

GIRL: And you will be a villain because you touch the hearts of no one.

PRIME MINISTER: Once more, exactly. Ours is a story from which the world will derive no benefit. The world is too stupid.

GIRL: But it has a heart.

PRIME MINISTER: And so?

GIRL: It may be touched.

PRIME MINISTER: By whom?

GIRL: The puppet, not the puppeteer.

PRIME MINISTER (*prepared to laugh*): Your father?

[123]

GIRL: Of course.

The PRIME MINISTER *laughs.*

Yes, how can you expect the public to be moved by your abstractions? They can only understand and feel the doubts and convictions shared by all who are left in the mainstream of life. You are misunderstood because you want to be. The rest of us wish to be understood, father more than any. He will command their hearts, he is the chief character.

PRIME MINISTER (*sarcastic*): Who are the other stars in the tragedy?

GIRL: Myself, and perhaps—

The door opens, and the PHOTOGRAPHER *enters.*

PRIME MINISTER: Ah, at last. Forgive me, my dear, for having to put an end to a most enlightening conversation. Perhaps you will make a convert in my absence. Unfortunately my self-imposed duty forces me to leave you for a moment. (*To the* PHOTOGRAPHER.) I think this time we will have a group.

GIRL: In order to push yourself to the foreground in the evidence?

PRIME MINISTER (*shrugging his shoulders. Pleasant*): Well, after all, you may be right . . .

He goes. Pause, while the PHOTOGRAPHER *sets up.*

GIRL: Have you noticed a change in me?

PHOTOGRAPHER: Since when?

GIRL: Since yesterday, of course.

PHOTOGRAPHER: Oh, I thought you meant since you were a child.

GIRL: You didn't know me then.

PHOTOGRAPHER: Yes, I did. I saw you first at your christening. Lord, how I cursed you. The service went on for a small eternity, and it was pelting with rain. I remember turning to one of my colleagues, the man from the *Evening Announcer*, and remarking on the fact that aristocratic families gave their children too many names. It's unfair to everyone, the priest, who has to memorize a whole string of queer sounds that will never be used, the civil service, who have quite enough desk-work as it is, and the poor reporters shivering in the cold. How many names have you? Twelve, isn't it?

GIRL: Thirteen. My father had become superstitious in battle.

PHOTOGRAPHER: Thirteen? My memory's not what it was. Thirteen's an odd number for a superstitious man to choose.

GIRL: The old man's stubborn. He won't admit he's superstitious. His weakness takes the form of grimly walking under ladders, and generally a proud, unfruitful courtship of disaster. (*Cosily.*) Yes, I'm called Beatrice, after my mother; Marguerite, after my father's sister, who hated mother; Olivia, after a favourite mistress of my father's; Penelope, because he admired faithfulness in soldiers' wives; Brunhilde, because Wagner wrote the only music loud enough for him to appreciate; Mary, after the Virgin, because he's religious; Diana, after the goddess, because he believes that Christianity marked the end of disciplined civilization; Sabina, because he has an exaggerated idea of soldiers' privileges; Virginia, because the ideal of purity is sacred to him; Josephine, because he admired Napoleon's outflanking movements; Gloria, because he deserved a daughter with such a name; George, because I should have been a boy, and—there's one more I've forgotten—oh, yes, Cordelia—I don't know why—I suppose because I was a girl.

PHOTOGRAPHER: And your mother had no say in the matter?

GIRL: No. She was dead. Father had everything his own way, as usual.

PHOTOGRAPHER: Yes, of course, she was dead. Foolish of me. I was at the funeral. The sun was shining, and the umbrellas looked out of place.

GIRL: When did you next see me?

PHOTOGRAPHER: Let me think. My memory's not as good as it used to be. You won a gymkhana, jumping tiny fences on a pony the size of a wolfhound.

GIRL (*smiling*): Yes, father was furious that I was only a girl on that particular day. There were a lot of cavalry officers present.

PHOTOGRAPHER: Then there were occasions at the opera, of course, escorting Maggots.

GIRL: Maggots?

PHOTOGRAPHER: I'm sorry, but that's the press name for your father.

GIRL: That's very rude.

PHOTOGRAPHER: The press is very rude. And then there was one occasion quite recently, just before the disaster.

GIRL: Where?

PHOTOGRAPHER: I caught you in the park, walking . . .

GIRL: With my fiancé.

PHOTOGRAPHER: Yes . . .

GIRL: Did I look happy?

PHOTOGRAPHER (*after a slight pause*): Yes.

GIRL: I was.

    Pause.

GIRL (*very quiet*): Do you ever expect to see me happy again?

[125]

PHOTOGRAPHER: I never expect anything, and therefore I am never disappointed.

GIRL (*sincere*): That must be terrible.

PHOTOGRAPHER (*sincere*): It is . . .

> *The door opens. Outburst of conversation. The* MARSHAL *is pushed in by the* NURSE. *The* VICTOR *follows with the* PRIME MINISTER. *The* FOREIGN MINISTER *brings up the rear, and closes the door.*

All ready, sir?

PRIME MINISTER: Yes, now if we could place the Marshal in the centre, with His Excellency Our Conqueror on his right, shaking him by the hand . . . then I suggest that I go here, with the Foreign Minister on the Marshal's left. Nurse, could we wake the Marshal?

PHOTOGRAPHER: Just a minute, sir. What kind of picture do you want?

PRIME MINISTER (*a little irritated*): Use your initiative, man. We employ you because you're supposed to be an expert. I shouldn't have to tell you what to do.

PHOTOGRAPHER: I prefer pictures which are unrehearsed, sir.

PRIME MINISTER: Now, now, now, we really have no time for you to air your preferences.

> *The others are already in a group.*

PRIME MINISTER: I suggest . . . (*smiling to the* VICTOR.) . . . if you agree . . . that we take one shot which will show the public solidarity, determination, righteous indignation . . . (*Merrily, to the others.*) Are there any other ideas to help this good fellow out of his quandary?

VICTOR: Ruthlessness . . .

PRIME MINISTER: If you like.

FOREIGN MINISTER: Nobility.

PRIME MINISTER: Certainly . . . (*He looks at the* PHOTOGRAPHER.) You don't seem impressed.

PHOTOGRAPHER: I took a photograph some years ago of the Finance Minister who was later discovered embezzling State Funds.

PRIME MINISTER: There is no need to remind us of that. (*Sudden anger.*) Is that a criticism of us?

PHOTOGRAPHER: No. Not necessarily. He was a man of great personal popularity, and under instructions I photographed him in a way redolent of all those virtues you wish me to ascribe to your group. Later his crime was discovered, and the same noble photo was reproduced in the press to denounce him, little arrows pointing to features of his face which psychology had prescribed to be criminal. The grim stable jaw became kleptomaniac, the honest unswerving eyes became paranoiac, the lofty intellectual forehead, primitive, and all owing to the assistant editor's genius for journalism. You can so easily become his victims too.

PRIME MINISTER: The assistant editor seems to be your bogey, but we can allow ourselves the luxury of far more hideous bogeys. Don't forget, it is we who tell the editors what to do. It is only events which are occasionally disobedient.

The others in the group laugh and smile at the PRIME MINISTER'S *skill.*

PHOTOGRAPHER (*shrugging his shoulders*): As you wish.

PRIME MINISTER: Then, after that, we ought to have one demonstrating pleasure and happiness at our new alliance—just for safety. Nurse, will the Marshal be able to react in these two different ways?

NURSE (*smiling*): Well, sir, I was just hatching a rather naughty plot.

PRIME MINISTER (*amused*): Out with it then.

NURSE: I couldn't help noticing that the young lady has brought the plums as usual.

PRIME MINISTER: Yes.

NURSE: Well, if we were to deny him the plums at first, after showing him that they are in the basket, you would get your first mood, and then after that we can give him a plum, which would make him happy, and you'd have your second mood.

PRIME MINISTER: How do you think of these things, Nurse?

NURSE: Oh, sir, I've dealt with children all my life.

She goes to fetch the plums. The GIRL *rises silently, and goes out, taking the plums with her.*

PRIME MINISTER: You are not so skilled with adolescents.

NURSE (*upset*): Oh, sir, I don't know what he'll say. He expects his plums at this time every day.

PRIME MINISTER: He will be disappointed. A pity. But still, his disappointment will have its value. Now. Ready, Photographer? Nurse, wake the Marshal.

NURSE: Wake up, dear.

The MARSHAL *grunts.*

Wake up. Rise and shine.

MARSHAL: Hm? (*He yawns.*) Ghastly dream. One long cavalry charge for hours and hours. Never got to the enemy. Unfortunate. Still, mustn't grumble. (*He yawns again.*)

[127]

NURSE: Is there anything you want, dear?

MARSHAL (*after a moment of reflection*): Yes. A plum.

The NURSE *signals the* PHOTOGRAPHER *with one hand as the others freeze into heroic poses.*

NURSE: They haven't arrived, dear.

MARSHAL (*angry*): Haven't arrived?

The others all adopt grim and determined expressions. Suddenly the MARSHAL'S *mood changes. He smiles.*)

MARSHAL: Well, after all, plums won't win a war, will they?

The PRIME MINISTER *makes frantic signals to the others to change their expressions. They all break into smiles. The* VICTOR *grasps the hand of the beaming* MARSHAL. *There is a flash.*

PRIME MINISTER: How was that?

PHOTOGRAPHER: Excellent. The assistant editor will be delighted.

As the PRIME MINISTER *begins to stage-manage another grouping*
. . .

THE CURTAIN FALLS

ACT III

Four years later. The same room in the early hours of the morning. The placing of the actors and the circumstances enveloping them should strike the observer as being strongly reminiscent of the beginning of the play. The PRIME MINISTER *is about to take an injection. The* FOREIGN MINISTER *is weeping unashamedly. The* VICTOR *manifests impatience, though his face is deathly pale. Terrible tension under the sombre green lights.*

VICTOR: This hysterical behaviour will lead us nowhere.

FOREIGN MINISTER: Ssh!

    Pause.

VICTOR: What's the matter?

FOREIGN MINISTER: I thought I heard gunfire.

VICTOR: Nonsense. They're miles away.

FOREIGN MINISTER: There it is again! Not the high, sharp note of our artillery. The deeper rumble of theirs.

PRIME MINISTER: May I just crave a moment of silence while I actually take my injection? After four years I am still not quite used to the idea of it, and it needs a little courage.

VICTOR: Courage! Outside people are losing arms and legs, and you can talk of courage when you prick yourself with a hypodermic!

PRIME MINISTER: You forgot to mention that some of them are also losing their lives. (*He smiles.*)

FOREIGN MINISTER (*shocked*): Really, sometimes I think you have no heart.

    Slight pause.

PRIME MINISTER: How often have we had this conversation?

VICTOR: Never.

PRIME MINISTER: I was talking to my colleague. This situation may be new in your experience. It is not in ours.

VICTOR: It is deplorable. Entirely unforeseen.

PRIME MINISTER: Are you suggesting that you are surprised?

VICTOR: Surprised? I am thunderstruck, both by the situation, and by your inexplicable attitude.

PRIME MINISTER: You ought to be even more used to defeat than we are. After all, you lost the last time too. At least we have won one recent war.

[129]

VICTOR: That is an outrageous remark.

PRIME MINISTER: No, no. You don't really object to the remark, because tempers are frayed. In such times you are accustomed to people saying things they don't really mean. What you object to is my calm.

The VICTOR opens his mouth.

Cynical is the word you are about to use.

The VICTOR shuts his mouth.

Pause.

VICTOR: I wish my government had never listened to your appeals for clemency. We should have occupied this infernal country of yours. A reign of terror would have taught you a lesson. Death is the best deterrent to your damned national impertinence.

PRIME MINISTER (*smiling*): All you would have done is to raise our standard of living. Twenty million live more comfortably than forty million. No, if you had been really cruel, you would have destroyed our cathedrals, our castles, our historical monuments—blown every stone over a hundred years old into the air. That is what I should have done in your shoes.

VICTOR: Why?

PRIME MINISTER: Why, he asks. It would have been a blow from which we could never recover in time of peace. It would cripple us entirely. (*Sly.*) I don't believe you realize how much we rely upon our tourist industry. Our gastronomy, our artistic sense, in a way, our culture, are geared to that need. (*Afterthought.*) I hope that after your defeat my successor will have the sense to teach you that lesson. I hope they annihilate every edifice you hold dear, the tombs of your ancient kings, the portraits, the altar-pieces, the great fortresses that cling so desperately to their pinpoints of rock throughout your country—very beautiful they are—I do watercolours as a hobby. I am glad to note that a great many of your showplaces have already suffered under aerial bombardment.

FOREIGN MINISTER: That is an atrocious hope!

VICTOR: Whose side are you on, in any case?

PRIME MINISTER (*loud and comic*): My own!

VICTOR (*cold*): You are foolish to take our defeat for granted.

PRIME MINISTER: You are even more foolish not to take it for granted.

The FOREIGN MINISTER is weeping noisily.

How many gallons of tears can you have shed in the past five years?

FOREIGN MINISTER: You are a traitor!

PRIME MINISTER: And what are you? Of course you should have flown the country, with our patriotic generals. You should have gone then, and salved your personal conscience. But you were weak, so you listened to me. If I am a traitor, at least I have the courage of my lack of convictions. You are a traitor out of cowardice.

FOREIGN MINISTER: What did you say? (*Supreme effort.*) It is not too late to die with honour.

PRIME MINISTER: The flags are still there, waiting to decorate your repulsive martyrdom. Only is suicide worthwhile now? It is only an escape, a consummation of your cowardice. You listened to me, and you will be remembered as a national disgrace. Listen . . .

    Louder gunfire.

The guns are louder. Your tears are numbered.

    The VICTOR *consults his watch, as the* FOREIGN MINISTER *collapses on to a chair.*

VICTOR: The car will be here in five minutes. It would serve you right if we were to leave you behind.

PRIME MINISTER (*smiling*): As you wish. My part is played. Now it is only a question of time.

VICTOR: My personal aeroplane is only supposed to carry four. (*Thinks.*) Myself, the Pilot, the Marshal, the Foreign Minister . . . and then there's you.

PRIME MINISTER: You put yourself first.

VICTOR: I am of more value than the rest of you. I put the pilot second, for the same reason.

PRIME MINISTER: Leave us behind then. Take the Marshal's nurse and his daughter, if you have room.

VICTOR (*stiff*): It's an idea.

    Enter the MARSHAL'S DAUGHTER—*visibly older.*

PRIME MINISTER: Ah, I wondered if you'd turn up to put a climax to your endless pleading. There is no need. You have won the final battle. We two traitors are being left behind so that you and the nurse can accompany the Marshal.

VICTOR: You have no right to make decisions on my behalf.

PRIME MINISTER: I have a right to make a sacrifice.

GIRL: I don't want you to make that sacrifice. Graceful gestures do not suit you, and then, I wish to stay.

FOREIGN MINISTER: I shall stay too!

PRIME MINISTER (*sly*): And give up the fight while there is still hope?

FOREIGN MINISTER: You said yourself——

PRIME MINISTER: I am only a civilian. I have no right to make decisions on behalf of the military. You heard me being reprimanded. But I am sure His Excellency Our Conqueror holds out a high hope for our future. The less guns he disposes, the more convinced he is of final victory. That's what patriotism does for a man. I should plead with him if I were you. Plead for a seat in the aeroplane. Plead for standing room in the last ditch.

FOREIGN MINISTER: I will stay!

PRIME MINISTER (*tender*): You make me smile. (*To the* VICTOR.) Very well then, take the Marshal. Satisfy this young lady's pleading at last.

GIRL: No. My father must stay here.

PRIME MINISTER: What?

GIRL: He must stay, and pray for death as never before.

PRIME MINISTER: It is really extraordinary. The ship is sinking, as you so wisely said four years ago, and here we are with the water lapping at our ankles, demonstrating the most exquisite courtesy in front of the last lifeboat. "After you, after you."

GIRL: The lifeboat's leaking.

PRIME MINISTER: Yes.

VICTOR: The Marshal will return with us.

GIRL: As a hostage?

VICTOR (*shocked*): As an ally.

GIRL (*calm*): No, you must leave him here.

VICTOR: You doubt our victory?

GIRL: That is not the point.

VICTOR (*impatient, looking at his watch*): What is the point?

GIRL: He is growing younger by the hour. Responsibility gave him a new youth, and he is beginning, slowly, to understand.

VICTOR: Well?

GIRL: If he is to die, kindly, by nature, or cruelly, by a firing squad, at least let him die mad. If he discovers what you have done to him, the pain of humiliation will be too terrible to bear. I want a quick end for him, painless and unexpected.

VICTOR: I cannot agree that he is growing younger, or that there is any risk of a return to sanity.

The NURSE *enters, dressed for travelling.*

Ah, is he ready?

NURSE: Oh, sir, I'm so worried. I really will have to give up my

[132]

place, I think. I can't bear it. And he's so strong. Nearly broke my arm.

PRIME MINISTER: Why?

NURSE: I offered him a plum, and he seized the dish from my hands, and threw it on the ground. Then he crushed each fruit under foot, one by one, shouting and swearing, and then gripped my arm, and asked me if the plums were bribery. Well, I didn't know what he was talking about. Luckily he still forgets, and the train of thought went, and he let me go. But look at my wrist. Great red marks.

PRIME MINISTER (*slowly*): Asked you if the plums were bribery?

The MARSHAL *enters, walking slowly with the aid of a stick. He has recovered a deal of energy in his four years. Lengthy pause.*

MARSHAL (*slow and quiet*): I have lost my taste for them.

PRIME MINISTER: Taste? For what?

MARSHAL: Don't ask me questions? It is I who have ten years of questions to ask. It is I who must lose myself in a cloud of answers. Why, I ask you?

VICTOR: Why what, Your Excellency?

MARSHAL (*loud*): Why?

VICTOR: I don't understand.

MARSHAL (*very loud*): Why?

PRIME MINISTER: Is there anything you wish to know?

MARSHAL (*shouting*): Why? Why? Why? Why? Why?

Pause.

MARSHAL (*quiet*): You sit there like a photograph. Might as well cry out one's questions to a piece of paper. You have the eloquence of statues. Bad statues, commemorating ill-managed wars.

VICTOR (*clearing his throat*): If you are ready—the aeroplane is about to leave.

MARSHAL: Then let it leave. Let it fly backwards with its tail between its legs. A fate it deserves. It's like everything else. No stability, no solidarity, just plums and little acts of treachery.

PRIME MINISTER: And yet it has a heart of gold.

MARSHAL: Aeroplanes don't have hearts, they are too much like men. You must be mad if you think they have, and deserve nothing more than a destiny of endless flight.

VICTOR (*trying to change the subject*): Nurse, is everything ready?

MARSHAL: Everything is ready. Only the corpses of a tray of guilty fruit lie rotting and unburied. There's that to do.

VICTOR: Then let's go.

[133]

MARSHAL: Where to? Away? Here? There? (*Shouts again.*) Why? Why?

VICTOR: There is a reason.

MARSHAL: Explain it to me in the language you reserve for children. A B C D E F G and so forth.

VICTOR: Nurse——

MARSHAL: You explain. You. I don't need interpreters. My soldiers have always understood me, because I mingled with them in the trenches. I am great, because I trust nobody, and because they all trust me. You tell me.

VICTOR: Mr Prime Minister.

PRIME MINISTER (*smiling*): You tell him.

MARSHAL: An ally—and that's no compliment.

VICTOR: We must evacuate the capital.

MARSHAL: Why? Were my orders obeyed?

VICTOR: In . . . their broadest sense.

MARSHAL (*terrible*): To the letter?

VICTOR: Events took a hand.

MARSHAL: Yesterday you reported to me that victory was in sight.

VICTOR: It was, yesterday. To-day—it still is to-day.

MARSHAL: Did the Nineteenth Corps attack this morning?

VICTOR: Yes . . . no.

MARSHAL: Two answers are too many for one question.

VICTOR: Yes.

MARSHAL: And were the objectives reached?

VICTOR: No.

MARSHAL: Why not?

VICTOR: We were defeated.

MARSHAL: By what?

VICTOR: A . . . a superior body of the enemy.

MARSHAL: According to your reports there was no superior body of the enemy left.

VICTOR: We were surprised.

MARSHAL: By what?

VICTOR: We . . . miscalculated. Those responsible have been punished.

MARSHAL: And the 212th Division?

VICTOR: The battle's still in progress.

[134]

MARSHAL: What battle? I ordered you to withdraw them from the line.

VICTOR: . . . They could not disengage.

MARSHAL: Why not?

VICTOR: The enemy attack was pressed home with too great a vigour.

MARSHAL: What enemy attack?

VICTOR: Their surprise attack.

MARSHAL: What surprise attack?

VICTOR: They delivered a surprise attack.

MARSHAL: With what forces?

VICTOR: A division.

MARSHAL: On a front held by three of our divisions? And the 4th Army?

VICTOR: It is re-forming.

MARSHAL: Where?

VICTOR: Behind our lines.

MARSHAL: How far behind our lines?

VICTOR: Some kilometres.

MARSHAL: How many kilometres?

VICTOR: Eighty.

MARSHAL: Eighty? On the left or right flank of the armies?

VICTOR: . . . Right.

MARSHAL: How far to the right?

VICTOR: The extreme right.

MARSHAL: And yet yesterday the 4th Army was successfully fighting a battle of annihilation on the extreme left flank. In other words, an Army of four Army Corps, twelve divisions, thirty-six brigades, one hundred and eight thousand men with all their equipment, heavy guns, horses and mechanical contrivances was moved from the extreme left flank to the extreme right flank, a distance of nine hundred and seventeen kilometres, in the space of eight hours and forty-three minutes.

Tense pause. He continues with bitter sarcasm.

Organization has certainly improved since my day. I must congratulate you. And no doubt this extreme administrative brilliance accounts for the fact that whereas victory was assured yesterday, we are evacuating our capital to-day.

Another pause. Then the MARSHAL *shouts stridently.*

Lies!

[135]

VICTOR (*flushed*): Are you accusing me——?

MARSHAL: All of you. Everything. Lying to me. Smiling at each other. Winking. Murmuring in corners. The corners murmur back. They are your counsellors. They have seen more than you have. Corners, and curtains to shut out the daylight. The curtains are agents of darkness. They have eyes and ears.

VICTOR: Perfectly preposterous.

The PHOTOGRAPHER *appears for a moment from behind the curtains, picks up his camera which is lying on a table at the back, and vanishes behind the curtains again.*

MARSHAL (*desperate*): Tell me, have I died? And is this some revenge of a supreme power for my disbelief? Are we all dead? Why do I remember so many faces? Are my armies armies of ghosts?

VICTOR: I have no time to waste on this sort of nonsense. If any of you wish to accompany me, you may. Now is the moment to choose. I'm going.

MARSHAL (*barring his way*): You will answer my questions.

VICTOR: I do not understand your questions.

MARSHAL: Why? Why? Why? Isn't that enough?

VICTOR: You are beginning to irritate me, Your Excellency. Four years of this sort of conversation have told on my nerves.

MARSHAL (*terrible*): I do not irritate. I destroy or I cherish.

VICTOR: I feel——

MARSHAL: You have no authority to feel!

VICTOR: Kindly don't interrupt.

MARSHAL: I do not interrupt. I am constitutionally incapable of such a triviality. It is you—you who interrupt every time you ventilate your insipidity.

VICTOR: I am tired of this.

MARSHAL: I order you to keep quiet!

VICTOR (*losing his temper*): You listen to me! Lies, you said? Yes, of course, you are right. It is a game I was willing to play at the beginning, when I respected you, when I was hypnotized by the awful sight of greatness in decay. Now, I don't care, because you are a nuisance.

MARSHAL (*pale*): What did he say?

GIRL (*to* PRIME MINISTER): Are you going to allow this?

PRIME MINISTER (*unmoved*): It is the tragedy I invited.

NURSE: Oh dear, oh dear.

FOREIGN MINISTER (*to the* VICTOR): Are you not ashamed of yourself?

VICTOR (*furious*): Ashamed of myself? What the devil do you mean? How do you permit yourself such insolence? I am sane, and for four years I have been the slave of lunacy.

> *He kicks a pile of stacked boxes, which fall over, showering tin soldiers on the floor.*

For four ghastly years I have been watching him play with tin soldiers, moving them over the map, pretending to take his idiotic manoeuvres seriously, obeying his farcical orders, and all in the interests of internal concord. It is a job for a nurse, not for a soldier. And then to be asked imbecile questions! Where is the 212th Division? Here it is, Marshal, on the floor, with its tin head broken. (*He steps on a toy soldier.*) Where is the 4th Army? Here it is, Your Excellency, taking to its heels. (*He kicks some more tin soldiers.*) Where is the 19th Corps? Here you have it, sir—— (*He picks up some tin soldiers.*)— Exploded on a landmine!

> *He throws the tin soldiers into the air. As he does so, there is the flash of a magnesium bulb. The* VICTOR *stops dead.*

What was that? Where did it come from?

PRIME MINISTER (*urgently*): From here, from the curtains.

> *The* PHOTOGRAPHER *opens the window and vanishes on the ledge.*

VICTOR (*running over*): Stop him! Destroy the camera!

> *The* GIRL *places herself deliberately in the way of the* VICTOR.

Why did you stop me?

GIRL: How else can I protest?

MARSHAL (*who has picked up one or two soldiers. Heartbroken*): You have killed my soldiers . . .

VICTOR: How can we catch that photographer?

PRIME MINISTER: You never will.

MARSHAL (*louder*): You have killed my soldiers!

VICTOR (*livid*): Killed? I have destroyed your soldiers!

MARSHAL (*in a transport of rage*): Killed! You have killed them! You have opened their veins! You did not reckon with their leader!

> *The* MARSHAL *belabours the* VICTOR *with his stick.*

MARSHAL: This is the reward for your treachery!

VICTOR (*seizing the stick*): You old idiot!

> *The* GIRL, *the* FOREIGN MINISTER *and the* NURSE *prevent a fight.*

PRIME MINISTER (*calm*): I am leaving . . . in your car.

VICTOR: What?

PRIME MINISTER: The gunfire is uncomfortably close.

A klaxon sounds desperately.

VICTOR (*to the* MARSHAL): How lucky you are that I have to go.

MARSHAL: Red weals across your back. It is a worse punishment than death. The punishment is to be alive . . . and suffer.

PRIME MINISTER (*to the* GIRL): Goodbye.

GIRL (*guarding the* MARSHAL): Goodbye. Good luck.

PRIME MINISTER: A thoughtless wish. You know I need more than that.

GIRL: I know. That's why I said it.

PRIME MINISTER (*smiles. To the* FOREIGN MINISTER): Will you join us?

FOREIGN MINISTER: I shall stay here . . .

There is a tremendous cannonade.

VICTOR: Follow me . . .

He takes his belongings and goes, rapidly.

PRIME MINISTER (*with a smile and a wave*): Die bravely . . .

The PRIME MINISTER *goes. Pause.*

GIRL (*calm*): Go with them, Nurse.

NURSE: Oh, no, miss. I couldn't leave him now.

GIRL: It's too late for devotion.

NURSE: Too late? I only did my duty.

GIRL: To whom?

NURSE: Well, after all, he was Prime Minister, dear.

GIRL: And?

NURSE (*embarrassed*): It's funny how frightened you are when you see someone in the flesh that you've only seen in pictures. . . .

GIRL (*to the* FOREIGN MINISTER): Go with them.

FOREIGN MINISTER: I shall stay with my chief.

GIRL (*bitterly*): Which one?

FOREIGN MINISTER: The . . . this . . . the only one.

GIRL: The only one at the moment. Will you refuse the handkerchief when they come to bind it round your eyes?

FOREIGN MINISTER: I . . . I shall know how to die.

GIRL: Will you protest your innocence?

FOREIGN MINISTER: I am innocent.

GIRL: If you think that, you will scream and shout. Only the guilty die with dignity.

[138]

FOREIGN MINISTER: What have I done?

GIRL: Nothing. Nothing of value to anybody. And because of that your death will seem useless to you, and you will hear your own voice screaming, and be powerless to prevent it. The soldiers, all of them nervous, and hating their duty, will gain courage when they hear your voice, because it will give their work a meaning. Put the poor animal out of its pain, they'll say, and fire to get a bit of peace and quiet. . . .

FOREIGN MINISTER (*terribly nervous*): Men are not beasts.

GIRL: They become cruel when they see a culprit clinging too desperately to life. It degrades human nature, and insults their own humanity. If you make too much noise, you'll lose all sympathy, and they'll shoot you with pleasure.

After a wordless moment, the FOREIGN MINISTER *rushes out. The* MARSHAL *has stood transfixed, gazing at his broken toys.*

NURSE: Why did you do that?

GIRL: What does he deserve?

NURSE: Well, after all, he is Foreign Minister.

GIRL: Oh, poor Nurse . . . (*She crosses to the* MARSHAL.) Father. . . .

MARSHAL: Look at the battlefield. Why are some of us gifted in the art of slaughter?

NURSE: They're only tin, dear.

GIRL: Ssh! (*Imploring.*) Let his madness return, for pity's sake. . . .

The MARSHAL *stoops to pick one of the soldiers up. The* GIRL *picks it up for him.*

MARSHAL: That's not the one I want.

GIRL: There.

MARSHAL: Look at him. (*He holds the broken toy soldier.*) 46th Infantry of the Line. You can see by the scarlet facings and the silver lanyard. What was he—corporal or sergeant? My eyes are not what they were.

GIRL: Sergeant.

MARSHAL: That's worse. An elaborate training gone to ruin. (*He gazes at the debris.*) So much burying to do.

GIRL: Shall I pick them up?

MARSHAL: Pick them up? What kind of talk is that? Cover their faces with their greatcoats . . . lift them on to stretchers . . . and carry them at a slow march to their resting-place . . .

He sits heavily, and drums his fingers on the table.

Muffle the drums, muffle the drums . . . and share our silence with them for a span of sacred seconds . . .

[139]

The GIRL *and the* NURSE *very quietly pick up the soldiers while the* MARSHAL *sits in silence.*

There. Honour's done. We, the survivors, must regretfully return to life. . . .

> *Pause.*

Tell me—you are my daughter, are you not?

GIRL: Yes, father.

MARSHAL: Strange, you look so much older than a daughter.

GIRL: I am . . .

MARSHAL: Tell me, am I alive? I believe I am, because death could hardly be so painful.

GIRL: It will soon be over.

MARSHAL: Those shadows? Those mocking eyes? The room's peaceful now that they've gone. (*He looks at the walls.*) But I still feel its bosom-full of sorrow. It's a bad room. Ungenerous to the old. Curtains that burst into flame. Words that have no meaning disguising thoughts which have—a glut of horrid, sidelong meaning. And then, here is my fatal battlefield; here on the floor, between the leg of a board-room table and the hoof of a gilded reception chair, the cream of my armies lie dispersed. That's enough for me to hate it. The carpet will grow flowers, red flowers fertilized by the blood of better men than we. (*He looks at the three green lamps.*) The sun, the moon and that unrecognizable star will go out presently in a bursting of bulbs, and my little world will be dark as death. Bulbs can't last for ever. They go out when you least expect it, like life . . . but if you stare at them, and wait, they will fill a brief eternity with cruel light.

> *One lamp goes out.*

Ah! There's hope! The sun has petered out—(*Worried.*)—but it's still a light night—too light for sleep. I must wait . . . must wait. (*Sudden violence—to the* GIRL.) Leave the dead where they are! They are too lucky for burial. I can be cruel too. Give me the living to drill. I'll make their life a hell. Left, right, left, and no time to take a breath. Up here on the table.

> *Suddenly he grips the* GIRL'S *wrist.*

What have they done to me?

GIRL: They have left us behind.

MARSHAL: In peace. I know that, I know. But before . . .

GIRL: They asked your advice.

MARSHAL (*sly*): But did not take it. Why?

> *Pause.*

Tell me, my darling, tell me.

GIRL: Forget them. They are evil men.

MARSHAL: I know, but I don't understand why. Evil, very evil, all of them, but I had only my eyes to tell me so. What did they do? And why is Nurse crying?

GIRL: You call her Nurse again?

MARSHAL (*simple*): That's what she is. She is a nurse. To look after me. I must be looked after.

Loud machine-gun fire.

They're still beating the drums. More must have died than I had realized. (*Smiles.*) Look at Nurse. Her nose is running, just as mine sometimes does. Give her my handkerchief, or she'll be embarrassed— as embarrassed as a school-mistress who has punished a pupil for not knowing the answer to a question she doesn't know herself.

Quiet, while the GIRL *gives the* NURSE *the handkerchief.*

The answer to a question. Why? Why? Why? . . .

Great burst of gunfire very close.

The GIRL *runs to the* MARSHAL.

MARSHAL: Are you frightened?

GIRL: No.

MARSHAL: It is your duty to be frightened, you are a woman. It is not being fair to the gentlemen if you are not frightened.

GIRL: I am frightened then, father.

MARSHAL: Nurse, are you frightened?

NURSE: Yes, dear.

MARSHAL: Then come to me. I will look after you, and absorb the cannonballs like the ocean. (*He sits with his arms round them.*) It is growing darker.

The GIRL *looks up hopefully.*

NURSE (*surprised*): It is growing lighter, dear.

GIRL: Ssh! Yes, it is growing darker, father.

MARSHAL: We never know everything, and as we grow older we forget more than we ever learned. There's not much left for me to forget now. Faces, memorials, ribbons, flags, medals, swords, drill, ballistics, trajectories. Behind them, intentions, prejudices, bigotries, ignorances. And underneath it all, the naked body, what we begin and end with, our prison and our tyrant, a twisted mass of tubes, a grimace for recognition, a heart which beats on obstinately, a living nerve. I cry "Halt" to my heart, but it goes on marching. I try to break the bars of my cell, but they have grown tougher with the years . . .

[141]

GIRL: Shut your eyes, and pray as you have never prayed before
. . . for death.

NURSE: That's blasphemy.

GIRL: For you, because you are innocent. You just pray.

> *Pause.*

Father . . .

MARSHAL: I am praying . . .

GIRL: I will too . . .

> *Sudden tumult in the streets. A shout. Massed voices begin to*
> *sing an anthem. The* MARSHAL *opens his eyes and tries to struggle*
> *to his feet.*

GIRL: Father!

MARSHAL: The anthem! To your feet!

GIRL: Father, sit down. The anthem's like your flags and swords.
You've left it behind.

MARSHAL: I was trained to rise to it.

GIRL: You've no time left. Pray, pray.

> *The* MARSHAL *falls back in his seat.*

MARSHAL: I am too tired to do my duty . . .

GIRL: Sleep, and forget to wake.

MARSHAL: The world . . .

GIRL: Don't talk.

MARSHAL (*an echo*): Why?

GIRL: Ssh . . .

> *Pause. The* MARSHAL'S *head slumps on his chest. The* NURSE
> *rises and gasps.*

NURSE: He's dead!

GIRL (*elated*): I hope so.

> *As the* NURSE *feels the* MARSHAL'S *pulse, the door opens slowly,*
> *and the* GENERAL *enters, his tunic covered in dust, and his arm*
> *adorned with armbands denoting his resistance to the existing*
> *order. The* GIRL *looks up at him. Then she and the* NURSE *rise.*

GENERAL (*quiet, weary*): Why didn't you try to escape?

GIRL: There is no escape from the decision I made.

GENERAL: The decision you had to make?

GIRL (*forthright*): The decision I made.

GENERAL: I shall have to arrest you.

GIRL: Obviously.

GENERAL: Not you, Nurse. Go into the street. You will be useful there. The wounded are lying on the pavements.

NURSE: I shall be useful here . . .

GENERAL (*to the* GIRL): You haven't changed.

GIRL: Oh, yes. Fundamentally. You look well.

GENERAL: Four years, over, it's been.

GIRL: How is . . . ?

GENERAL: Well. Twice wounded.

GIRL (*concerned*): Badly?

GENERAL: No. I advise you not to try and see him.

GIRL: Oh . . .

GENERAL: He is a hero of the liberation, decorated with the highest orders.

GIRL: There's too much between us in any case.

The door opens, and a STRANGER *bursts in with a message. Full battledress. He stops dead. Moment of tension.*

I mustn't embarrass you by calling you "darling," but that is what I want to call you. Don't try to smile.

GENERAL: Shall I . . . ?

He is restrained by the STRANGER, *who stands with his back to the audience.*

GIRL: Your face is so covered in dust, I can't tell what you're thinking—but then I never could tell that. It was your fascination. There's nothing to say, is there? We did our duty. Now father's dead. I have nothing. But I saw it coming. . . . I saw it . . . just as though a fortune-teller had told me the date of your home-coming, I could prepare very carefully, very quietly for . . . this.

Pause.

I hear that you were wounded?

Pause.

We always imagined we'd retire to the country when you were a Colonel, when you'd done your duty to your family . . . and live a quiet life, a good life. Now I can see that you're ambitious, and as for me . . .

Pause.

(*Very tender.*) I haven't heard your voice yet. Won't you shout an order? Won't you call them to arrest me, just so that I can hear it?

Pause.

[143]

Won't you just sigh, or clear your throat . . . or . . . is it too much to hope? . . . Won't you just spare a moment from your duties and tell me that you loved me once? (*She is in tears.*) Refresh my memory . . . you're crushing it as you stand there . . . please, please tell me that you loved me once . . . I'm only a girl . . . a woman . . . I have been brave for so long . . . I am not like that . . . not made of ice . . . not calm, resigned . . . I am a woman . . . if I must die, at least remind me that I once had hopes . . . it will hurt, but pain is better than silence . . . it proves I am alive. . . .

> *Pause.*

Won't you even shout at me, hate me? Won't you beat me for my treachery? Won't you be kind, take your gun, and kill me? Then, as I died, I could think it was for love? . . .

GENERAL (*moved*): Speak to her.

> *Quickly the* STRANGER *goes out.*

I'm sorry . . .

GIRL (*broken*): Heroes have no time for charity.

GENERAL: Is charity what you want?

GIRL (*flashing*): No! I too can be cruel. Give me your revolver.

GENERAL: No.

GIRL: I've had enough. The only life I want is in his conscience. Give it me.

GENERAL: I can't.

NURSE (*in agony*): Give it her.

GIRL (*amazed*): Nurse!

GENERAL: Why?

NURSE: I have my reasons. Let her go.

GENERAL: I can . . . leave it on the table . . . out of forgetfulness.

GIRL: Do it then.

> *The* GENERAL *places his revolver on the table.*

You are kind.

GENERAL: You have talked to me like a soldier, and that is the greatest compliment I can pay.

> *The* GIRL *lifts the revolver. At that moment, the people in the street begin to sing the anthem. The* MARSHAL *stirs in his sleep, and suddenly rises to his feet, his eyes lunatic and brilliant, and begins to sing the anthem. With a howl, the* GIRL *drops the revolver.*

NURSE (*agonized*): I knew he wasn't dead. (*Hopeless, to the* GENERAL.) Oh, sir, we are too late!

Sadly the GENERAL *crosses to the door, and calls out, dispassionately:*

GENERAL: Guards.

The GENERAL *turns to face the* MARSHAL, *and says, with military precision:*

You are under arrest, sir.

Very slowly the MARSHAL *turns and begins to walk towards the door, as—*

THE CURTAIN FALLS

ACT IV

Some weeks later. The courtyard of an island fortress. Ramparts run round the back wall, with a flight of steps leading down to the ground from them, CENTRE. *Slightly to the* LEFT, *a large wooden gateway with a smaller door let into it. Over the gate, a central elevated crenellation with a flagpole. Small doorway,* RIGHT. *Everywhere spikes and barbs. The sky is cold but clear.*

The curtain rises on an empty stage. Then the NURSE *comes quickly in from the small door and hurries across to the gate, mumbling to herself agitatedly. She tries to open the inset door, but the bolt is stuck.*

NURSE: Sergeant! Sergeant! (*No reply. More intimately.*) I'll open it, dear.

> *She makes a superhuman effort, and pulls the bolt. The little door groans open.*

(*Exhausted and tender.*) Come in, my dear. Thank you, boatman.

> *The* GIRL *comes in, a shadow of her former self. Her hair seems shorter, and is unkempt. Her clothes are old and soiled. She carries a small suitcase bound with string.*

GIRL (*tender, weary*): Nurse . . . Nurse . . .

NURSE: Oh, my dear . . .

> *They embrace.*

Come in. I have made some coffee. You'll be able to sit down and rest yourself.

GIRL (*with peculiar emphasis*): I want to stand, Nurse . . .

NURSE: Let me look at you.

GIRL (*clutching her*): No, no, don't look at me. Where are the warders? I expected so many.

NURSE: Poor boys, they are all so bored. They don't like it here, and so spend their time playing cards.

GIRL: They do that on the mainland too.

NURSE (*suffering for her*): Oh, dear child. Here they leave the doors unlocked. They have no discipline. Being sent on to an island, they feel they're being punished, and resent it.

GIRL: I expected to be met by them.

[146]

NURSE: No, dear, it's Saturday. There's a football match on the radio.

GIRL: But how did you know I was coming up the path?

NURSE: I saw the boat from the ramparts. It was a speck on the horizon at midday. Then it grew and grew and I followed it all the way into the harbour.

GIRL: The boatman says he senses thunder.

NURSE: I saw the clouds, and hoped you'd get here first.

GIRL (*looking up*): The ramparts?

NURSE: Yes, it's nice up there when the wind isn't too fresh.

GIRL: Can the wind ever be too fresh?

NURSE: Don't remind yourself, my dear. It must have been too terrible. A child like you in prison. I can hardly——

GIRL: Please, Nurse. I couldn't open my eyes for a week when I came out. (*She wanders to the stairs.*)

NURSE: I shouldn't go up there, dear.

GIRL: Why not?

NURSE: He's up there.

GIRL: He? (*Sudden realization.*) Can he climb the stairs?

NURSE (*sadly*): Without the aid of a stick.

GIRL (*shattered*): Oh, no . . .

    Pause.

Does he realize what has happened?

NURSE: Thank God, no.

GIRL: But his trial?

NURSE: He can't remember. He thought he was asleep, and dreamt about his subordinates' ingratitude.

GIRL: Is he . . . reasonable?

NURSE (*sad*): No. Life is a battle to him.

GIRL: A battle?

NURSE: Yes, and the sea is just dry land.

GIRL: He never liked the sea.

NURSE: He saw your boat, and thought it was a squadron of horses. The wake he thought a cloud of dust. He gave the order to open fire.

GIRL: And when no one did?

NURSE: He was satisfied. A victory was won in his brain. He forgot the rest.

GIRL (*pathetically, tentative*): Will he recognize me?

NURSE (*tactful*): He may not. You may be a messenger with vital dispatches, or a general on his staff. I hope you're not a prisoner they've just brought in—that's a very difficult one to get out of.

GIRL: But I'm a woman.

NURSE: That doesn't matter. The warders are too bored to humour him, or at least, when they are in a mood to, they do it so maliciously that I have to ask them to stop. He's short of soldiers, so that I have to play his whole army for him, and when I'm not there he's satisfied with the shadows on the wall. I've heard him.

GIRL: How can you bear it?

NURSE: My darling, you get used to it. It seems almost normal to me now. I don't take it too much to heart, and so it becomes quite fun.

MARSHAL'S VOICE (*off*): Colonel . . .!

The GIRL *starts as she looks up.*

NURSE: Be gentle with him. Don't insist you are his daughter. Not at first . . .

The MARSHAL *appears on the ramparts, his white hair disarranged by the wind. He wears a plain tunic, and a golden belt with a scabbard on it.*

MARSHAL: Colonel!

NURSE: Yes, sir.

MARSHAL: There was a delay in your answer.

NURSE: I beg your pardon, sir.

MARSHAL: Slovenly, slovenly. That troop of cavalry was dispersed with the first whiff of powder. Commend those responsible for their shooting, only don't praise them. It doesn't do to praise soldiers. Commend them, but make it clear with the inflexions of your voice that they ought to have done better. The night is closing in. Post double sentries. Reveille at five. No bugles. Let the enemy underestimate our strength.

He turns slowly and sees the GIRL. *Long pause. She hopes desperately for recognition. At length he speaks.*

The emissary from our advance guard. Why did you not report immediately on arrival?

NURSE: Say anything.

The GIRL *is unable to speak.*

MARSHAL (*frightening*): Well? Are words so fragile that they must be whispered? Or have you news of some disaster?

NURSE: He's a very young officer, sir.

[148]

MARSHAL: And we must be indulgent with the young. They are even farther from death than we are. Are your casualties high, young man?

GIRL: Yes . . .

MARSHAL: Yes? Yes? Yes? Yes, what?

GIRL: Yes, sir.

MARSHAL: How high?

GIRL: A . . . thousand, sir.

MARSHAL: A thousand? You call that high? A nation, a race, would be moderately high. A thousand's a mere thimbleful of blood, a handful of crosses, a stain on the soil.

NURSE: He meant a million, sir.

MARSHAL: A million's more like it. There's a foretaste of sacrifice in that. Sacrifice! Have you any idea what sacrifice means? There are things more terrible than loss of life. (*He beats his breast.*) All my decorations went into the making of a cannon!

NURSE: They were cruel to take away his medals . . .

MARSHAL: My epaulettes became a fragment of a bullet! There's sacrifice! (*Different tone.*) Have you a sword, young man?

GIRL: No, sir.

MARSHAL: No sword, no symbol of honour? And a young man at that, ripe for learning? Here, take mine, your helplessness overrides my need for it.

> *He pulls an imaginary sword out of his scabbard, reverses it, and mimes the surrender of it.*

Come and fetch it then. You don't expect me to come down and give it you. My vigil here is endless. I may not leave my post.

> *The* GIRL *begins slowly, painfully, to climb the stairs.*

Quick, quick, at the double! (*Resentfully and sadly.*) You move as slowly as the years.

GIRL (*gazing at him closely. Softly*): Father.

MARSHAL: You are an orphan, sir!

GIRL (*louder*): Father!

MARSHAL: The sword! Take it!

GIRL (*crying*): Father!

MARSHAL (*shouting*): The sword I say!

NURSE (*urgent*): Take the sword and leave him his oblivion. It's what you wanted.

GIRL (*taking the imaginary sword*): I am so lonely now . . .

MARSHAL: The living stand naked in a waste land. Their solitude's their skin.

GIRL: He understood!

MARSHAL: The sky's a curtain; behind it the actors stand prepared. What will the rising of the velvet drapes reveal? The footlights of the sinking sun surrender no secrets. The curtains bulge with the passing of men behind them. The overture is ending as the wind dies down and the clouds go black with premonition. Will it be cavalry, sweeping across the plain like a scythe? Will it be artillery, lobbing its unseen but undeniable message through the air with little, casual whistles? Will it be infantry, plodding its weary way over the shelter-less land, a forest of marching targets? Whoever they are, whoever fills this pregnant emptiness with fury, they will find us prepared. Young man, we stand on the confines of massive and melancholy times. Grip your sword, trust God, the God on our side, not on theirs, and follow me . . .

He walks out warily. The GIRL, *with an agonized look at the* NURSE, *follows him round the ramparts. The* NURSE *has only time to register her mood with a wan shake of the head before the* PHOTOGRAPHER'S *head appears over the ramparts,* LEFT.

PHOTOGRAPHER: Psst! Nurse!

NURSE (*recovering from her shock*): What? You again? Where do you always spring from? Come down from there before the old man sees you.

Nimbly the PHOTOGRAPHER *climbs over the wall, and then leaps lightly from the parapet without bothering about the stairs.*

NURSE: How did you get in?

PHOTOGRAPHER: I used to be a clown. Followed in my father's footsteps. I could do three somersaults in the air when I was six; walk on a wire when I was seven; feel at home on the trapezes when I was nine. Then I grew and grew and grew. As I was his only son, Father never forgave himself for marrying a tall woman.

NURSE: But how did you get to the island? Look out!

It is clear that the MARSHAL *is looking back in the* PHOTO-GRAPHER'S *direction. The* PHOTOGRAPHER *holds himself flush with the wall. In a moment, the danger passes. He emerges.*

PHOTOGRAPHER: I bribed the boatman. He hid me under a coil of rope.

NURSE: He had no right.

PHOTOGRAPHER: The bribe was substantial. My newspaper gives me a generous dispensation for bribery. It is almost twice my salary.

NURSE (*resentfully*): They ought to leave the poor old man alone. It's the least they can do after the way they've treated him.

PHOTOGRAPHER: They have treated him in the way they treat all traitors.

NURSE: Are you suggesting that he *is* a traitor?

PHOTOGRAPHER: To the vast majority who read the papers, who see my pictures, certainly.

NURSE (*hostile*): Then what do you want to do here?

PHOTOGRAPHER (*laughing*): Why do you ask? How can you protect him?

NURSE: I can call the guards.

PHOTOGRAPHER: I have not spent all my bribe-money. The wretched guards are underpaid. If you have their interests at heart, call them now.

He takes out a wad of notes.

Slight pause.

NURSE: At least you cannot bribe me.

PHOTOGRAPHER: I wouldn't try. There's no point. You never go on leave, and here there's no point in having money.

NURSE (*fearful. On her guard*): What kind of man are you?

PHOTOGRAPHER: A menial, like you. And we are lucky, Nurse.

NURSE: What do you mean?

PHOTOGRAPHER: We can never commit the gravest modern crime, a crime of which the Marshal is flagrantly guilty.

NURSE: And what is that?

PHOTOGRAPHER: The crime of being important.

NURSE: Important.

PHOTOGRAPHER: The great crime of the Marshal was to win those famous national victories twenty-five years ago, for which he was decorated, honoured, and given his baton. He also won importance, and there his catastrophe began.

NURSE: Importance is a fine achievement.

PHOTOGRAPHER (*with unexpected vehemence*): Not in a world in which all things are relative, and in which morality is the most relative thing of all.

NURSE (*frightened*): Those are big and terrible words.

PHOTOGRAPHER (*calm again*): Big, terrible and commonplace. Oh, the field of my photography! Nurse, if you had seen the world through my view-finder, you would understand me better. No, you wouldn't.

You are a person with a tiny, rigid honour of your own, the honour of a faithful dog. You form your attachments, right or wrong, and stick by them. I am a coward, a vacillator, a prostitute. I have nothing to say, nothing to defend. My service is to the horrible fragments of arrested time in my lens, and I sell these bits of evidence for profit, adding and subtracting nothing of my own. I am a worthless and a dangerous man.

NURSE (*with instinctive kindness*): Don't you perhaps take your work too seriously?

PHOTOGRAPHER: Seriously? I don't take it seriously at all. That's the trouble. I daren't. But the effect it has in the hands of the editor! That man, who has the audacity to be important!

NURSE: You mentioned him before.

PHOTOGRAPHER: I mentioned the assistant editor, but it's all the same. Both he and my former editor are dead, shot for collaboration with the enemy. I have a new pair, patriots, men of temporary honour, until they too pay the price of their importance with the next vacillation of national morality. Everyone seems delighted with the new appointments; I don't notice the difference.

NURSE (*ingenuous*): Are you very bitter?

PHOTOGRAPHER: Bitter? No. Illusions must be shattered for bitterness. I never had any.

NURSE: Have you never been in love?

PHOTOGRAPHER: I have too great a pity for people.

NURSE: Oh, you have pity?

PHOTOGRAPHER (*surprised*): Of course. A terrible pity. How could I avoid it? When I was photographing that heroic group of ministers, how could I avoid pitying the Marshal, who didn't know what was happening, and how could I avoid pitying the Prime Minister, who knew too well. He knew he would die, and he did, just as he said. I photographed his death. He was shot with his eyes bandaged, because he explained quietly that he was squeamish, and that was all he said. And how could I avoid pitying the Foreign Minister, who struggled so desperately with his cowardice. He died screaming platitudes about the Republic. And how could I help pitying the Marshal's daughter, and you.

NURSE: Me? Why? I have my work to live for. I look after the sick. That's enough for me. I want occasional affection, not pity.

PHOTOGRAPHER: I pity everyone, without exception.

NURSE: But have you nothing to live for? Have you no aim?

Pause.

[152]

PHOTOGRAPHER (*slow*): Yes. I have one vast, one unreasonable ambition.

NURSE (*awed by his gravity*): What is it?

PHOTOGRAPHER: I want to take a photograph of such eloquence that the assistant editor will find it impossible to distort. I want one moment of truth after the decades of lies. That's why I appealed to him to let me come here.

NURSE: It was your idea?

PHOTOGRAPHER: Yes.

NURSE: Why?

PHOTOGRAPHER: I have my intuition.

There is a distant roll of thunder.

NURSE: Thunder. Now the trouble will begin. Go and hide.

PHOTOGRAPHER: No. I shall take part in the battle.

NURSE: But you don't know how to play the game.

PHOTOGRAPHER: I know better than you can imagine.

NURSE: Oh, dear. It's begun to rain.

Another roll of thunder. The MARSHAL *reappears.*

MARSHAL: The attack has begun. Every man to his post.

The GIRL *follows him, distraught, leaning heavily on the parapet. The* MARSHAL *examines the horizon.*

There they come! A cloud of cavalry! Hold your fire, but sound your bugles! Give the men heart!

He goes off again, shouting:

All howitzers, 4,000 metres. Mortars, 1,000 metres. Hold your fire . . .

NURSE: Darling . . .

GIRL: I can't bear it any longer . . .

PHOTOGRAPHER: But you will hold on bitterly, to the end.

GIRL: Why are you here?

PHOTOGRAPHER: I've followed the story from the beginning. I am indispensable to the end.

GIRL: The tragedy . . .

NURSE: Ssh! Stop talking such nonsense. Come down here, dear, out of the rain.

GIRL: I like the rain. And it's hardly raining at all.

NURSE (*holding out her hand*): The most dangerous kind of storm, a storm without much rain.

The MARSHAL *returns.*

MARSHAL: Why are you all standing around like dummies? The whole horizon is galloping. Move, move, move to your stations.

Big roll of thunder.

MARSHAL (*to the* GIRL): Why do you stand there, staring? What's your regiment?

GIRL: Leave me alone, please . . .

MARSHAL: What way is that to talk?

NURSE: He's hurt!

MARSHAL: What?

NURSE: He's wounded!

MARSHAL: Already? Our first?

NURSE (*desperate, to the* PHOTOGRAPHER): Say something!

PHOTOGRAPHER: The bishops are here, Your Excellency, to bless the troops!

MARSHAL: Let them save their murmuring for the burials. I'll have no holy men in my camp. I speak to God without their agency.

PHOTOGRAPHER: The politicians are here, Your Excellency, to give their advice!

MARSHAL (*roaring*): Put them against the outer wall, and let the enemy shoot them. I'll not waste our bullets on them.

PHOTOGRAPHER: They have brought you a medal!

MARSHAL: Take the gold from their teeth, the rims from their spectacles, the caps off their fountain pens, and melt them down for bullets! Open fire!

Big roll of thunder.

PHOTOGRAPHER (*to the* NURSE): The sky's in the conspiracy. It's obeyed his order.

MARSHAL: Look at them, rolling off their horses, tripping up those who follow!

NURSE: It's the mist on the sea.

MARSHAL: Fire!

Silence.

Fire! Where are my gunners?

PHOTOGRAPHER: The sky's turned cruel.

MARSHAL: Fire, I say!

Roll of thunder.

The artillery's asleep! (*To the* GIRL.) Run and wake them up!

NURSE: I'll do it!

MARSHAL: Stay where you are! I selected this runner! (*To the* GIRL.) Are you dead?

GIRL: No . . . only dying . . .

MARSHAL: Then, while there's life, run, run, obey my orders!

NURSE (*distraught, to the* PHOTOGRAPHER): For God's sake!

PHOTOGRAPHER: The prisoners have been brought in, Your Excellency.

MARSHAL: Question them, promise them life, and then kill them. Let us have the honour of honourable men. Give them hope before you blacken their world. Lift them high in the air before you drop them. Show them the sun through a needle's eye, and bring them fresh air in wine-glasses, every hour. Let their food be a smell of soup from the next room. Let them drink their tears to quench their thirst. (*To the* GIRL.) Meanwhile, I have not forgotten. I gave you an order . . .

PHOTOGRAPHER (*urgently*): Our dying are laid out in the hospital, Your Excellency.

MARSHAL (*delighted*): Bring in the bishops, you fool, like the clowns. Let them die to the sound of holy mumbling, their growing darkness lit by flickering candles. Give them a good memory of existence to take with them into sleep. Superstition, ritual, gravity, solemnity, let's have all of it. Emphasize the emptiness. Underline the vacuum. Stress stupidity!

Roll of thunder, very loud.

(*Furious.*) I gave no order to fire!

NURSE: I gave the order!

MARSHAL: You?

He comes down the steps menacingly.

GIRL (*clinging to the parapet. Desperate*): If only it would rain!

MARSHAL: Since when are there two commanders?

NURSE: Forgive me, Your Excellency.

MARSHAL: The firing-squad will forgive you, a hedge of dull grey barrels. I can no longer forgive. Compassion lies shipwrecked on an island.

PHOTOGRAPHER (*urgently, to save the* NURSE *from physical violence*): Your Excellency, that officer is seeking to protect your soldiers. It was their enthusiasm which is to blame. They fired of their own accord.

MARSHAL: Then punish them all for disobedience! The minimum punishment, death, not the maximum punishment, life.

[155]

PHOTOGRAPHER: But the battle must go on! We must have soldiers!

MARSHAL: Fight with thoughts! Arm the sentiments! Pass the ammunition to the conscience, and let it shoot through the ranks of responsible men. Bury the corpses in the realm of shame. Let bitterness be their sacramental wine, remorse the bread of their devotion. Invade oblivion with reason, let it chase men from every pillow, and occupy sleep with the silly logic of existence. Make night as vile as day.

Remoter thunderclap.

They have fired again!

PHOTOGRAPHER: I gave the word.

MARSHAL: You did? Come here, and let me strangle you with my own hands.

The PHOTOGRAPHER *skips out of the way.*

Why d'you run away?

PHOTOGRAPHER: I don't want to be strangled. Is that so strange?

MARSHAL: What a mere man wishes is an incidental . . . He has no will. He is driven.

The PHOTOGRAPHER *escapes again.*

MARSHAL: Come here. Stop dancing about like a clown.

PHOTOGRAPHER: I am a clown.

MARSHAL: So they have even mobilized the clowns. They have no need of laughter.

PHOTOGRAPHER: They laugh too well without us.

MARSHAL: Buy your freedom then. Make me laugh.

PHOTOGRAPHER: I don't know any jokes.

MARSHAL: I know too many. D'you know the one about the fossil they dug from its graveyard daydreams to lead a nation of living men to the fathomless depths of victory? (*Laughs.*) D'you know the one about the room full of men who tried to clean their hands in dirty water? (*Laughs.*) D'you know the one about the curtains which knew all the secrets, but couldn't find a mouth to tell them with? (*Laughs.*) D'you know the one about the dish of poisoned plums which gave sight to a man who was so happy blind? (*Savage.*) I can make myself laugh, sir. You're a fraud.

PHOTOGRAPHER: Aren't we all frauds? I don't believe you're a real Marshal.

MARSHAL (*delighted*): Of course, you're right. We're just the naked masquerading. I am here to lead this emptiness to glory.

NURSE: Emptiness?

MARSHAL: Do you see anybody?

NURSE: Why yes, all these soldiers.

MARSHAL: Where? All I can see are walls, and the earth, and the sky.

Distant rumble of thunder.

And there . . . there . . .

NURSE: The battle's over. We've won. The last cannonade.

MARSHAL: The battle's over. We've lost. The last roll of thunder.

GIRL (*with a cry of agony*): It never rained.

MARSHAL: You can't expect kindness.

GIRL: No rain. No freshness. Just the prison of sanity, and . . . the heart, talking in whispers . . .

NURSE (*concerned*): Darling . . .

MARSHAL: Ssh! Give the girl her hearing . . .

NURSE: Girl?

MARSHAL: Who is she?

GIRL: I must let go . . . regretfully . . . my will's . . . not my own . . .

She collapses.

NURSE (*rushing forward*): Oh, no . . .

MARSHAL (*stern*): Nurse, leave her alone. She is my responsibility.

NURSE: Do you know who I am?

MARSHAL (*beginning slowly to climb the steps*): Haven't I known you for years . . . for centuries?

Pause until he reaches the top of the steps. He lifts the GIRL *into his arms.*

The battle was real . . . we have had a casualty . . . the sea's undisturbed . . . the sun's struggling with a horde of clouds . . . but we have had a casualty.

NURSE: Is she . . . alive?

MARSHAL (*carrying the* GIRL *with a supreme effort*): No. There's a frown of anguish on her face, but in spite of that, she's not alive.

He begins to come slowly down the stairs.

She's safe. She's safe at last.

NURSE (*approaching them*): But do you know who she is?

MARSHAL: Keep away from us. We belong together. Don't you know better than to disturb a courting couple?

NURSE (*anguished, to the* PHOTOGRAPHER): Get your camera ready.

[157]

PHOTOGRAPHER: It's in my hand.

The MARSHAL slowly carries the GIRL in his arms, and kneels down on the ground.

NURSE (*in tears*): Get up off the ground, dear, it's damp.

MARSHAL: And will the damp harm this young lady? Is it worse for her outside the tomb than in?

NURSE: But are you sure——

MARSHAL: Quite! The heart has stopped. She is all repose and reticence.

Pause, while he looks at the GIRL.

Tell me frankly, as frankly as you can, for you are human beings, is she my daughter?

NURSE (*weeping*): Yes . . .

MARSHAL (*quiet*): I thought she was from the beginning, but didn't wish you to think me mad . . .

Pause.

So now I am alone. In my right mind, and alone.

The NURSE is leaning against the wall, weeping helplessly.

The wall's the wall. My body is sensitive. I feel a draught.

The sun breaks through the clouds.

Now the sun's broken through the clouds. I know it is the sun. It's not the face of God, or a burning city, or a bursting shell. It is the sun. And my nurse is crying her eyes out. Why? Has she pricked herself, or burned herself as she was ironing my shirts? Why?

Slight pause.

And here I am as I entered the world, without responsibility, owning nothing. I had soldiers once, I had a monument unveiled. One? Fifty monuments. I had a house and an orchard. I was not a man, I was an oracle, a voice which spoke among the fluttering flags and the stuttering drums, a hope or condemnation as the need arose . . . and I had a daughter, a bundle of humanity, my eyes transposed, my ears, not my mouth or forehead . . . I made concessions there . . . she was the simplest message I had to give . . . but they did not understand it . . . they distorted it, as they distort everything . . .

He looks at the GIRL, and begins to weep himself.

Stop crying, Nurse . . . oh, please stop crying . . . she is not crying, look . . . she is brave . . . takes the news of her death with fortitude . . . why do you frown, though? . . . Are you angry with me? . . . Have

I forgotten to say thank you for your present of plums?... And why am I alive ... and naked ... a child again, a white-haired child, holding his hope in his hands like a broken toy?... Why?... Why? ... Why?... Why?... Why?...

> *As the* MARSHAL *intones his question, the* PHOTOGRAPHER *lifts his camera to his eye. There is a flash. The* MARSHAL *continues his soft intonation, the* NURSE *weeps more controlledly, and the* PHOTOGRAPHER *smiles a smile of serene elation.*

SLOW CURTAIN

BEYOND

A Play in One Act

FOR
NOEL WILLMAN

CHARACTERS
(in order of appearance)

JOHNNY LA FORCE, *Poet*, 85
CHARLEY MALLORY, *Inventor*, 84
COLONEL RADLEY, *Unknown Soldier*, 83
A NURSE

Action takes place in a home for old men.

———

First performed on 21 March 1943, at The Arts Theatre, London.

THE CAST

CHARLEY MALLORY	Tarver Penna
JOHNNY LA FORCE	Denys Blakelock
COLONEL RADLEY	Marcus Barron
THE NURSE	Dorothy Primrose

Directed by ALEC CLUNES and in décor by MAISIE MEIKLEJOHN.

A simple room decorated in the Victorian manner. Dark brown walls, upholstered furniture. A fire burning. Outside, Autumn. Trees and mist.

COLONEL RADLEY, *an unknown soldier of 83, is gazing out of the window. He is tall, wistful, resigned and very robust for his years; of a serious disposition.*

CHARLEY MALLORY, *the inventor, is sitting by the fire. He gazes into the flames, and they light up his hard, sombre, humourless face.*

JOHNNY LA FORCE, *the poet, sits to the left of the room in a rocking chair, covered with a rug. He looks incessantly from* RADLEY *to* MALLORY *in apparent anxiety. His is a broad sensitive face with watery, staring, blue eyes. The second movement of Tchaikovsky's Fifth Symphony crackles through the minute wireless by his side.*

Pause.

JOHNNY (*wistful*): Another Autumn . . .

CHARLEY (*after a slight pause. Irritated—with no great conviction*): Don't be so damned patient about it . . .

JOHNNY (*hopeless*): What else can I do but sit here and wait and count the days passing by. . . . You won't listen to my poems . . .

RADLEY (*kindly, from the window*): Ah, now, don't take that to heart . . . it doesn't do to be too sensitive . . .

JOHNNY (*surprised*): But I'm a poet!

RADLEY (*philosophical*): I know, old boy, I know . . . but I've had sensitive people in the Army . . . in Africa . . . poets and so on. . . . I daresay they saw more beauty in the jungle than we did . . . they eulogized about everything they saw . . . panthers, pigmies, ground-nut trees . . . everything . . . they even wrote satirical stuff about White settlers . . . you know the kind of thing . . . well, it was all very well, but, by jingo, those blighters suffered. . . . We saw pigmies when pigmies arrived, but they saw, I forget what it was . . . sun-tanned relics of an age gone by, or something of the sort . . . well, it didn't do . . . I mean, it was of no use . . . they didn't get on with Africa . . . too sensitive . . . wouldn't do . . .

JOHNNY (*exasperated*): Do stop telling me what would and wouldn't do . . . I am a poet . . . I draw up my own code of behaviour . . . I am sensitive, yes, and proud of it . . . it makes me see beauty in the simplest things . . .

[165]

RADLEY (*stupidly, as if he had won his point*): Ah, yes!

JOHNNY: What do you mean by that? I am sensitive, yes . . . and that makes life bearable for me . . . as for Africa . . . I have never been there . . . I have no connections with it, sentimental, pictorial, or even climatic . . . and I never want to go there . . .

RADLEY (*incredulous*): Never want to go to Africa! I'd give my right arm to get back . . .

JOHNNY (*smiling*): At your age?

RADLEY: At my age. I've always wanted to die a violent death, Johnny. . . . After my retirement from the Army I was a very disappointed fellow. . . . I knew better than the military authorities my worth as a soldier, but they retired me . . . (*Rather agonized.*) I was never much of a social hog . . . suppose that was it. . . . Spent most of my time alone, studying military history. . . . I had ambitions to be a General . . . (*Hardly able to bear it.*) They put me on the retired list as a Lieutenant-Colonel . . . (*Numb.*) I cheat, and pretend I'm a full Colonel in order to make myself believe I was nearly as successful as I once hoped I would be . . . but it doesn't work . . . you can't cheat yourself for ever . . . it gives you moments of mock-pride . . . and moments of dismal shame . . . resentment . . . (*Hardly audible.*) It doesn't do . . .

JOHNNY (*sighing—bored*): We've heard that story so often before.

RADLEY (*with a trace of a smile*): We don't listen to your poems— you don't listen to my biography. Charley's the only sensible one . . . keeps his mouth shut . . .

CHARLEY (*with surprising vigour*): I'm sick of this existence. . . . All my life I've tried to give the human race the benefit of my knowledge . . . of my invention . . . I've just been unlucky . . . I thought of wireless just after Marconi . . . I got the telephone in a few days after Edison . . . I came out with television a matter of hours after Baird . . . (*Bitterly.*) There's luck for you . . . I know more about electricity and magnetism than any one living man . . . and yet they won't listen to me in this world. . . . Perhaps . . .

JOHNNY: Yes?

CHARLEY (*sombre*): Perhaps it's no use trying here any longer . . . perhaps we had better just die as quickly as possible and trust to luck that we'll evolve to a world where electricity hasn't been discovered . . . I *would* start with an advantage then, wouldn't I? (*A little sad.*) If I remembered . . .

JOHNNY (*sighing*): It is depressing how we say the same thing day in, day out . . .

CHARLEY (*irritated*): Do turn the wireless off . . .

JOHNNY (*does so, but goes on talking*): Every morning I put the wireless on, and we stand in these positions until lunch-time, when we are herded downstairs by a nurse to take lunch with two hundred other dotards. . . . After lunch we sleep for an hour, and then return to these positions . . . and every day we wring the same painful confession from the Colonel . . . every day we hear the same philosophical bitterness from Charley . . . (*Aggressively.*) Word for word . . . (*With a sigh.*) And every day you refuse point-blank to hear my poems . . .

RADLEY (*smiling*): It won't do, will it?

JOHNNY (*earnestly*): No, it won't . . . (*New voice.*) A fortune-teller once told me that I should die at the age of forty-five . . . a violent death, she said . . . a catastrophe on the funiculaire . . . but I'm still here . . . forty years overdue . . . (*Afterthought.*) I must admit superstition always prevented me from going up a mountain on a funiculaire . . . (*As there is silence.*) I have never been up a mountain on a funiculaire . . .

CHARLEY (*agonized*): We've had that one before, too . . . Yesterday . . . before yesterday . . . every day . . .

JOHNNY (*sighing*): There doesn't seem anything left to talk about, does there?

RADLEY (*frank admission*): No.

JOHNNY (*after a pause*): Another Autumn . . .

CHARLEY: We get that one all the year round . . . even in mid-winter sometimes . . .

JOHNNY (*reasonably*): Ah, yes, but with a different inflection . . . now, it is a statement . . . "Another Autumn" . . . then, in winter it is a lyrical outburst of longing and wistfulness . . . "Another Autumn". . . .

CHARLEY: Yes, but you always get the inflections the wrong way round . . . in Autumn you say "Another Autumn", and in winter you say "Another Autumn".

JOHNNY (*amazed*): Do I?

    Pause.

RADLEY: Have you quite exhausted that topic of conversation?

JOHNNY: I'm afraid every topic of conversation has been exhausted . . .

    Pause.

JOHNNY (*shyly*): Let's talk about death . . .

CHARLEY (*dreary—fed up*): We've exhausted death . . .

JOHNNY (*apologetic*): Oh, hardly . . .

CHARLEY (*decisive*): We've absolutely exhausted it . . .

    Pause.

[167]

JOHNNY (*distant*): What will you most hate leaving behind when you go?

RADLEY (*dry—definite*): Africa.

CHARLEY (*serious*): The dreams and aspirations of my youth.

JOHNNY (*still more distant*): And I shall regret the passing of those memories whose glories I immortalize in my verses . . . memories of another age . . . fragrant and volatile . . .

> Pause. *They all begin talking together and stop. They apologize. Then . . .*

RADLEY (*taking the initiative*): I loved Africa. (*A little embarrassed.*) She was my wife and my inspiration . . . (*Laughing a little.*) Africa will always be my better half . . . couldn't bear the negroes though . . . smelled . . . I liked the wild life . . . the sport of it all . . . the animals, not caged up, but loose, roaming on the plains and in jungle, challenging man's supremacy . . . (*Reminiscent.*) I've spent my whole life meeting challenges and overcoming my assailant . . . on the field of battle . . . in the jungle . . . over the chess-board . . . now . . . (*Difficult.*) They've all forgotten me . . . the elements . . . the wild beasts . . . the chess-champions . . . nobody challenges me any longer . . .

JOHNNY: I'll play you chess, Colonel . . .

RADLEY: You're so bad, Johnny, I always beat you in about two moves . . .

JOHNNY: I can always put up some kind of show though . . . (*Reflection.*) I loathe the game . . .

RADLEY (*smiling sadly*): Sorry, old lad, it wouldn't do . . .

CHARLEY: I have always wanted to overcome the elements . . .

RADLEY: My desires are more modest than that . . . I just want some kind of adversary . . . of any kind . . . the need to conquer is inherent in my nature . . . I am just wasting my time here . . . there's plenty of life in the old dog yet . . . (*With some irritation.*) I'm much too young for an institute of this sort.

JOHNNY (*sighs*): Oh, dear . . .

RADLEY (*sly*): Look . . .

JOHNNY (*hopeful*): What are you going to show us?

RADLEY (*he has gone to his cupboard and fetched an old revolver of a type used in the Boer War*): My gun . . .

JOHNNY: Good heavens! How did you get it in here? A weapon of violence . . . how disgraceful . . .

RADLEY (*warm*): I never showed it you before . . . I trusted you both, but there was always a sneaking terror in my heart that you might tell Nurse about it in a moment of forgetfulness . . . I couldn't lose this . . . because . . . (*Secretly.*) I imagine that it has eyes and a memory . . . and shares Africa with me . . . I believe that . . . and it shares the strange atmospheres of the veldt with me . . . it remembers the evenings . . . the dawn . . . the perils . . . the mountains . . . the . . . the continent . . . (*Tragic.*) Africa and this gun have been my only loves . . .

JOHNNY (*nervously*): I hope it's empty . . .

RADLEY (*smiling sadly*): Oh, yes . . . it has no dangers . . . and no uses any more . . .

CHARLEY: Let's see it . . . (*Takes it.*) H'm . . . it's constructed on a very elementary principle . . . must be old . . . I invented a revolver once . . .

JOHNNY: Why?

CHARLEY: For the love of it . . .

JOHNNY (*aghast*): You love to design weapons of death?

CHARLEY (*serious*): If my mechanical genius leads me to the design of weapons of death, I must obey it . . .

JOHNNY: I write poems about peace . . .

RADLEY: Look here, Johnny . . . you suggested death as a subject of conversation a moment ago . . . now you treat it with horror and so on . . .

JOHNNY (*earnest*): I approve of death at that great natural moment of dying . . . I hate premature death . . . and I detest . . . I simply detest retarded death . . .

RADLEY: Are you frightened of death?

JOHNNY (*definite*): No . . . I don't believe many human beings are frightened of death . . . nearly everyone is frightened of the last moments of life . . .

RADLEY (*honest*): Yes . . . yes . . . that's perhaps why I have always prayed for a violent death . . . a bayonet through the heart . . . dramatic . . . brave . . . clean . . . (*With satisfaction.*) . . . very desirable . . .

JOHNNY: I want my death to be something rather gentle and noble . . . like an incident in an eighteenth-century opera . . . I want a few tears and many, many flowers . . . I admit it . . . the thing I long for most is a splendid funeral . . . with all those hired mourners . . . all those top hats . . . gilded hearses . . . patent-leather shoes . . . (*Malicious.*) I hope it rains . . . and that I may be there in spirit . . . sheltering under Sir Henry Newbolt's umbrella . . .

RADLEY (*smiling*): You expect him there? . . .

JOHNNY: Oh, yes . . . (*New thought.*) I have had very bad luck . . .

I have lived much too long to be a really successful poet . . . successful poets die at thirty . . . of cancer, consumption, double pneumonia, love, or a Turkish cannon-ball in the breast . . .

RADLEY: You're thinking of Byron . . . the warrior-poet . . .

JOHNNY: I'm thinking of Chopin, Byron, Shelley, Pushkin—all poets in their own way . . . a galaxy of them . . . they were raped from the human race . . ., we love them because we are still in mourning for them . . . we still feel guilty for their wasted talents . . . their martyrdom at the hands of their fellow-mortals . . . at our hands . . . (*With a new bitterness and sombre tragic voice.*) . . . and I'm thinking of the bearded men who boast titles and orders achieved through their verses . . . cracked, nimble heads, crowned with laurel leaves, and filled with solemn, blind conceit and facile, skin-deep rhythms . . . we revere them, and they die before their deaths . . . the others we drown or see them killed doing work not their own . . . and when they literally die before their deaths, we recognize our shame . . . I hate it all . . . the crazy logic of this world . . . and the ruthless, ironic pattern of that logic . . .

CHARLEY: There is nothing to be afraid of in death if life itself has given you nothing . . . I saw all the bitterness the world has to offer, and now, weary, and perhaps with a longing for change and adventure, I wait day by day . . .

RADLEY (*a little tentative*): All the same . . . there is no guarantee that Africa will die with me . . . I am pretty damn loth to leave her . . .

JOHNNY: Well, what do you expect to find in death?

RADLEY: I expect . . . I expect to be congratulated on having tolerated so much . . . I expect to be awarded and knighted for the battles I might have won . . . and I should like to be billeted in that part of Heaven where all lovers of Africa live . . . (*With childish longing.*) I hope they hunt in Heaven . . . in other words, what I want in death is a new lease of life . . . see what I mean . . . I want adventure . . . endless, eternal adventure . . . (*He sits heavily.*) That would do . . .

JOHNNY (*sad*): Strange to pass into the land of peace, a warrior . . . do you yearn for the clash of arms, Charley . . . more bustle, more heroics . . . even beyond?

CHARLEY: No, I long for death though.

JOHNNY (*whimsical*): Yes, I agree . . . I feel we have rather outstayed our welcome here . . . it is as though God had forgotten about us . . .

CHARLEY: I wouldn't be a bit surprised . . .

Pause.

JOHNNY: It is very silent here . . . I have never felt so forgotten, so overlooked in all my life . . .

Pause.

JOHNNY (*new vigour*): About Africa, Radley . . . (RADLEY *is asleep in his seat.*) Is he asleep?

CHARLEY: Radley! . . .

JOHNNY: Ssh! Don't wake him . . . sleep is so rare nowadays . . .

CHARLEY (*looking at him*): He's . . . not asleep . . . (*Rises, and goes over to him. Looks up.*) Radley's dead.

JOHNNY: Good God!

CHARLEY (*begins going quickly to the door*): Nurse!

JOHNNY: No . . . pssht! . . . Charley! . . . Come back!

CHARLEY (*coming back, surly*): What is it?

JOHNNY (*smiling radiant*): Don't you realize? God's remembered . . . He remembered Radley . . . He must remember us . . . he was younger than we . . . it'll be our turn soon . . . Come on . . . sit down . . . He may be able to help us . . .

CHARLEY (*undecided*): Well . . . I had better . . .

JOHNNY (*frantic—fervent*): No, no . . . sit down . . . here . . . anywhere . . . be silent . . . be silent . . . think . . .

CHARLEY *sits down. Pause.*

JOHNNY: . . . At this moment . . . now . . . Radley is being told whether he can have Africa up there . . . whether he can campaign among the clouds . . . and charge with heavenly horses through the stars . . . his new life is being made for him . . . pray God he will not forget us, languishing here on earth . . .

CHARLEY (*conventional*): I hope he gets what he wants . . .

JOHNNY (*smiling—electric*): He will . . . we will, both of us, achieve our aims . . . you will start anew with your inventions . . . they will need you wherever you go . . .

CHARLEY (*very slow—tortured*): They must need me . . . I have a . . . a timeless feeling . . . as if I had passed through many worlds completely useless . . . I feel as if I am standing on the edge of a great precipice . . . I can feel the wind on my forehead . . . there is darkness and light before me . . . there are no dimensions . . . logic has crumbled . . . (*Climax.*) I can see . . .

He slumps forward . . . motionless.

JOHNNY (*smiling—transported*): And now me! . . . Me!

Pause. He breathes heavily—shouts up to Heaven.

[171]

JOHNNY: Don't forget me . . . please, please . . . I am eighty-five. Radley was eighty-three . . . Charley eighty-four . . . I should have gone first . . .

Pause. Soft. Ardent.

JOHNNY: . . . Don't make this moment unendurable, dear God . . . let it come like a thunderclap . . . let there be noise . . . clamour . . . let me follow them into the land of everlasting peace . . .

Pause.

JOHNNY: Surely my time has come now . . . a matter of a few minutes . . .

Pause. Agonized.

JOHNNY: Hurry, hurry . . .

Gazing at the ceiling transfixed.

JOHNNY: Don't turn your eyes from me . . . (*Hysterical, with wild, stupid poetry.*) Why does the music grow softer? . . . Sound the bells for my coming . . . I shall sing as I rise through the clouds . . . (*Screaming.*) Do not shut the gate . . . Hear me! Hear me! . . .

Quite out of breath, he looks down, twitching and sweating. Suddenly throws off the rug, and totters to the cupboard, groaning. He stoops low, and brings out RADLEY'S *revolver.*

JOHNNY (*ardent*): If only . . . if only . . .

He aims at the ceiling, and absently pulls the trigger. There is a loud report, and some plaster falls from the ceiling.

JOHNNY (*transported*): It is . . . (*Looks up, hastily.*) . . . forgive me for what I am about to do . . . I dare not be forgotten now . . . and I am only anticipating my deliverance by a few seconds. Forgive me, . . . forgive me . . .

He places the revolver to his temple, shuts his eyes, and pulls the trigger. Nothing happens. His eyes open. He pulls again . . . then again and again in desperation. Noises outside. A NURSE *rushes in.*

NURSE (*hysterical*): Did that noise come from here?

JOHNNY (*simply*): Yes . . .

NURSE (*sees revolver and the two dead men, and screams—then retreating*): You . . . killed them . . .

JOHNNY (*like a disappointed child*): No . . . I didn't have to . . . they cheated me . . . they left me all alone . . .

NURSE: Is that loaded?

JOHNNY: Do you think I would be here, if it was?

NURSE: Did you try to . . . (*She is overwhelmed by the idea.*)

JOHNNY (*weary*): I tried to feel the wind on my forehead . . . there was none . . . I tried to see darkness and light before me . . . they were not there . . . (*Bitterly.*) I tried to make logic crumble . . . it wouldn't . . .

NURSE (*not by any means recovered*): But how did they die?

JOHNNY: I wish I knew.

NURSE (*overwhelmed*): Oh, how . . . awful.

    Pause.

JOHNNY (*infinitely sad*): Yet another Autumn . . . and another Autumn . . . and another . . . and not so much as a glimpse . . . beyond . . .

CURTAIN

THE LOVE OF FOUR COLONELS

A Play in Three Acts

THE LOVE OF FOUR COLONELS was first presented by Linnit and Dunfee Ltd. (by arrangement with Bronson Albery) at Wyndham's Theatre in London on 23 May 1951. The play was produced by John Fernald, the settings were designed by Fanny Taylor, and incidental music was by Antony Hopkins. The cast was as follows:—

COLONEL DESMOND DE S. RINDER-SPARROW	Colin Gordon
COLONEL WESLEY BREITENSPIEGEL	Alan Gifford
COLONEL AIMÉ FRAPPOT	Eugene Deckers
COLONEL ALEXANDER IKONENKO	Theodore Bikel
THE MAYOR OF HERZOGENBURG	Paul Hardtmuth
THE WICKED FAIRY	Peter Ustinov
THE GOOD FAIRY	Gwen Cherrell
THE BEAUTY	Moira Lister
MRS BREITENSPIEGEL	Patricia Jessel
MME FRAPPOT	Diana Graves
MRS RINDER-SPARROW	Mary Hignett
MME IKONENKO	Mona Lilian

THE LOVE OF FOUR COLONELS was first produced in the United States, in a somewhat modified form, at the Sam S. Shubert Theatre in New York, 15 January 1953, by the Theatre Guild and Aldrich & Myers. It was staged by Rex Harrison and scenery and costumes were by Rolf Gerard. Karl Nielsen was production stage manager. The cast was as follows:—

COLONEL WESLEY BREITENSPIEGEL	Larry Gates
COLONEL DESMOND DE S. RINDER-SPARROW	Robert Coote
COLONEL AIMÉ FRAPPOT	George Voskovec
COLONEL ALEXANDER IKONENKO	Stefan Schnabel
MAYOR OF HERZOGENBURG	Reginald Mason
THE MAN (Wicked Fairy)	Rex Harrison
DONOVAN (Good Fairy)	Leueen MacGrath
BEAUTY	Lilli Palmer
CHAMBERLAIN	Reginald Mason

SYNOPSIS OF SCENES

ACT I: *The Office of the Allied Administration at Herzogenburg.*

ACT II: *Within the Castle.*

ACT III: *The same. A few minutes later.*

AUTHOR'S NOTE

It should be carefully noted that the cast in the English production of this play differs considerably in some respects from that of the American production. Since the text printed in this book is that of the English version, the cast of the English production is the one to be followed here.

The characters of Mrs Breitenspiegel, Mrs Rinder-Sparrow, Mme Frappot and Mme Ikonenko do not appear in the American version.

In the American version, the same actor who plays the Mayor plays the Chamberlain.

ACT I

The offices of the Allied Military Administration at Herzogenburg, a village in the Hartz mountains, disputed by Britain, France, America and Russia after the Great War of 1939-45. As a consequence of this dispute on a high level, this innocent and charming spot is cursed with an abundance of Colonels, charged by their governments to carry on the friction on an intimate, domestic level. The scene of the battleground is a drab room giving every evidence of near-destruction, but rendered habitable by a liberal dispensation of plywood, cardboard, and asbestos. The furnishing is as functional as only military interior decoration can be. There is a trestle table, four chairs, a few ingenious filing systems in cupboardlike containers. The walls are covered in old notices, all of them either urgent or important. There is also a large photograph of a naked woman being coy with a beach ball, a drawing of a bulldog with young, a reproduction of an Utrillo street scene, and a framed portrait of Joseph Stalin. The window at the back gives over a forest. The upper turrets of a castle can be dimly perceived rising from the jungle.

Door LEFT. *Door* RIGHT.

As the curtain rises, COLONEL WESLEY BREITENSPIEGEL *is lying back dangerously in his chair, his feet on the table, smoking a cigar. He is a bald man with rimless glasses.* COLONEL DESMOND DE S. RINDER-SPARROW *is sitting forward on the very edge of his chair, puffing at a pipe, his eyes glazed in the manner of an Empire-builder hypnotized by his greatest enemy, the horizon. There follows the longest pause in theatrical history, towards the end of which the audience should be convinced that the actors have been the victims of some administrative disaster. The pause is terminated after the adequate time for embarrassment has elapsed.*

DESMOND: We seem to have run out of conversation.

Another long pause.

WESLEY: Yeah . . .

DESMOND: What?

WESLEY: Yeah . . .

DESMOND: Yes . . .

Pause.

WESLEY: Have you ever contemplated suicide?

DESMOND (*deeply interested*): Lord no. Have you?

WESLEY: No.

DESMOND: I say, old man, you're not . . . I mean . . .

WESLEY (*a little irritated*): What are you so embarrassed about?

DESMOND: Well, I hardly like to say.

WESLEY: Then don't.

DESMOND: You've not anything rash in mind?

WESLEY: No. Unless you call playing golf with you rash.

DESMOND: That's very far from what I meant. This sudden mention of suicide . . .

WESLEY: O, no. Good God, no. My wife would be furious.

    DESMOND *laughs*.

What are you laughing at?

DESMOND: You bringing the wife into it.

WESLEY: My wife's not funny. She's very far from funny. But then I don't go for laughter much. I'm a romantic at heart.

    DESMOND *laughs again*.

What are you snickering at now?

DESMOND: I always imagined a romantic as tall and emaciated, with long hair.

WESLEY: Do you mean to say you haven't even gotten the imagination to conceive of a bald romantic?

DESMOND: I've never given the matter a thought, to tell you the honest truth.

WESLEY (*robust*): Then it's time you did! You have before you a man who dreams of only one thing—to disobey an order in the most glamorous possible way.

DESMOND (*shocked*): Disobey an order?

WESLEY: Yes . . . I'd like to have led the Charge of the Light Brigade against all expert advice.

DESMOND (*possessive*): You'd have to have been a British officer to do that.

WESLEY: You're as possessive as a woman.

DESMOND: I'm quoting facts.

WESLEY: O.K., O.K. I'll leave the Charge of the Light Brigade to you.

DESMOND: I don't particularly want it.

WESLEY: And you grudge me having it?

DESMOND: Oh, you can have it if you like.

WESLEY: Now I'm sore. I don't want it any more.

DESMOND: I'm sorry. I didn't mean to be difficult about it.

WESLEY (*defiant*): I still have Custer's Last Stand.

DESMOND: Yes, I suppose you have.

WESLEY: Listen, I'll tell you just how romantic I am.

DESMOND: Are you positive you haven't told me before?

WESLEY: You know, you're the one man who's ever made me lose my taste for conversation.

DESMOND: I've always preferred silence myself.

WESLEY (*vindictive*): In that case, I'm sorry to disappoint you.

DESMOND: I'm used to disappointment, old fellow.

WESLEY: Well, I'm not. My romanticism is entirely personal and selfish. It is, according to my psychiatrist, ingrowing, largely owing to the inadequacy of my father.

DESMOND: He seems to have been adequate enough to bring you into the world.

WESLEY: He was counter-balanced by the overadequacy of my mother, and of a certain Doctor Purkiss.

DESMOND: Was he the family doctor?

WESLEY: In more ways than one.

DESMOND: Good gracious me.

WESLEY: A compromise was reached. My second name is Purkiss.

DESMOND: How very unusual.

WESLEY: My psychiatrist assures me it is absolutely usual, and that it is wrong to conceal such things, as a lack of ventilation alone breeds complexes. Have you a psychiatrist?

DESMOND: In England we can't afford them. Thank God.

> COLONEL AIMÉ FRAPPOT *enters. Short and a little sour, a dead cigarette always in his mouth.*

Hello, Aimé.

AIMÉ: Ikonenko not here yet?

DESMOND: No sign of him.

AIMÉ: The conference should have begun five minutes ago. I hoped I would be late.

DESMOND (*smiling*): Not looking forward to it?

AIMÉ: Enormously. Last week we all talked in French. For once I could relax and tell you all what I thought of you with no fear of contradiction.

DESMOND: It beats me why we should have to talk French when all of you know English.

AIMÉ: It is a question of honour. English may be more convenient, but it will not be used if there is the chance of the French language being slighted.

> *He feels in his pocket for a match, and not finding one, goes over to* DESMOND, *who is lighting his pipe.*

May I?

> DESMOND *gives him a light.*

WESLEY: Next week we all have to speak Russian.

AIMÉ: It's then that Ikonenko pushes all his legislation through, and we get into trouble.

WESLEY: Yeah. The bastard.

AIMÉ: He's not a bad fellow.

DESMOND: Clever.

AIMÉ: We mustn't be ungenerous enough to grudge him that.

WESLEY: After all, we're all clever in our own way.

AIMÉ (*with a smile and a glance at* WESLEY): Yes. (*Slight pause.*) It's strange how I hate this place, and yet I know in advance I'll be sorry to leave it.

DESMOND: Yes, it is strange.

AIMÉ: No, not really. It was stupid of me to say it was strange. Have you never noticed how, in life, hatred is as binding a tie as love? The pathos of leaving a detested school, or a mistress who has begun to bore you?

DESMOND (*charming*): Heavens, I always begin to bore them first.

AIMÉ (*a little disarmed*): I must remember that. It's a perfectly charming remark.

DESMOND (*surprised*): Is it?

WESLEY: Why did you go into the Army, Aimé?

AIMÉ: My father said it was the best entrée into politics. He was a man hypnotized by his own mediocrity.

DESMOND: Oh, I say. Those are hard words for anyone to use about his old man. What was he?

AIMÉ: He was Minister of Agriculture for ten minutes in 1912.

> *The others laugh.*

You know, Desmond, you look like a man who has never had the embarrassment of a choice in his life.

DESMOND: Well, in my case it was a toss-up between the Army and the Church. Luckily there were more vacancies in the Army at that particular moment, so my mind was made up for me. I wasn't very bright, you understand.

AIMÉ (*with tact*): I understand entirely.

DESMOND (*suddenly laughing*): Before you came in, Wesley said he was a romantic.

AIMÉ: I know he is.

DESMOND (*unsure now*): Is he?

AIMÉ: Yes. He's a romantic. I'm a realist. And you . . . you're a thoroughly nice fellow.

DESMOND (*barely audible*): Thanks.

AIMÉ: That's why we get on so badly. Think of us, for a moment, and reflect on the stupidity of our employers. We have been here ever since this disputed zone was created, two and a half years ago, and in that time we have decided nothing except that we wish to transfer our headquarters from here to that overgrown palace. (*He gazes at it through the window.*)

WESLEY: I've had the latest reports in from the troops trying to get through to the castle.

AIMÉ: Any result?

WESLEY: No. Lieutenant Coppermaker reports that at first he thought the weeds uprooted during the day were being replaced in some mysterious way by the local population during the night. Now he's convinced the plants are growing together by themselves during the hours of darkness. He then indulges in some useless speculation on the effect of the atomic explosion on flora and fauna, and suggests finally that Washington should send a man.

DESMOND: Is it going to?

WESLEY: If you knew Washington, you'd realize that that is the silliest thing to ask it to do. What I've done is to send Lieutenant Coppermaker to the psychiatrist for a start.

AIMÉ (*smiles*): You are sceptical because you are a romantic. I, being a realist, am prepared to accept Lieutenant Coppermaker's report.

WESLEY: What do you mean?

AIMÉ (*agreeable*): I believe in fairies.

DESMOND: Well, you know, in Ireland——

WESLEY: I know, leprechauns, giants. Listen to me——

The door opens, and COLONEL IKONENKO *enters. An entirely*

[183]

expressionless man carrying a brief case. There is an electric silence occasioned by his entrance.

You're late.

> IKONENKO *doesn't answer. He just sits at his place, spreads his papers out, opens his fountain pen, and then says:*

IKONENKO: Now you're late.

> *The others all make haste to sit down.*

Colonel Breitenspiegel, I wish to bring to your attention as Chairman for this week that I am Chairman by rotation next week, and that the official language for the seven days commencing (*He consults a diary*) on the 18th will be Russian.

WESLEY: There's no need to rub that in.

AIMÉ: Colonel Ikonenko, may I permit myself the honour of bringing to your kind attention the fact that during the week commencing (*He consults a diary.*) the 2nd, that is, eight days after the conclusion of your term as Chairman, I shall be in the Chair, and the recognized language will be French.

IKONENKO (*stiff*): That is generally understood.

DESMOND: I trust no one is forgetting that—(*Flicking the pages of his diary.*) Where are we?—Yes—that on the 25th it's my turn, and we all speak English.

AIMÉ: On behalf of my Government, I agree.

WESLEY: There's no need to put all this to the vote, I trust.

IKONENKO (*secretive*): It may be better.

WESLEY: But heavens, we all agree.

IKONENKO: You never know.

WESLEY: Well, I'm against it. It's ridiculous. It's a waste of time.

IKONENKO: I must insist.

WESLEY: In that case, I propose that this Committee does not wish to vote on the agreement of the agreement, owing to the redundancy of so doing. Will all in favour of not voting kindly signify their viewpoint in the usual way?

> WESLEY, DESMOND *and* AIMÉ *raise their hands.*

Now will all in favour of voting raise their hands?

> IKONENKO *lifts his hand.*

The Committee has voted by a majority of three to one not to vote.

> IKONENKO *packs all his documents, and leaves the room.*

Crazy guy.

AIMÉ: He'll be back in a minute.

DESMOND: Extraordinary waste of energy.

Pause. IKONENKO *re-enters, and replaces all his documents expressionlessly.*

IKONENKO: What is next on the agenda?

WESLEY: You haven't given me much time to look up my notes, have you?

IKONENKO: Is there any report on the state of the castle yet from your subordinate?

WESLEY: Yes. All in good time.

IKONENKO: I must take it on myself to press for a decision.

WESLEY: Another matter comes first on the agenda.

IKONENKO: I must press for a reversal in the order of the agenda.

WESLEY (*angry*): Why?

IKONENKO: I have received a report on the situation independently of yours. Lieutenant of the 3rd Grade Bulganov——

WESLEY (*livid*): That is a direct contravention of our agreement that the duty of investigating and clearing the undergrowth surrounding the castle devolved on United States arms. Lieutenant Coppermaker was acting not in the interests of the U.S., but in the interests of the——

IKONENKO (*firm*): Lieutenant of the 3rd Grade Bulganov's word is above suspicion. He is a Hero of Stalingrad, a Hero of Labour, and holder of the Suvorov Medal of the 2nd Class.

WESLEY: That has nothing to do with it! Lieutenant Coppermaker is an accredited member of the New York Stock Exchange, and an old Princeton alumnus. His report is the only valid report, and the matter will be dealt with in the order of the agenda.

AIMÉ: I thought you said he had been sent to the psychiatrist?

WESLEY (*faltering*): On a social call. The psychiatrist is an old personal friend of his.

AIMÉ: From the Stock Exchange?

WESLEY: No, from Princeton.

IKONENKO: You refuse to change the order of the agenda?

WESLEY: As Chairman for the week, I formally refuse your request.

IKONENKO *gathers all his papers together, and leaves the room.* Will you get him!

DESMOND: It's damn bad form, you know.

AIMÉ: He believes in exercise.

IKONENKO *returns, expressionless, and lays his documents on the table.*

IKONENKO: What is the next subject for discussion?

[185]

WESLEY: I'm going to give way to you, Ikonenko. We're going to discuss the castle after all. I'm sick and tired of you, and I'm going to have this out with you, here and now. I will begin with Lieutenant Coppermaker's report. Mummummummum . . . (*He skips passages which seem to him irrelevant.*) . . . "In that I am convinced after three days' work on the undergrowth, during which we employed not only picks and shovels, but also bulldozers and tractors, that some botanical phenomenon is restricting our progress. However many weeds we dug up during the day, they were without exception deep in the soil again next morning. It is clear to anyone with an elementary knowledge of gardening that the reconstitution of the weeds is far neater and more accurate than could be achieved by human labour. I therefore feel . . ." mummummummum . . . that is Lieutenant Coppermaker's report in a nutshell.

IKONENKO: Colonel Breitenspiegel, we are here to put our cards on the table. There is no room in our relationship for nutshells. Why, Colonel Breitenspiegel, were you mumbling?

WESLEY: Red tape, Colonel Ikonenko. Unadulterated military red tape, with which, for reasons of a surprising charity, I did not wish to try your patience!

IKONENKO: Your attitude is deeply unpleasant to me. Rather than argue with you, I will set you an example. Contrary to the hysteria shown by Lieutenant Coppermaker, the report of Lieutenant of the 3rd Grade Bulganov is both brilliant and to the point. (*He opens a document.*) Mummummummum . . . "It is easy to understand that the lack of progress in the clearing of the undergrowth is due to—(1) the lack of will to work shown by American soldiers unversed in Socialist doctrine, (2) the consistent sabotage exercised by Reactionary Diversionists and Fascist hyenas . . ."

WESLEY *opens his mouth to reply, but is too late.*

DESMOND: Nobody with a working knowledge of the hyena would ever credit it with any political opinions.

WESLEY (*angry*): Desmond, for God's sake don't interrupt. What was the meaning of all *that* mumbling, Ikonenko? Here's something I want to put to the vote, fellows.

IKONENKO: I object.

WESLEY: I move that this meeting deplores the underhand, surreptitious and dishonest nature of the Soviet tactics on the occasion of the report over the operations to free the castle from its surrounding jungle. Will all those in favour kindly raise their hands?

WESLEY *and* DESMOND *raise their hands, but* AIMÉ *rises and goes towards the door. There is immediate tension. All half-rise.*

[186]

IKONENKO: Does this move of yours reflect the official French attitude?

AIMÉ: What?

WESLEY: Does this mean a split in the Atlantic bloc?

AIMÉ: Why?

IKONENKO: I must telegraph Moscow immediately.

AIMÉ: For what reason?

WESLEY: I warn you, this action may affect United States Economic Aid.

AIMÉ: What action?

DESMOND: Remember Verdun, old son. Don't let us down now!

AIMÉ: Who am I letting down?

WESLEY: Us. By walking out of the conference now, of all times.

AIMÉ: There comes a time during the day when even the most strongly constituted of us has to leave the room. I'll be back in a minute.

> AIMÉ *goes out.*

WESLEY: There are times when nature reasserts herself, Ikonenko, and laughs in the face of all governments. That should be a chastening thought for you.

IKONENKO: The Soviet Government has never attempted to deny the presence of nature in the world. On the other hand, we are the pioneers of Socialist-Realism, and the dishonest manner in which Colonel Frappot left the room reflects the mocking and decadent state of contemporary French so-called civilization.

DESMOND: How does a Socialist-Realist spend a penny?

IKONENKO: I do not understand the question.

WESLEY: What would you have done?

IKONENKO: I should have made my intention clear.

DESMOND: How terribly embarrassing.

WESLEY: Speaking then as a Socialist-Realist——

IKONENKO: But you are not one.

WESLEY: O.K. Speaking as a—what is it? Pluto-Democrat——

IKONENKO: You condemn yourself!

WESLEY: It's rather fun. I like it. Speaking as one of those, I think Stalin stinks.

IKONENKO: I think the same of Truman.

WESLEY: So do I. I'm a Republican.

> AIMÉ *returns.*

[187]

AIMÉ: The Mayor is waiting outside . . . did any one of you summon him?

WESLEY: I did, yes.

IKONENKO: Without consulting us?

WESLEY: Have him come in. (*To* IKONENKO.) If you walk out now, you'll miss the fun.

> AIMÉ *goes to the door, and returns with the* MAYOR OF HERZO-GENBURG. *Very old, very benevolent.*

Dr. Busch, why come right in.

MAYOR (*beaming*): So nice. (*He shakes* WESLEY *by the hand.*) Oberst Breitenspiegel. Your name I remember. It's a good old German name.

WESLEY: We're descended from the Counts of Breitenspiegel.

MAYOR: This I didn't know. But once we had, when I was small, a man who was sharpening the knives in the village. He had exactly this name of Breitenspiegel.

WESLEY: Yes . . . well, you know Colonel Frappot.

MAYOR: Oh, yes. (*In appalling French.*) Chay eu l'honneur de vous regontrer . . . em . . . decha . . .

AIMÉ: En effet, M le Maire.

DESMOND: Good evening, Mr Mayor.

WESLEY: Colonel Rinder-Sparrow.

MAYOR (*laughing*): You must forgive it to me. Such a name I can't not so remember. Breitenspiegel——

WESLEY: Colonel Ikonenko.

> IKONENKO *doesn't look up.*

MAYOR (*determined to make an impression*): Da, da, da. Nitchevo. Ya Vas Lublu.

WESLEY: Won't you sit down?

IKONENKO: I must make my position clear. I am opposed to your visit here.

MAYOR: Why?

IKONENKO: I was not consulted.

MAYOR (*pityingly*): Is that the only reason?

WESLEY: Others will occur to him later on. Come on, sit down. Have a cigar. Now, Herr Busch, we'll come straight to the point.

MAYOR (*with the infinite indulgence of the older man*): You wish to ask questions from the castle, naturally.

DESMOND: How do you know?

IKONENKO: Nothing is confidential in this place.

MAYOR: Oh, my dear boy, why should it be? I have been an officer in an army of occupation myself—Galicia, 1914. No, dear boys, if you have secrets, you keep them from each other, not from me.

THE COLONELS *shift nervously.*

WESLEY: Suppose you tell us about the castle?

MAYOR: Forget the castle. I have seen your soldiers working, and I even saw a Russian officer sitting in the bushes looking at them, and I thought to myself, "So much sweat wasted, and that poor officer can sit in the bush all night, he will find nothing. Nothing."

WESLEY: Why nothing?

MAYOR: Don't ask me. Even if I knew——

IKONENKO: He's bluffing.

MAYOR (*strange*): I know nothing about it.

WESLEY: But you do know that the weeds around it behave in the strangest way.

IKONENKO (*loud*): He knows? He is responsible for it!

MAYOR: I know it is difficult to reach the castle . . .

WESLEY: Difficult? It's damned impossible!

MAYOR: I have never tried it myself.

WESLEY: Why not? I should have thought that human inquisitiveness alone would have——

MAYOR: In these parts we know better than to try. We leave it to the others.

AIMÉ (*intrigued*): Which others?

MAYOR: The officials. People like you. There was a Gauleiter who came here eight years ago. He saw it in the distance and wanted it as his office. He tried to enter, and failed.

DESMOND: Good heavens, we're not in Tibet. What is all this mystery?

MAYOR: Before him, there was an officer of the Gestapo who came here. Once again he tried, and once again he failed. He is now in a lunatic asylum.

WESLEY: Why?

MAYOR: It was the shock of failure on a mentality at that time accustomed to success.

IKONENKO: Herr Busch, you have spoken to us in a deeply suspicious and incomprehensible manner, and your attitude, even though it is impossible to understand, does you no credit. I must warn you against the terrible danger of being incomprehensible in the future.

MAYOR: I am not afraid of you, dear child. Why do you want to take what does not belong to you?

WESLEY: That's no way to talk, Mayor. You must understand that Germany has been thrashed, and that we're here as an occupying force. You've got no right to argue with us.

MAYOR: You have defeated Germany, but you have not defeated me, and you have not defeated the past, and you have not defeated the soil.

DESMOND: Now look here, Mr Mayor, you inferred, if I understood you aright, that we are thieves. As I understand it, that castle doesn't belong to anyone—who then are we robbing?

MAYOR: You are robbing history.

DESMOND: That's nonsense.

AIMÉ: But it's extremely poetic.

IKONENKO: Poetry should be left to poets.

AIMÉ: Why?

IKONENKO: It is their duty. Our duty is administration. Regardless of any decision of this Council, I shall give the order to-night for Soviet troops at my disposal to begin operations for the occupation of the castle at dawn to-morrow, so that it may pass back into the hands of its legitimate owners, the people!

   The MAYOR *laughs.*

Your laughter may have serious consequences.

MAYOR: You say the castle belongs to the people. How will they all get into it?

AIMÉ (*who has been pacing agitatedly*): I ask you, mon Colonel, to reconsider your order to your troops.

IKONENKO: Actions are more comprehensible than words!

AIMÉ: And more dangerous.

IKONENKO: The victors must educate the defeated. Our position here has been made ridiculous by (1) the lack of initiative shown by American troops in clearing the undergrowth, and (2) the Wall Street tactics of——

WESLEY (*jumping up*): I've had enough of this!

DESMOND (*jumping up*): May I appeal for some good sound British common sense?

IKONENKO: What have you to say?

DESMOND: Nothing as yet, but I'm thinking furiously.

WESLEY draws some pills out of his pocket, and an inhaler. Quickly he takes the pills.

MAYOR (*soft*): Dear boys, you are making yourselves ill, and all for such silly reasons. You must take care of yourselves. Are you married? Colonel Ikonenko?

IKONENKO: I do not discuss my affairs in public.

MAYOR: Your wife is an official secret also?

WESLEY inhales deeply, shutting first one nostril, then the other.

AIMÉ: I am married. We are all married.

MAYOR: And you are happy?

AIMÉ: Speaking personally, she is the mother of my children.

MAYOR: And that is all?

AIMÉ: I live with an actress. She lives with a haulage-contractor. Apart from that we are inseparable.

MAYOR: But your children?

AIMÉ (*simply*): I love them.

DESMOND: What has all this to do with the castle?

MAYOR: A great deal, Colonel. Have you a wife and a home?

DESMOND: Yes, and three dogs.

MAYOR: And you love them?

DESMOND: Yes, I breed them. Dingos. Wild dogs, you know.

MAYOR: And I presume that Herr Breitenspiegel is also married?

WESLEY: Don't talk to me. The doctor told me I've got to be free from all worry.

MAYOR: Then as you all have something worth living for, children, I beg you not to continue asking questions about the castle. Be happy you are alive, and leave it at that. I appeal to you before it's too late!

DESMOND: Too late? Too late for what?

MAYOR (*very soft*): . . . All I know is that when I was telling the Gauleiter what I had heard about the castle, the door opened slowly without us noticing it . . .

The door begins to open slowly.

AIMÉ: And who came in?

MAYOR (*his voice filled with wonder*): Nobody . . .

IKONENKO suddenly laughs.

IKONENKO: Brilliantly dramatic!

DESMOND: Who opened that door?

[191]

IKONENKO: The wind.

AIMÉ (*at the window*): Look at the trees. There's no wind to-day.

MAYOR (*agonized*): Oh my dear children, change the subject!

AIMÉ: What happened then?

MAYOR: A bell rang. A terrible, cracked church bell.

IKONENKO (*after a pause. Triumphant*): Silence!

> *A distant church bell rings a discordant note.*

MAYOR (*vehement*): You fools!

AIMÉ (*shouting*): What happened then?

> *The figure of a MAN appears silently at the door, dressed as a tramp. He is very tall, thin, and he smiles. The MAYOR expresses the greatest terror, cowers, crosses himself, places his hat on his head, and prepares to escape.*

MAN (*calm*): Guten abend, Herr Busch.

> *The MAYOR lifts his hat.*

MAYOR: Guten abend . . .

> *He runs out.*

IKONENKO: Who are you? And have you a permit?

MAN: I have many permits to do many things, but I can afford to ignore them.

IKONENKO: No, my friend, you cannot afford to ignore them. You may not circulate without a permit, and you may not enter this office without an appointment.

MAN: I have an appointment.

IKONENKO: We never make appointments during conference hours.

MAN: All you need do is to look in your appointment book.

IKONENKO: No use, I know we have no appointments. Now will you kindly leave before I call soldiers.

MAN: Your soldiers are all asleep. I passed them on the way up, sleeping like babies.

IKONENKO: What? You're lying!

MAN: Oh, you nasty man. What a horrid thing to say!

DESMOND (*who has been fingering the appointment book*): I say, it's quite true.

IKONENKO: What?

DESMOND: There is an appointment here.

WESLEY: For whom?

DESMOND: I don't know. It's in Russian.

IKONENKO: Let me see.

DESMOND *passes the book.*

Professor Diabolikov. I did not write this.

DESMOND: It's in your handwriting, old son.

IKONENKO: Diabolikov. Is that your name?

MAN: It was a nickname Catherine the Great gave me . . . to please Voltaire. They shared the joke. I never thought it very funny.

IKONENKO: I must warn you——

MAN: Against the dangers of incomprehensibility. I know.

IKONENKO: What? (*Fresh start.*) Are you a Russian subject?

MAN: Not predominantly.

IKONENKO: I expect a specific answer.

MAN: I expect an intelligent question, duckie.

DESMOND: I regret to say the fellow's English.

MAN: Not unqualifiedly, I'm just talking English because this is the week for talking English. If you had inspired a visit next week, I should have talked Russian with pleasure.

AIMÉ: How did you know about our ruling?

MAN: How did I know . . . and love . . . Catherine the Great?

AIMÉ: Love?

MAN: In my way . . .

AIMÉ: Vous l'avez aimé?

MAN (*in perfect French*): A ma façon . . .

IKONENKO: You have not yet produced a satisfactory permit.

MAN (*searching in his vast coat*): You really are most difficult to convince. What's this?

He pulls out a scroll.

Oh, no. This is permission from Nero to taunt the lions before their dinner of gospellers. Here we are. No. A front-row ticket for Robespierre's execution. A disappointing affair. The weather was far from perfect. There's a special kind of weather which is ideal for executions, you know—you need an autumn morning, really, to surround the scene with an aura of poetic melancholy, and just enough of an orange sun to catch the blade. For lions, on the other hand, you can't do better than your midsummer heat, in which the poor beasts are torn between an oppressive lethargy and their greed for blood. Such leonine quandaries drag out the agony of the gospellers deliciously. (*With a giggle.*) But what am I doing, talking about it as though it still went on to-day. No, alas. (*He sighs.*) The taste for

[193]

THE LOVE OF FOUR COLONELS

limited horror was dissipated. A decadence set in. Our love of quality was polluted by a love of quantity. Nowadays we do things on a majestic scale, with guns and bombs and gases, and it's surprising how the human species obeys our every whim in this respect . . . (*Looking at the* COLONELS.) All dressed up in their little boiler suits, with bits of gold and silver braid to mark the degree of their guilt. (*He laughs.*) Oh dear, oh dear . . .

IKONENKO (*terrible*): Where is the permit?

MAN (*feminine*): Oh, do stop nagging, Sasha! I've got it. Look. Signed by you. (*He gives* IKONENKO *a permit.*) This man may go anywhere, do anything, and say anything at any time. Signed Ikonenko.

IKONENKO (*his hand trembling*): This permit is a forgery, and is confiscated.

MAN: I don't mind. I've got plenty more. Look, here's the same signed by Stalin, on official paper.

IKONENKO *seizes it.*

IKONENKO: This permit is likewise——

MAN (*sinister*): Be careful what you say! Do you dare to suggest that this is a forgery too? (*In terribly accurate and menacing Russian.*) Astarojna, Tovarisch Polkovnik! (*He wags a finger.*) Astarojna! I may well be an officer of the M.V.D. You never can be sure.

IKONENKO: The situation is open to review.

WESLEY: What does that mean?

IKONENKO: This is a purely Soviet matter.

DESMOND: I damn well *hope* it is.

IKONENKO: The conditions in this town are perilous for visitors. I therefore take the liberty of placing you in protective custody until it is safe for you to circulate.

He rings a bell.

MAN: I told you the soldiers were asleep. Nobody will answer that bell.

IKONENKO: We shall see.

MAN (*offering* DESMOND *a pouch*): Tobacco, Colonel?

DESMOND: Thank you so much. I only smoke my own brand.

MAN: McPherson's Fine Old Curly Shag.

DESMOND: How did you know?

MAN: It's the only kind I have.

DESMOND: But it's unobtainable outside the Shetland Islands.

MAN: I know. Isn't it a bore. (*He gives* DESMOND *the pouch. To* WESLEY.) Cigar?

WESLEY (*challenging*): I bet you don't have my brand.

MAN: Cherokee Blues?

WESLEY: Well, what do you know?

    The MAN *throws it over.*

MAN: Mon Colonel, Gauloise Bleue?

AIMÉ (*pleasant*): Je ne dirai pas non.

MAN (*giving him the packet of cigarettes*): Voilà. Comrade Colonel.

IKONENKO: I don't smoke.

MAN: I have even catered for you. I have brought you nothing.

    IKONENKO *rings the bell again, viciously.*

DESMOND: I say, I've been thinking.

MAN: Yes?

DESMOND: It's just occurred to me . . .

MAN: Yes?

DESMOND: Who are you?

MAN (*sighing sadly*): It's a long story.

AIMÉ: How long?

MAN (*a little surprised*): Very, very long.

AIMÉ: I have no light.

MAN: Oh, I'm so sorry.

    He pulls out an enormous and elaborate table lighter from his robes which gives a flame like a blow-lamp. They all gaze at it in astonishment. With some trepidation AIMÉ *lights his cigarette from it. Pause.*

AIMÉ: Do you know who I think you are?

MAN: No.

AIMÉ: The devil.

    The MAN *practically drops the lighter.*

MAN (*falsetto*): Who?

AIMÉ (*charming*): The devil.

MAN: Why, do I look like him?

DESMOND: I say, steady.

AIMÉ: I don't know. I've never met him. But he's someone I've always wanted to meet. We have so much in common.

MAN: I'm glad you've never met him, dear, because I've never heard that I look like him before, even from those who know us both very well. I don't want to seem catty, or say anything behind his back which could give offence, because I have the very, very highest regard for him, but I don't think looks are his strong point. Dear me, no.

DESMOND: This is perfectly preposterous. I suppose the next thing you'll be telling us is that you know God.

MAN (*sore point*): I always go out of my way to smile at Him, but He *always* cuts me dead.

IKONENKO (*who has been ringing furiously*): This man is mad. I am going to fetch the soldiers.

MAN: Sorry if I've been boring you about God and the Devil—I beg your pardon, the Devil and God.

IKONENKO: I recognize no such people.

He stamps out.

AIMÉ: But then, who are you?

WESLEY: He's come straight out of an asylum.

DESMOND: How d'you explain all those tricks of his? How d'you explain the tobacco?

WESLEY: He's a conjuror who's gone crazy. Yeah, that's it, the guy's a crazy conjuror.

DESMOND: It goes deeper than that, I'm afraid Wesley. This tobacco. It's the genuine article. Marvellous. It takes a lot to convince me, but now . . .

AIMÉ: What has he convinced you of?

DESMOND: I don't know yet . . .

They look at the MAN *fixedly. He becomes coy.*

MAN: You're making my ears tingle, talking about me like that.

WESLEY: Why did you come here?

MAN: In answer to a summons.

WESLEY: Who summoned you?

MAN: I came to take you to the castle.

DESMOND: The castle!

IKONENKO *returns.*

IKONENKO: All the soldiers have been drugged! This is sabotage and counter-revolutionary activity of the most dangerous sort. (*To the* MAN.) You are under arrest.

MAN: Don't be silly.

The MAN *rises.*

IKONENKO: Stay where you are!

MAN: I want to stretch my legs.

IKONENKO (*draws a revolver. He shouts*): Stay where you are!

DESMOND ⎤ Ikonenko!
WESLEY ⎬ Put that away!
AIMÉ ⎦ I forbid it!

MAN: Don't worry about me. (*Approaches* IKONENKO.) Now, don't make a fool of yourself, there's a love.

> IKONENKO *shoots once; twice; then four times in rapid succession. The* MAN *scratches his stomach.*

(*Feline.*) It's terrible how bullets tickle.

IKONENKO (*appalled*): He's alive! (*He collapses on to a sofa.*)

DESMOND (*military*): Explain yourself.

MAN: Who?

DESMOND: You, sir.

MAN: Me?

DESMOND: Yes, indeed, sir. Why aren't you dead?

MAN: Why should I be?

DESMOND: Don't side-step the issue, sir. This is the most inconsiderate behaviour. After all, we are in some sense allied to the Russians, and look what you've done to my friend over there.

> IKONENKO *is in a state of collapse.*

He's in a perfectly ghastly condition. What you've done, sir, is neither fair nor funny. I can only put it down to a lack of breeding. Now, out with it!

MAN: Out with what? I have it on the devil's authority that English women are the easiest of victims, while Englishmen are quite impossibly difficult in practically every respect.

DESMOND: I will not tolerate remarks of a questionable nature about my countrywomen from the devil or anyone else. Kindly apologize to Colonel Ikonenko this instant, and if indeed you have drugged the soldiery, I would ask you to bring them to a state of consciousness with all due dispatch.

MAN: I've never been so bullied in all my endless life! Why should I apologize to Ikonenko? He called me names, and I'm very sensitive indeed. As for the soldiers, they're asleep, not drugged.

DESMOND: Then wake them up. If they sleep any longer they'll miss their tea. As for Ikonenko, I must appeal to what sense of honour you have to realize that there's a great difference between an officer doing his duty and a fellow assing around with live bullets inside him and refusing to lie down.

MAN: No, I won't apologize. I'm sulking.

DESMOND: In that case, I have no alternative, but to place you under arrest pending investigation. (*To his colleagues.*) Do you agree with me?

WESLEY: I guess so, but I don't like it. Say, how do you do it? You'd have had a great future in Chicago in the 'twenties.

MAN (*laughs*): I'd have had a great future! Splendid muddle of tenses for a mere mortal! What you mean to say is, I had a great past. (*In a faultless American accent.*) I was always at Al Capone's shoulder, and I was with Dillinger when he died.

WESLEY: That I don't believe.

DESMOND: The next thing you'll be saying in your damned irresponsible way is that you were there when Caesar crossed the Rubicon.

MAN: No, I wasn't. But then I didn't like Caesar personally, and when I don't like people, they've had it. What are you doing?

DESMOND *rings the bell.*

DESMOND: Ringing for Sergeant Daniels.

MAN: But you saw what happened before. The men are all asleep.

DESMOND: They'll come if I ring.

AIMÉ: Tell us about the castle.

DESMOND: I advise you not to talk to the fellow.

AIMÉ: I want to know. You see, I think we ought to arrest him, but I don't think we can.

MAN: Bravo. The castle? Yes. I'll take you there if you're very, very good.

DESMOND: If I go, I go alone.

MAN: You won't get in. You see, it is not a castle like any other. It is a castle touched by magic.

A very beautiful, but very prim A.T.S. GIRL *appears at the door.*

GIRL: You rang, sir?

MAN (*horrified*): You? Here?

DESMOND: Who the devil are you?

GIRL: Private Donovan. Your new driver, sir. Reporting for duty.

DESMOND: I told you they'd come if I rang. But look here, what's happened to Private Nash?

GIRL: Went sick, sir.

MAN (*violent*): Why did you come here? Just as I was getting on so well!

DESMOND: Donovan. D'you know this man?

[198]

GIRL (*sadly*): Yes, sir.

DESMOND: Who is he?

GIRL: I've known him for years, sir.

DESMOND: Eh? Where?

GIRL: Everywhere.

DESMOND: For years? How many years?

GIRL: About six thousand.

DESMOND: Donovan, I warn you. I'm in no mood for jollity.

GIRL: I'm telling the truth, sir. I've brought the car.

DESMOND: What for?

GIRL: To drive you to the castle.

DESMOND: I didn't order it.

GIRL: You were going to, though, sir.

DESMOND: But you haven't answered my first question yet. Who is this fellow?

GIRL: He's an old enemy. (*Fresh thought.*) You'll have plenty of time to find out, sir, at the castle.

MAN (*sad*): Are you coming too?

GIRL: I'm driving you.

MAN: There goes my fun.

AIMÉ: Fun? What fun?

GIRL (*seeing* IKONENKO, *who is still in a state of collapse*): Oh, the poor colonel! (*She takes him in her lap, and rocks him, administering smelling salts which she produces from her pocket.*)

DESMOND: Donovan, will you kindly put the Colonel down, and inform me first of all about yourself and then about this man.

GIRL (*smiles*): How are your dogs, sir, Ranger, Thunderbolt and Black Havoc?

DESMOND: Extremely fit, thank you, by the latest reports. How do know about them?

GIRL: Ah, Colonel Breitenspiegel, you were wrong to trust your wife's pyschiatrist.

WESLEY: Why?

GIRL: He's taking advantage of your absence. He took your wife to the Stork Club last night, and then——

WESLEY (*rising with a howl*): What!

MAN: Spoilsport!

GIRL: And you, Colonel Frappot. It was sinful of you to tell the Mayor that your wife was living with a haulage-contractor while you

[199]

are living with an actress. It's true that you live with an actress, but your wife is utterly faithful to this day, and lives in hopes . . .

AIMÉ (*unsurprised*): One tells little lies to appease one's conscience—and then, my wife's fidelity has always seemed to me so embarrassingly un-French.

GIRL: Or just embarrassing?

AIMÉ: Or just embarrassing.

IKONENKO (*stirs*): Where am I?

GIRL (*going to him*): You've been a bad boy, Colonel Ikonenko, shooting at a man.

IKONENKO: Is he dead?

GIRL: No.

IKONENKO (*writhing*): I have failed! I have failed!

GIRL: No, dear Colonel, you have not.

IKONENKO: My life is finished. I must go to Moscow and confess.

GIRL: You're coming to the castle with us.

IKONENKO: The castle . . .

GIRL: Yes, to visit the Sleeping Beauty.

DESMOND: What's that?

GIRL: Yes, sir, it's the castle where the Sleeping Beauty has been asleep for a hundred years.

DESMOND: Donovan, I warn you. I'm sure you're an excellent driver, but I won't have romancing.

WESLEY: Romancing!

AIMÉ: La Belle Au Bois Dormant.

DESMOND: What?

AIMÉ: The Beauty of the Sleeping Forest.

IKONENKO: Tchaikovsky.

AIMÉ: But then, who are you, Miss Donovan?

DESMOND: Just call her plain Donovan, Aimé. She's in uniform.

AIMÉ: She is too beautiful for such familiarity, at least at the beginning. . . . Dear Miss Donovan, please tell us who you are.

The GIRL *looks round for a moment, in a quandary.*

MAN (*hurt*): Might as well tell them now. The harm's done. Thanks to you, you silly immortal bitch.

GIRL (*smiles radiantly*): In the visible world I have many names. In pre-history, I was the angel charged with the painful duty of chasing Adam and Eve out of the Garden of Eden. (*Racked with remorse.*) Oh, if only I had been there first, I could have warned them . . .

MAN (*mocking*): But you weren't.

GIRL (*sad*): I wasn't. And in the world of dreams and legends, they call me the Good Fairy.

AIMÉ (*softly*): And what do we call you?

GIRL (*with a shrug and a charming smile*): Donovan.

MAN (*piqued*): Well . . . is nobody going to ask me who I am?

DESMOND: We have done so consistently, sir. I can only take it as a reflection on your character that you have to be provoked into a confession by Donovan's good example. (*Aside.*) Full marks, Donovan.

MAN (*scoffing*): Good example, my magic wand! I, too, have many names in the foolish world of things and facts and figures. In pre-history, I won my first victory over Donovan, in that same Garden of Eden where she first learned what she was up against. Yes. (*Vindictive.*) I was the Serpent who gave Eve the forbidden apple. The devil was absent. He didn't realize the importance of the occasion. Since then, Donovan and I have been struggling for the driving reins of this ramshackle carriage they call humanity—a carriage in which all the living recline and jostle each other on the rough road they travel. I can tempt, and so can Donovan, and you, gentlemen, are our battleground. You and Eve and the Sleeping Beauty, and all the peoples and dreams of the world. (*Suddenly agonized.*) And you have the wonderful possibility of choosing . . .

AIMÉ: Choosing? Why do you think that should give us such pleasure? Personally, I welcome an escape into that world of dreams and legends where Donovan loses her prosaic name and becomes the Good Fairy. You did not tell, mon serpent, what is your name in that sweeter world?

MAN: Me? (*A peal of laughter, followed by an elaborate gesture.*) Silly boy, I'm the Wicked Fairy!

CURTAIN

ACT II

Within the castle. When the curtain rises, all is dark. All that can be heard is a sound, which may be music, of a deep, mysterious and atmospheric sort. Trees rustle and sigh. The noise of a car can be heard. Brakes are applied. Doors slam. A jumble of voices.

WESLEY'S VOICE: Come on, in here.

AIMÉ'S VOICE: Ow!

DESMOND'S VOICE: What is it? Oh, drat!

IKONENKO'S VOICE: A step, two steps, ai!

> *A torch appears.*

WESLEY (*overawed*): Can you see anything?

> *As the* COLONELS *file in, he shines his torch on the set, which reveals nothing but a forbidding screen of sagging gauzes.*

Kind of eerie.

WICKED FAIRY: It's what you asked for.

DESMOND: Can we have some light?

WICKED FAIRY: How do you expect me to produce light?

DESMOND: Magic.

WICKED FAIRY: So you do admit of such a thing?

DESMOND: I'm not one to look a gift horse in the mouth.

> *The front of the stage becomes lighter.*

IKONENKO (*eyes gleaming*): This looks the kind of castle where jewels lie hidden.

AIMÉ: Do I hear the people's representative hoping to find jewels?

WICKED FAIRY: The people's representative stole a diamond-studded watch from a German duchess.

IKONENKO: It's a lie. I exchanged it against a Soviet cuckoo-clock.

AIMÉ: Where will you take us from here?

WICKED FAIRY: You're boys at heart, the four of you. You'd much rather explore than be shown anything, wouldn't you?

WESLEY: Sure. Speaking for myself.

WICKED FAIRY: Go on, then. I'll show you all you want to know when you have found nothing.

WESLEY: Come on, fellers.

[202]

DESMOND: Where are you going to be? You won't leave us here alone?

WICKED FAIRY: We won't. I just want a word with Donovan.

DESMOND: Have I your word?

GOOD FAIRY (*entering*): You have my word.

DESMOND: Good enough for me, Donovan.

IKONENKO: I shall try the floorboards . . .

They go.

GOOD FAIRY: You want a word with me? Why?

WICKED FAIRY: I hardly know where to begin. That's odd for me, isn't it?

GOOD FAIRY: Are you trying to be sincere?

WICKED FAIRY (*looking away from her*): Isn't it embarrassing?

Pause.

You see, in a strange way, these four idiots have touched me . . .

GOOD FAIRY: What game are you playing now?

WICKED FAIRY: My dear child, if I was playing a game, I'd do it in the usual way. I'm too old, too hidebound, for innovations. (*Softer.*) I mean what I say with all the very limited sincerity at my disposal.

GOOD FAIRY: Why should these four have touched you, when you have ridden roughshod over the dead, and even worse, the dying? When throughout our immortality you have spent your sleepless existence gloating over misery and vice?

WICKED FAIRY: That's just it. I'm beginning to tire. (*Pause.*) Oh, Donovan, if you knew, if you could guess . . .

GOOD FAIRY: What?

WICKED FAIRY: How I am dying to do a good deed!

GOOD FAIRY: Ssh! (*Nervous.*) Be careful what you say . . .

WICKED FAIRY: I've become quite reckless. I sometimes can't bear to do the obvious. I'm such an expert in evil that there's no challenge any more. I dream of new worlds to conquer. I dream of one day saving a life . . . or at least of upholding a fidelity. Can you understand?

GOOD FAIRY: Too well! If you knew how the mawkishness of inhuman kindness had begun to pall! Perfection is a stagnant thing. Oh, Serpent, I'm longing to be bad. Just for once.

WICKED FAIRY: Now I could almost forget who I am, and fall in love.

GOOD FAIRY: With me? Surely not.

[203]

WICKED FAIRY: Yes. One kiss would bring me peace for centuries. I could drain a little goodness from your lips, and it would linger through the years, tingeing the mind with sweetness, and making a memory of that empty space I call my heart.

GOOD FAIRY: And I could sense the poison of your tongue. I would be stung by the sadness of the world, and drown for a moment in the savage pallor of your eyes. Then I would taste of that bitter thing they call reality.

They are standing very close to each other.

Dare we?

WICKED FAIRY (*heartcry*): No!

GOOD FAIRY (*breaking away*): It was a silly game to have played.

WICKED FAIRY: If the extremes collided they would crush the whole of life between them. (*Quiet and bitter.*) We have our duty.

GOOD FAIRY: How I envy mortals.

WICKED FAIRY: They can choose between us. We have no choice.

GOOD FAIRY: We must return to our predestined positions.

Pause.

WICKED FAIRY (*gentle*): Donovan . . .

GOOD FAIRY: Mm?

WICKED FAIRY: Would we be failing in our duty if we agreed not to interfere for once?

GOOD FAIRY: What are you thinking of?

WICKED FAIRY: The four idiots.

GOOD FAIRY: They are good men.

WICKED FAIRY: Idiots.

GOOD FAIRY: You mean, if when we show them the Beauty, we let them try to awaken her love, each in his own way, without our influence?

WICKED FAIRY: Yes.

GOOD FAIRY: Is that possible? What could men do without good and evil? They too would lose the joy of strategy, the possibility of choice.

WICKED FAIRY: But love is stronger than choice. Love has made laughing stocks of us both. Remember how we struggled over Romeo and Juliet, Paolo and Francesca, the whole damned cohort of star-kissed lovers who escaped from us into a blameless and enviable death? Love is our only common enemy.

GOOD FAIRY: Love is my friend.

WICKED FAIRY: Carnal love?

GOOD FAIRY: Spiritual love.

WICKED FAIRY: And the love that leads to suicide? No, my dear, we don't know where we stand with love. After all, it has even affected both of us. . . . You are the conscience, I, the primitive desire. We may struggle for the heart——

GOOD FAIRY: But it is a battle neither of us can ever win.

WICKED FAIRY (*suffering*): That is something these poor mortals must never know. That is our ghastly secret . . .

GOOD FAIRY: But can we trust ourselves not to interfere?

WICKED FAIRY: You mean, can you trust me?

GOOD FAIRY (*shy*): Yes . . .

WICKED FAIRY: I'll try to behave. I can't say more than that.

GOOD FAIRY (*tender*): No, you can't . . .

> *She makes an instinctive movement towards him, but breaks away when the voices of the* COLONELS *are heard. The four* COLONELS *return.*

WESLEY: This place is like a maze.

AIMÉ: Of what period is the architecture?

WICKED FAIRY (*abstracted, gazing tenderly at the* GOOD FAIRY): Modern . . .

AIMÉ: What?

WICKED FAIRY (*recovering*): Oh, I beg your pardon. Comparatively modern. Thirteenth century. It was built by Otho, First Grand Duke of Burg zu Burg-Burg von Herzogenburg. A charming man.

GOOD FAIRY: A brute.

WICKED FAIRY: His successor, Willibald, was a relatively weedy boy of seven foot two, who was a perfect pest.

GOOD FAIRY: He relieved me of a great deal of worry.

WICKED FAIRY: Yes, he was the first man to fit a primitive equivalent of a Yale lock on to a chastity belt.

IKONENKO: May we visit some other rooms?

WICKED FAIRY: You will do better. You will see the Sleeping Beauty. She will wake up soon.

AIMÉ: But the legend says she will wake only when Prince Charming kisses her, at the end of a hundred years.

WICKED FAIRY: This will be a temporary awakening for your benefit. She will have to sleep again later. That is—unless *you* succeed.

IKONENKO: Succeed?

WESLEY: What are we waiting for? Is she yummy?

WICKED FAIRY: Is she what?

WESLEY: Has she got "it"?

WICKED FAIRY: What?

DESMOND: Is she personable?

AIMÉ: Est-ce qu'elle a du chien?

WICKED FAIRY: Du chien?

IKONENKO: Is she sexually attractive?

DESMOND: He's damned coarse, this fellow.

WICKED FAIRY: Now, I must ask for complete silence from you gentlemen. The next step is fraught with technical difficulties. No time to explain now. . . . Donovan!

> *The two* FAIRIES *stand with their backs to the audience and raise their arms. As they do so, the stage grows dark, to notes of a glacial music. When the lights come up again, they reveal the proscenium of a Court Theatre of the early nineteenth century. It is elaborate and golden, with all the attendant symbolism of this type of erection. Small Royal box,* LEFT. *In it the King and Queen, asleep. The King leans drunkenly over the parapet. The Queen, lies back, sleeping and aghast. Box on the right, empty. On the stage, a fantastic and elaborate bed, in which lies the veiled and fragile figure of the* SLEEPING BEAUTY. *The music stops.*

IKONENKO (*suddenly filled with wonder*): It is exactly as I had always imagined it.

AIMÉ: No, it is as I have often seen it in illustrations, and therefore not as I had imagined it. The French genius is the genius of mistrust.

DESMOND: Plenty of time for philosophizing later. Donovan, put me in the picture.

GOOD FAIRY: Yes, sir. We are in the Court Theatre of King Florestan the 24th, which was added to the castle in 1816. In spite of the Queen, whom you see sleeping up there, he had a . . . a morganatic arrangement with an actress.

WICKED FAIRY (*laughs mockingly*): He liked to call himself a King. He was only a Grand Duke really.

GOOD FAIRY: It happened a hundred years ago to-day. It was Aurora's birthday, and I was among the guests. My friend here, Carabosse—

DESMOND: Who?

WICKED FAIRY: Me. Carabosse. Not my real name. A kind of nom-de-fée.

DESMOND: I see. Go on, Donovan.

GOOD FAIRY: Carabosse was, for obvious reasons, not in the King's engagement book, and he was not invited to the Christening—

IKONENKO: But any child knows this story!

DESMOND: Any child may, but there are still a few colonels who do not. Donovan.

GOOD FAIRY: He determined to be revenged, and therefore uttered a terrible curse on this house.

WESLEY: What do you know?

GOOD FAIRY: The curse was that should Aurora ever prick herself with anything sharp, she would die. Naturally, we kept everything remotely sharp away from her. It worked, until this terrible day. (*Self-effacing.*) In my infinite innocence——

WICKED FAIRY (*with a cackle*): Bravo!

GOOD FAIRY: In my infinite innocence, I wrote a play, a pastoral piece in rhyming couplets, gentle and sweet as the first ray of dawn—

WICKED FAIRY: Sickly as a piece of Turkish delight.

GOOD FAIRY: In it I foolishly placed a spinning-wheel. However, this was a play, a little diversion, a make-believe, an unreality. The needle was made of twisted silver paper, and could not hurt a fly. (*Remorseful.*) I was not to know that the Chamberlain, who is now asleep in the wings—I was not to know that he was unreliable. He was charged with the stage management, and he substituted the paper needle with a—

WESLEY (*emotional*): Oh no, don't tell me!

GOOD FAIRY: With a real one.

WESLEY (*suffering*): Oh no, oh no.

GOOD FAIRY: The rest of the story must be clear to you.

IKONENKO (*on his usual warning note*): It is not exactly as it is in the ballet.

GOOD FAIRY: Very few things are. Aurora pricked herself in the third act, when the entire court was charmed by her exquisite purity. She died. I brought her back to life, but she fell into a deep sleep, and here she lies . . .

WICKED FAIRY: The rest is up to you.

WESLEY: What can we do?

WICKED FAIRY: Win her heart. Tempt her, as I tempted Eve—only I warn you, your task will be more difficult, as she is not yet married.

WESLEY: She'll never look at us.

WICKED FAIRY: Why shouldn't she?

WESLEY: Well. Look at me, for instance. *And* I need glasses to read.

WICKED FAIRY: Don't you think that after a perfumed existence, in which beauty has become a commonplace, a myopic man might be a rarity, and consequently a thing of loveliness?

WESLEY: What? Me, a thing of loveliness? That's effeminate talk. I'll knock you down if you—

> WESLEY *adopts a threatening attitude. The* WICKED FAIRY *raises his hand, and* WESLEY *is frozen into belligerent immobility. As the others stare at* WESLEY, *the* WICKED FAIRY *continues unperturbed.*

WICKED FAIRY: Or Aurora may prefer the sparse carroty whiskers of Colonel Rinder-Sparrow, or the garlic-flavoured breath of Colonel Frappot, or the porous nose of Colonel Ikonenko. These attributes are rare as radium in fairyland.

> *The* GOOD FAIRY *sees* WESLEY.

GOOD FAIRY (*annoyed*): Carabosse!

> *She blows on* WESLEY *gently, and he is released from the spell. The others gather round him.*

DESMOND: Are you all right, old chap?

WICKED FAIRY (*to* GOOD FAIRY): May they go and look at her, do you think?

GOOD FAIRY (*to* WICKED FAIRY; *schoolmasters discussing the future of the boys*): I see no harm in it, so long as they don't touch her.

WICKED FAIRY: No, they mustn't touch her. (*To the* COLONELS.) All right, go and look at her, but don't touch her.

> *The* FOUR COLONELS *clamber on to the stage.*

GOOD FAIRY: What shall we do next?

WICKED FAIRY (*cruelly*): Why do you ask me?

GOOD FAIRY: Evil always has the initiative.

> WESLEY *emits the conventional low whistle.*

You see. I am only the one who prevents you from achieving your aims.

WICKED FAIRY: Sometimes.

GOOD FAIRY (*sad*): Sometimes . . .

WICKED FAIRY: Well, as a matter of fact, I have a brainwave.

GOOD FAIRY (*full of doubt*): Mm. Let's hear it.

WICKED FAIRY: We will continue with the theatrical performance after an interval of a hundred years. We will give a performance couched deeply in the Colonels' imagination.

GOOD FAIRY: I don't understand.

WICKED FAIRY: Look at them up there, prowling round her like wolves round the sheep's pen. To them she is the ideal. They all see her in different ways. Only lust is common to them all.

GOOD FAIRY (*suffering*): Yes.

WICKED FAIRY: Then let's bring Aurora back to momentary life, and—

WESLEY (*calling from the stage*): Hey, Fairies, I'm in love.

WICKED FAIRY: What did I tell you?

DESMOND: She's damned attractive. A lovely, fair-haired English rose.

WESLEY: Fair? She's got red hair, like flame.

AIMÉ: Red? She's the type of dark Mediterranean beauty like one finds in Marseilles.

IKONENKO: Dark? A typical distortion. She is flaxen, like the farm girls in the Ukraine. Her face betrays deep convictions and a desire for immediate motherhood.

WICKED FAIRY: You are all in love with her?

WESLEY (*with boundless enthusiasm*): Sure!

DESMOND: I must say she strikes a chord in me that has not been struck since my cadet days.

AIMÉ: I don't know whether I have the capacity for a love which is free from the selfish manoeuvres of a carnal attachment. However, I am not a fool. I would like to sleep with her.

IKONENKO: I have already made my position clear in this matter.

WICKED FAIRY: Very well. But first, gentlemen . . . (*He goes up to the centre of the stage, and beckons the* COLONELS *to gather round him. Secretive.*) A word in your ear about . . .

> The WICKED FAIRY *points to the* BEAUTY. *He appears about to impart a confidence to the* COLONELS, *who cluster round him in the centre of the stage, by the footlights. Suddenly the curtain-within-a-curtain falls, leaving the* COLONELS *outside. The* WICKED FAIRY *cackles with laughter. The* COLONELS *are caught unawares and are angry.*

WESLEY: Hey, what's happened to the girl?

WICKED FAIRY: You shall see her, if you behave. (*The* COLONELS *struggle to penetrate the curtains.*) No, you can't get through there, I'm sorry.

> The COLONELS *come down from the stage.*

AIMÉ: What do you wish us to do?

WICKED FAIRY: You're interested, aren't you?

AIMÉ: Very. My life has been an experiment. I have explored the byways of the senses and almost arrived at a conclusion. The last thing I wanted was to arrive at a conclusion.

GOOD FAIRY: You have searched too hard, and reached the wrong conclusion!

AIMÉ: That we are animals tortured by a thinking brain? That there is no lingering beauty, that it is a momentary flame, sweet, but with its very sweetness soured in advance by the knowledge of its filthy aftertaste? No, my dear, existence is a shocking business. And existence is love.

WICKED FAIRY: Go and prove it. But first, become the character you always hoped to be in your child's heart.

AIMÉ: I have no illusions. The only character I always hoped to be is myself.

WICKED FAIRY: Have you no favourite period in history at least?

AIMÉ: Ah, yes. That is different. The turn of the eighteenth century, when France was inundated with the sun, reflected off her sovereign's pride.

WICKED FAIRY: Will you go first?

AIMÉ: Where to?

WICKED FAIRY: To act your love to your ideal.

AIMÉ (*falters*): Here?

WICKED FAIRY: On the stage! Now! Go into the wings, you will find all there to fit your most private dreams.

AIMÉ: And she will appear?

WICKED FAIRY: As your ideal. As your hope. As what you left behind when you first knew a woman!

> *After a moment of hesitation,* AIMÉ *submits to temptation, and runs into the wings.*

Music!

GOOD FAIRY (*urgent*): Oh, don't wake the conductor! He only confuses the orchestra when he's conscious. He's so bad, the poor darling.

WICKED FAIRY: What do you suggest?

GOOD FAIRY: For the eighteenth century? Wake Herr Doktor Gimpel, the Harpist, Herr Doktor Straubel, the Flautist, and—Herr Professor Kampff, the Violinist.

WICKED FAIRY (*calling into the orchestra pit*): Herr Doktor Gimpel, Herr Doktor Straubel, Herr Professor Kampff! Music of the eighteenth

[210]

century, please! Hey Presto. Hey Lento, Hey Allegro—Ma Non Troppo!

> *Lights appear under the protective palm leaves. The lights in the theatre dim. The footlights go up. The three instruments begin to tune up.*

DESMOND: I say, what *is* going on? Are we to be treated to a theatrical performance? And if so, why?

WICKED FAIRY: It will be your turn next.

DESMOND: Mine?

WICKED FAIRY: Yes. You too will become upon the stage your secret self, in quest of your ideal. Now sit down.

WESLEY: Where?

WICKED FAIRY: Here. (*He indicates one of the boxes at the side of the stage.*) I will sit here—(*He indicates the box on the opposite side*)—and you, my dear, here. (*He fetches a gilt chair for the* GOOD FAIRY, *and places it in front of his own.*)

GOOD FAIRY: How kind of you to fetch me a chair.

WICKED FAIRY: So much of my time is spent with the upper classes.

> *The music begins.*

IKONENKO: I don't understand what this performance will prove.

WICKED FAIRY: Would you mind keeping quiet please! After all, you are in the theatre, gentlemen. Pray silence while we see the naked soul of a certain Aimé Frappot chasing the elusive bird which flutters in his heart. And may be catch it!

WESLEY: Just before we start, is this some form of psychiatry?

> *The* WICKED FAIRY *silences him with an impatient gesture. The curtain-within-a-curtain rises slowly. The sketchy set shows an interior of 1700.* THE BEAUTY *sits at a dressing table, making up her face. She is in corsets. Her black hair flows down her back, while her wig is on a wig-stand.*

DESMOND (*whisper*): Who's that?

GOOD FAIRY (*enchanted*): The Beauty. How lovely she looks in that costume.

IKONENKO (*loud*): That's not the Beauty!

WICKED FAIRY: Of course it is, idiot. Aimé's Beauty.

BEAUTY (*as the music stops*): Heigh-ho. It is but eleven o'clock in the morning, and already I am awake, for when a woman of the town must choose a husband, it is wise to rise early. (*She powders her face.*)

IKONENKO: Eleven o'clock is late, not early.

WICKED FAIRY: Sssh! Give your colleague a chance.

BEAUTY: Husband! What a tedious thing is man when he is called by the vile name of husband!—And yet, were there no husband, the little lapses that women of the town dote upon would lack of savour. (*Laughs.*) Yes, I have ribboned bonnets, a wardrobe as fine as the richest in Paris, periwigs and toys and baubles, pretty little dogs, black boys to serve chocolate, a Dutch milliner, an Italian dancing master, and all that elegance could wish. (*Melancholy.*) Yet now I lack a lover. But first, a husband, for without a husband to deceive, a lover's an empty pleasure. But hist, one comes. I shall dissemble.

> AIMÉ *enters, immensely romantic in the costume of the period, and winks at the audience.*

AIMÉ (*bowing deeply*): Mademoiselle, methought this to be a coffee-house.

BEAUTY: A coffee-house, sir? A coffee-house, sir? How came you by this notion?

AIMÉ: I know not, and it matters less. (*Aside.*) I had observed her through the window while in quest of a coffee-house. My taste for coffee was dispersed.

BEAUTY: A bold gallant, too good for husbanding. I shall pretend to hate him. (*To* AIMÉ.) Sir, that you were in search of a coffee-house, I doubt not. That you have found one, however, I doubt much. Now there's nothing in a man so odious as a mind which is ever, like a butterfly, fluttering hither and thither, from purpose to purpose, and therefore, sir, if you hope for my respect, I pray you turn about and *find* a coffee-house.

AIMÉ (*aside*): Which means she loves me. (*To her.*) If I were sure, Mademoiselle, that the coffee-house would hold such charms as these, still I would not go, for any journey would be irksome that carried the traveller away from you, and then, what fool would engender your respect, and not tarry to enjoy it?

BEAUTY (*aside*): I doubt that it is my respect he wants. Yes, alas, he is too good for husband, and too soon for lover! (*To him.*) Are you not afraid to incur my wrath, sir?

AIMÉ: No, Mademoiselle, for it is à la mode to hate in public those you would tumble behind locked doors.

BEAUTY (*aside*): He speaks like a gentleman indeed. (*To him.*) Then I, sir, am not of the rule, for when I hate, I hate, and there's an end to't.

AIMÉ (*aside*): She loves me more with every phrase she utters. (*To her.*) Then, madam, I am here to a double purpose.

BEAUTY: Nay, nay, why do you call me "madam" now?

[212]

AIMÉ: You have a short wind for raillery, madam, which betokens that you are but lately brought to bed by a husband, and have not yet wearied of his palsied face upon your pillow.

BEAUTY (*aside*): Now could I love him. Were't better to admit I am a maid, or, sighing, say, "Alas, sir, what you suppose is true. I have a husband."

AIMÉ (*aside*): See, she sighs and moans, and each heaving of those twin rotundities doth seem to beckon me.

BEAUTY: Sir, I am indeed cursed with husband, as hideous a vaporous wretch as was ever purg'd by physick, for indeed all he touches, or breathes upon—or fondles—has upon it the cloying stench of Pharmacy.

AIMÉ: Ha!

BEAUTY (*aside*): I have affected him.

AIMÉ (*aside*): I will approach her.

BEAUTY (*aside*): Heigh-ho, how sweet is the lot of woman when it is not miserable. (*To him.*) Have you done prowling, sir?

AIMÉ (*aside*): So? She is impatient?

BEAUTY (*aside*): This then is the calm, which, preceding the storm, doth make the storm so very much more enjoyable.

   AIMÉ *seizes her. The other* COLONELS *rise from their seats in astonishment.*

BEAUTY: I shall scream, sir!

AIMÉ: Untruss, ma'am, untruss!

BEAUTY: I shall box your ears, sir!

AIMÉ: You conspire to add to their delight!

BEAUTY: I shall black your eye, sir!

AIMÉ: And surround your image with a coronet of stars!

BEAUTY: I shall smack your cheek, sir!

AIMÉ: To aid a lover's blush!

BEAUTY: I shall pummel you, sir!

AIMÉ: And I shall think it is the beating of your heart!

BEAUTY: Help, help! (*As he has almost stolen the fatal kiss.*) I am a virgin, sir!

DESMOND: Good God!

AIMÉ (*releasing her abruptly*): How? How's this?

   The other COLONELS *relax and go back to their seats.*

BEAUTY (*pouting*): I lied . . . a little lie, sir, to fan the flame of ardour.

AIMÉ (*with aloof savagery*): You call it a little lie, miss, to create a husband i' the mind as full of good, solid, husbandly vices as the million others of the cursed band? You call it a little lie to drive me on in the hope of theft, to find that you are ownerless? You call it a little lie to flatter me by breathing scandal of an imaginary spouse?

BEAUTY (*aside*): How he glowers! I must appease him, for he is a handsome enough coxcomb, and may have his uses. I will sing awhile. (*Aloud.*) La-la-la. Fol-de-rol-rol.

GOOD FAIRY: Oh, thank goodness.

IKONENKO (*exploding*): That's not the Beauty! Where are her motherly virtues?

DESMOND: I certainly can't call this lass innocent. Is that what he sees in her?

WESLEY: She sure knows her way around.

GOOD FAIRY (*sighs*): Yes, that's what he sees in her. But the fatal kiss was avoided, that's all I care about.

DESMOND: But Donovan, are you *sure* it's the same girl as I saw sleeping up there? Admittedly, there is a superficial resemblance, but—

GOOD FAIRY: It's the same girl, sir. You will see her in a different light when your turn comes.

IKONENKO: Have they finished? Has he failed?

GOOD FAIRY: Yes. Carabosse. (*Suddenly jumps up.*) Where is he?

DESMOND: Who?

GOOD FAIRY: Carabosse!

DESMOND: He's gone!

> *Not at all. He enters on the stage, as the very description which the* BEAUTY *gave of her imaginary husband.*

WICKED FAIRY: So soon abroad, my love, my chick, my doll? And hast thou drunk thy chocolate yet, and hast thou learned thy minuet and little songs, and hast thou pretty things to tell me? Hm? Eh?

GOOD FAIRY (*heartcry*): I knew he'd have to interfere!

WICKED FAIRY (*aside to* GOOD FAIRY): My nature was too strong for me!

GOOD FAIRY: You haven't beaten me yet!

> *The* GOOD FAIRY *runs off*, RIGHT.

AIMÉ: Oons! It is her father!

WICKED FAIRY: Zounds! I am her husband!

BEAUTY: My husband, say you?

AIMÉ. How? (*Aside.*) Thus was her lie no lie at all, but a strategy to draw out my anguish, and with my anguish, my delight!

[214]

BEAUTY (*aside*): That I have no husband I am sure, though I'm sure I'm eager to acquire one. This old fool is ugly enough—and blind enough, for if he mistake me for his wife now, he will again, or I'll see to't.

WICKED FAIRY: Madam, I pray you, tell me who is this gallant who appears to be studying the wall with such grave and scholarly attention?

BEAUTY (*with deep disdain*): That is my eunuch, sir.

WICKED FAIRY: An eunuch, madam?

BEAUTY: Yes, an eunuch from the Ottoman realm.

WICKED FAIRY (*aside*): Yea, straight from the ottoman, I'll warrant. Her hair is all unkempt, while he doth avert his eyes to cover his confusion. I'll talk with him. (*Aloud.*) Sir! Sir, I say!

AIMÉ (*falsetto*): Sir, I am your honour's most obliged, most devoted servant.

WICKED FAIRY (*aside*): There's truth in't then. (*Aloud.*) And I yours, sir, I assure you.

    The BEAUTY *pretends to faint.*

BEAUTY: Oh! I faint! Help!

WICKED FAIRY: My knick-knack! My bee! My grouse! My pigeon! My widgeon! What ails thee?

BEAUTY: A lack of breath, sir.

WICKED FAIRY: Which physick declares to be no more than an over-excess of vacuum.

BEAUTY: And a swimming of the brain, sir.

WICKED FAIRY: Ah! A case of inundation of the mentality.

BEAUTY: And a stopping of the heart, sir.

WICKED FAIRY: Or lack of movement in the sentimental regions.

BEAUTY: And a freezing of the hand, sir.

WICKED FAIRY: Yes, yes, an insufficiency of manual torpor.

BEAUTY: And a shivering of the limb, sir.

WICKED FAIRY: Cardinal! Capital! An instability of the pedestrian organ! Attend me, my nightingale, my owlkin, my nightjar. I'll fetch thee medicine straight.

    He goes. Immediately the BEAUTY *and* AIMÉ *fly into each other's arms. They are about to kiss, when the* GOOD FAIRY *enters, disguised.*

GOOD FAIRY: Hold!

AIMÉ (*out of character, faltering*): Jeanette ...

[215]

BEAUTY: What name was that?

AIMÉ *releases her.*

Thy wife?

AIMÉ: My mistress.

BEAUTY: How? Thou hast a mistress—and a wife? How have I been deceived!

GOOD FAIRY: Thy victims grow younger, chick, which is a sign o' the approach of hoary winter in a man.

AIMÉ: Hoary is well said, ma'am. For a man is like a ship which leaves the harbour. First is he set loose upon the calm waters of life, and spends his innocence in the mole's embrace. Then he comes to man's estate, and senses the ocean's subtle billows at the harbour mouth, and then, with age, his horizon does grow wider, until, out of sight of land, he believes the whole wild wilderness of water to be his, and all the great regiment of women in the world for him alone. There's the irony o' the world. When too young to know, he loves a woman, cruel and playful. When too old to be able, he loves the whole cursed sex. (*With dignified pathos.*) He has lost sight of land . . .

BEAUTY: Nay, then, sir, I will not love thee, for to be one of ten or twenty is to be in the fashion, but to be loved as one of an entire sex verges upon the indiscriminate. I'll none of your waves and billows, sir, your seascapes and marine fancies. I am of the land, sir, and with that send you packing. (*Aside.*) How handsome does his grief render him, his brow arched in noble melancholy, his eye upcast in pain. Now could I love him indeed.

AIMÉ (*aside*): Ah, how a refusal should spur me on! And yet——

GOOD FAIRY: Come then, sir, content yourself with a well-remembered face. The lines of sorrow upon it are your own.

AIMÉ *smiles at her.*

GOOD FAIRY: Canst see thy signature upon my cheeks, thy seal upon my lips? And canst see thy younger self reflected in my eye?

AIMÉ: Thou art like an old song, but ill-remembered.

GOOD FAIRY: And quick to learn again?

She holds out her hands to AIMÉ, *who seizes them and kisses them. The* BEAUTY *bursts into tears. The* WICKED FAIRY *enters.*

WICKED FAIRY: Here's medicine, my cake, my bun, my sweetmeat . . .

He senses the situation, loses all sense of character as well as his temper, and shouts:

Curtain! Bring it down! The play is over!

Consternation. The curtain falls.

[216]

DESMOND: What d'you make of it?

WESLEY: I didn't understand his motivation.

IKONENKO: He treated her like a swine.

WESLEY: Why did he want her to be married?

DESMOND: He's always given me the impression of a fellow who's a bit sick of women, but who can't leave them alone.

WESLEY: Yeah, but that doesn't explain why he throws over a girl as fresh as that for the second dame. She was one whole lot older.

DESMOND: Yes. She was a bit long in the tooth. What did he call her? Jeanette?

WICKED FAIRY (*looking through the curtains*): Colonel Rinder-Sparrow. How do you see yourself?

DESMOND: Eh?

WICKED FAIRY: What is the embodiment of your romantic self?

DESMOND: Goodness knows.

WESLEY: You probably see yourself as a golden retriever.

DESMOND: No need to be rude about dogs, Wesley. They're finer souls than you or I.

WESLEY: O.K. Go up there as one. See the Beauty as a pekingese.

DESMOND: Just a minute. There was a bloke who always fascinated me.

WICKED FAIRY: Who?

DESMOND: When I was small, and allowed to stay up late with the grown-ups, there was a family portrait just opposite my chair, and while my parents were talking about this and that, I used to stare and stare . . .

WICKED FAIRY: Who was it?

DESMOND: The first of the Rinders. My mother's a Sparrow, you see. He was the Private Secretary to Lord Burghley's Personal Choirmaster, and died of a cholic condition in the late spring of 1616 . . .

WICKED FAIRY: Colonel, will you come on to the stage please.

DESMOND: Wish me luck.

WESLEY: Oh no. I'll wish myself that.

DESMOND: That attitude, Wesley, won't get you anywhere.

He goes into the wings.

WICKED FAIRY (*calling into the orchestra pit*): Orchestra! The music of England's Golden Age!

A pavane is started. AIMÉ *enters, right, back in uniform. He seems weary. The* WICKED FAIRY *disappears once more behind the curtains.*

[217]

WESLEY: Ah, Aimé. We've been discussing the motivations.

AIMÉ: I failed. I knew I would.

WESLEY: But why in hell did you insist that she was married?

AIMÉ: Does it not disgust you when men of our age throw our shadow over youth and blissful inexperience? I am a lover, Wesley, not a corrupter.

WESLEY: Do you mean you were being unselfish?

AIMÉ: It is a relief when selfishness and unselfishness come to the same thing. I do not enjoy seducing youth. I can no longer bear to see the hope in its eyes. The hope of permanency—of eternity. It dazzles me, and leads me to behave like a fool. I like laughing at others, not at myself.

IKONENKO: But who is Jeanette?

AIMÉ: Jeanette? My mistress in Paris.

WESLEY: The actress?

AIMÉ: The actress. She is not beautiful, but she is sad, and I like sadness. She is also safe. We lost our illusions with our second kiss, and our third was more passionate than the first.

IKONENKO: Still, you made every effort to make love to the Beauty.

AIMÉ: I wonder if I did.

IKONENKO: Your attitude was clear to the spectator. Clear and reprehensible.

AIMÉ: I am so armoured against disappointment that I never make every effort any more. I am a man. She is beautiful. You might call her my ideal—and yet, as I have no ideals, my very love was tempered with misgiving. I saw Jeanette again with what was almost relief.

WESLEY: Tell me, as man to man, what do you see in Jeanette?

GOOD FAIRY (entering): What does any man see in his conscience?

IKONENKO (to AIMÉ): I fail to understand, Frappot, how you can have chosen as a favourite period the epoch of pre-revolutionary France.

AIMÉ: Why?

IKONENKO: The insincerities which led relentlessly to the revolution were already painfully in evidence.

AIMÉ (lively): Insincerities? By God, they said what they thought in those days, and said it wittily.

IKONENKO: Wit is unnecessary.

AIMÉ: So is life.

IKONENKO: No, my friend, you are wrong. Life is necessary, for without life, the world would be unpopulated.

[218]

AIMÉ: And a great relief.

IKONENKO: That is an offensive remark.

GOOD FAIRY: I quite agree.

IKONENKO: Without population, there could be no working class. That is in itself enough sufficient reason for population.

GOOD FAIRY: And where does God take his place in your conception?

WICKED FAIRY (*looking through the curtains*): Stop canvassing! Silence please. The play begins, I hope this time with satisfactory results.

GOOD FAIRY: That depends upon you.

> *The music stops. The lights go down. The curtain rises. Dim corridors of castle.* DESMOND *is discovered, bearded, and dressed in elaborate Elizabethan costume.*

DESMOND: The day speeds sullenly to its decline
And all's yet unachieved. There lingers in the mind
A vision of such galling purity
That I must defile it quick, or call myself
No more, Desmonio.
Five grey eagles cackled at my birth.
And the entrails of a wasp lay, by dint of magick,
At my moaning mother's feet, who, being brought to bed
Of a two-months' child, did presently faint,
And pine, and die, aweary of her sire's black reproaches,
Which, being the first sounds to play upon this Desmon's ear,
Did fill full his thoughts with hatred of all chastity.
Thus with the light of lately-dwindled moon
Did I pit my passion against an Illyrian nun—
"My vows, my vows", she cried, but 'twas in vain—
A maidenhead well lost's a mistress' gain.

> *Trumpets. He exits. The* BEAUTY *enters, sleepwalking. She is fair, lovely, and desperately Elizabethan.*

IKONENKO: This is more like the Beauty.

AIMÉ: It is ridiculous. This one had no temperament. I can see it already.

IKONENKO: Who is this Illyrian nun?

WESLEY: Don't ask me. I know he was in Yugoslavia just after the liberation.

> *The* BEAUTY *crosses the stage, sleepwalking, and exits.* DESMOND *enters from the opposite side of the stage.*

[219]

DESMOND: The Fates, those horrid beldams
Who do play at tennis with our fortunes.
Do just now score a point in their portentous game.
For here's Aurora, betrothed to chastity,
But robbed of her entire kin by agencie
Of poison in the sacramental wine.
I'll to her while her heart's enfeebled by her grief.
For when a man is bent on sin
His conscience does fly out, his lewdness in!

> *Exit. Trumpets. The* BEAUTY *comes on from the opposite side
> from which* DESMOND *has exited.*

BEAUTY: Ah, could I but while away the restless hours
Enshrouded in oblivion, then could the mind
Wander as a cloud, unanchored, midst th' uncharted stars,
And seek a refuge beyond imagination's reach.
Logic I abhor, and this woman's shape
A prison is. These hands, ten twigs, but petal-soft,
These arms, roads that lead into the air
From this all-too-solid dish of garnished bones
That men lust after. These breasts, that never will give suck,
But are as waterfalls dried up i' the heat
Of the desert sun, or as the eyes of one
With no more tears to weep. This face,
This outline of perfection, this sketch of beauty,
This mirror which, held up, reflects the nothingness within.
This belly, this empty cell, this resting place
Of the unborn, forever uninhabited, an echoing vault,
My goldless treasury, my starless night.
These legs, these slender columns which bind me to the earth,
These restless travellers whose path runs wild
From the nowhere of birth to the nowhere of death
Through the nowhere in between. I have grown
Weary of breathing. Patience, enfold me then,
And death, be kind.

DESMOND (*entering*): Death be kind,
But life be kinder first.

BEAUTY: What's he that enters? Art thou a ghost?

DESMOND: Nay, Aurora, but a geographie of rivers red
Which break their banks and rush for thee
In one cascading tide. Musick, ho!

> *Music.*

BEAUTY: How dulcet is the virginall.

DESMOND: And dulcet thou, of all most virginall.

BEAUTY: Art thou a man? For if thou art
Get thee to some more frolicksome abode
And do thy wenching there.

DESMOND: I shall stay here, and we will sink
Our frantick hearts in a sweet sleep.

> *He seizes her.*

BEAUTY (*livid, throwing him away*): Thou toad-spawn, thine own
second worser self,
Thou yellow-painted bauble, thou toy, thou gadfly,
Thou wasp without a sting, thou twilight of a man,
Thou yolkless egg, thou image of decrepitude,
I'll none of thee. Go sing thy amorous odes to statues,
Get with child a tree-stump. Marry a broomstick. Away.

DESMOND: Say you so? Then if I have thee not
Let no man have thee!

> *He draws a knife. The* WICKED FAIRY *enters as a Clown. The*
> GOOD FAIRY *rises precipitately.*

GOOD FAIRY: He's done it again! (*She rushes out.*)

WICKED FAIRY: Hold, sirrah! 'Tis of no avail to stab a monument.

DESMOND: A monument, say you?

WICKED FAIRY: Ay, marry, a monument, upon which mournful
pigeons sit,
And spill their droppings, which do go for tears.

BEAUTY: Oh, foolish fool.

WICKED FAIRY: How should I not be foolish, being a fool, for were
I not a fool, I would be wise, the less like thee, for thou, good lady,
art in no wise wise, and no wise foolish, and not foolish wise, and no
wit either, for to be without wit is to be neither, therefore thou'rt in
no wit wise and in no wise witty, and fall'st on thy bum 'twixt Gran-
dam Nature's twin stools.

BEAUTY: I am in no humour for mirth, boy.

WICKED FAIRY (*imitating her*): I am in no humour for mirth,
wench.

WESLEY: This must have amused the audiences of the time.

BEAUTY: I weep.

WICKED FAIRY: Nay, nay, an' thou weeps't, thou art no monument. Thou art a fountain, lady. I shall go abroad, and weep myself,
and say, "My lady is the breathing stuff of sprats, the nourishment of
frogs, the comforter of dogs, for they do cock their legs at her as I
do cock my snook." (*He pulls a long nose.*)

BEAUTY: My tears do turn to tears of laughter,
And I do hate thee for it.

DESMOND (*aside*): This boy doth serve my purpose well.

WICKED FAIRY: Hate me, madam, if it help thee know thyself, for I am much-hated Tom-a-Green, or Tickle-Rib, or Itch-Side, or Cackle-Face, or Grin-Jowl, or Chuckle-Head, or Wit-Nit, and I have as many names as I have faces, an' if there's one of me you hate, there's ten more left to love.

BEAUTY: Thou sayest true, boy, and I do love thee well.

WICKED FAIRY: Nay, lavish not thy love on me. There is another, worthier far, who is so fine and great a one, he does not walk but in a pavan, does not run but in a coranto, and does not stand still but in a gracious and tempestuous attitude.

BEAUTY: Why tempestuous, boy?

WICKED FAIRY: It is the longest word I know.

BEAUTY: Who is this suitor, boy?

WICKED FAIRY: His name, Desmonio.

BEAUTY: Desmonio. It is a name which doth
Make music of a moan. I'll to him straight.

DESMOND: But straighter he to thee.

BEAUTY: Desmonio.

DESMOND: How is my name lullabied upon that tongue,
And bathed in breath as sweet as rose's scent.
The name is not enough. The man must follow.

BEAUTY (*seeing him*): Art thou Desmonio, then?

DESMOND: The same.

BEAUTY: How have I wronged thee! Thy eagerness deceived.

DESMOND *holds* BEAUTY *in his arms.*

DESMOND: The veil of sorrow's lifted, all's well, Aurora.
Come into the halter of my arms, and shake not off
Thy new-found shackles till th' impudent sun
Does peep through his drapery of morning clouds
To tease young lovers out of sleep. Nay, speak not,
For silence is the language that we lovers speak.

BEAUTY: And yet I must. O sweet Desmonio, now
All nature is abuzz with living.
Summer and spring do lie within my heart
And play at paramours. I am invaded
With a love which knows no satisfaction,
For it would stretch to the farthest frontiers o' the senses

Like an all-consuming tide, and o'er-reaching itself at last,
Fall into a slumber as sweet
As is the word serenity.

DESMOND: Let's to't then.

The GOOD FAIRY *enters as a Ghost.*

BEAUTY (*shrieks*): It is my mother! All's ill wi' me!

DESMOND (*releasing her*): Th' Illyrian nun!

WICKED FAIRY (*transcendentally angry*): Oh, no! Curtain! Bring it down! Give me time to think!

THE CURTAIN-WITHIN-A-CURTAIN
AND THE MAIN CURTAIN
BOTH FALL

ACT III

A few minutes later. WESLEY *and the* TWO FAIRIES *are absent.* DESMOND *is there, back in uniform. There has evidently been a pause for sombre meditation.*

DESMOND: I say, was I awfully embarrassing? I mean, did I let a lot of cats out of the proverbial bag?

AIMÉ: Quite enough. Do you write poetry?

DESMOND (*embarrassed*): Oh, that. Just for fun. Not seriously.

AIMÉ: Like so many English, you are permanently embarrassed.

DESMOND: There's so damned much to be embarrassed about.

IKONENKO: Have you ever published a poem?

DESMOND (*laughs softly*): Yes, I have. Twice. One in the *Observer*, the other time in *Country Life*. I took a woman's name to write both, thought they'd have a better chance. I was right.

IKONENKO (*shocked*): A woman's name!

DESMOND: It doesn't do to have a Colonel writing about trees and flowers, not in England—not on the active list.

IKONENKO: Then you should not have written them at all.

AIMÉ: Don't be ridiculous. Desmond, you amaze me. I have often watched you, and I think I know you a little better now. God forbid, you will say. You don't really want to be known.

DESMOND (*embarrassed*): I don't mind.

AIMÉ: You are like so many of those strange and secret English, with a genius for reflection.

IKONENKO: Reflection? I fail to understand. How can one have a genius for such a passive quality?

AIMÉ: The English gaze at their countryside through a swirl of pipe-smoke, through the sights of a huntsman's gun, from under wet umbrellas, and they link all generations in their mind. History is a reality, for the gigantic oaks are living witnesses of it. The cliffs were already there to echo the trumpets of long-forgotten battles, while the mansions are but sleeping quarters for the dead. The supernatural holds no surprises for them in the sacred preserves in which they wander with such unspoken relish. Only the present, the realistic commonplace, shocks them, and they are driven to embarrassed silence by the events of every day. That is the reason why you, Ikonenko, are so profoundly shocking to them.

[224]

IKONENKO: I fail to see why I should be profoundly shocking.

DESMOND: That's your charm, old man.

IKONENKO: On the contrary, you have made certain statements which I suspect to be of a highly scandalous nature.

DESMOND: Such as?

IKONENKO: Who is this Illyrian nun?

DESMOND (*puffing at his pipe. Grave*): Oh, nothing. I just behaved rather disgracefully to a Yugoslav girl when I was there.

IKONENKO: A nun?

DESMOND: No, no. Just a girl. A young girl. I let her down. It was a caddish thing to do. Did I refer to her as a nun?

IKONENKO: Yes.

DESMOND: Well, it just shows what the conscience will do to force its way into the imagination.

AIMÉ: The romantic imagination.

DESMOND: Oh, for heaven's sake, leave romance to Wesley.

AIMÉ: I wonder what we shall see?

DESMOND: American Civil War, I wouldn't be surprised.

IKONENKO: Wall Street.

AIMÉ: That's probably more like it. I mistrust people who boast of their romanticism.

WICKED FAIRY (*through the curtains*): Orchestra! Cacophony, please.

He disappears. The orchestra plays a highly sentimental blues.

AIMÉ: That sounds promising.

DESMOND: It seems Donovan's going to stay up there.

IKONENKO: She has understood the full measure of Carabosse's duplicity.

DESMOND: Here we go . . .

The curtain rises on the outline of a honky-tonk bar. The BEAUTY *is sitting at the bar, an unmistakable street-walker, puffing at a long cigarette-holder. She gazes out with the idealized melancholy of her profession.*

DESMOND: Good gracious!

IKONENKO (*rising*): This is an outrage!

AIMÉ: Sit down, sit down. Wait for the hero of fiction. Here he comes . . .

WESLEY *enters, dressed as a clergyman.*

DESMOND: I say, he told me his greatest ambition was to lead the Charge of the Light Brigade.

[225]

AIMÉ: You took us by surprise, Desmond. You must allow him the same privilege.

WESLEY *sits at the single table, and lights a cigarette.*

IKONENKO: What sort of uniform is he wearing?

AIMÉ: He is a priest.

IKONENKO: A counter-revolutionary!

WESLEY: Cigarette? (*Silence.*) Cigarette?

BEAUTY: Are you talking to me?

WESLEY: Yeah, I guess I was.

BEAUTY: If you want me, I'll give you a price. I don't go for opening gambits.

WESLEY (*with a self-righteous smile*): I don't . . . em . . . want you. I was offering you a cigarette.

BEAUTY (*incredulous*): For free?

WESLEY: Sure.

BEAUTY (*staggered*): Hey, what kind of a fellow are you?

WESLEY: Can't you see?

BEAUTY: Yeah, I can see. I got eyes. Listen, you oughta be in church. This is no place for you.

WESLEY: You're wrong, kid. This is for me, and it's you ought to be right there in church.

BEAUTY: Yeah? You talk like my father.

WESLEY: Where is your father?

BEAUTY: Dead. Cold. Flat.

WESLEY: I'm sorry.

BEAUTY: Me, I'm glad.

   Pause.

WESLEY: What's your name, child?

BEAUTY: Hey, where d'you get that "child" from?

WESLEY: We are all——

BEAUTY: I know. God's kids. I got loaded with that boloney at Sunday School.

WESLEY (*laughing*): We're going to have quite a time putting you right, my dear.

BEAUTY: If you want to keep that purty smile on your kisser, you just won't try, that's all.

WESLEY: You haven't told me your name.

BEAUTY: What's it to you?

WESLEY: I'm Father Breitenspiegel. They call me the Fighting Father.

BEAUTY (*impressed*): Hey, are you Fighting Father Breitenspiegel? *The* Fighting Father Breitenspiegel?

WESLEY: Sure. The guy that started Girls' Town. Now will you tell me your name?

BEAUTY: Aurora-Mae Duckworth.

WESLEY: Aurora-Mae. Kinda cute name.

BEAUTY: They call me Rory.

WESLEY: Who's they?

BEAUTY: Guys.

WESLEY: Which guys?

BEAUTY: How do I know? I only see them once, if that.

The wail of a train's siren is heard.

WESLEY: What's that?

BEAUTY: The Cincinnati Chieftain, bringing them into town.

WESLEY: Bringing who into town?

BEAUTY (*with a shrug*): Customers.

WESLEY: Listen, Rory, I want you to know something.

BEAUTY: Something I don't know?

WESLEY: Sure. The world's not like you think it is.

BEAUTY: The world's tough like last week's steak.

WESLEY: Sure it's tough, but it's kinda great and beautiful, too.

BEAUTY: Brother, that's not my world. Keep it. You're welcome to it.

WESLEY: You, too, Rory, you're welcome to it.

BEAUTY: Thanks all the same, but I'm a working girl.

WESLEY: I want to take you away from here, Rory, but bad.

BEAUTY: Why don't you shut up?

WESLEY: Ever seen the sun rise over the Alleghenies, Rory? It comes up like a great big lantern in the sky, and seems to say, "Get up, get up" to all God's creatures. "I'm back again, folks," it says, "I've been keeping guys warm right the other side of the great wide world, but I've kept my promise to you, and now I'm right back here with you till my old pal the moon comes back to-night." And you'd kneel there, Rory, filling your billy-can by the brook, and say to it, "Thanks, sun, it's sure good to see you back. You're a pal." And the old sun'ud say, "Don't thank me, Rory, I'm just doing my duty, drawing my lantern from the mountains in the morning, and dipping it into the ocean at night. I'm doing my duty, Rory—are you?" And you'd think, and smile up at the old boy up there, and say, "Sure, Mr Sun, I've left the city lights way back of me"—and then you'd add, "Sorry, feller, I'll be seeing you. It's my turn to build the bonfire for breakfast at Girls' Town." "What's cookin', kids?" he'll call, "Waffles with maple syrup, ham, cornflakes, and real good coffee." Then, if it rains, Rory, you'll know it's just the poor old fellow's mouth watering.

AIMÉ: I have an irresistible desire to brush my teeth.

BEAUTY (*visibly moved*): I'm sorry, Father—you're too late.

The door opens, and the WICKED FAIRY *enters dressed as a gangster. His face is practically concealed in the upturned collar of his overcoat, beneath which can be seen the striped trousers of a convict.*

BEAUTY: Hey. Just go on talking to me, that's all.

WESLEY: What's wrong?

BEAUTY: Please. Pretend to know me.

WESLEY: Who is that guy, Rory?

WICKED FAIRY: Don't I get any service round here?

BEAUTY (*urgent*): Don't answer.

WICKED FAIRY: Anybody got ears?

WESLEY: Why yes, I have.

WICKED FAIRY (*swinging round*): Then keep them shut, if you know what's good. (*Smirking.*) Hiya, Rory. You didn't figure you'd see me again so soon, huh?

BEAUTY: What are you doing here? You got a ninety-nine-year stretch.

WICKED FAIRY: I came out on parole, honey, just to see you.

WESLEY: Hey, didn't I see your face in the newspaper?

WICKED FAIRY (*sinister, grinning*): Sure. I take good pictures, huh? Oughta be in Hollywood, playing heavies.

WESLEY: You're Tony Carabosse. You didn't come out on parole. You broke jail.

WICKED FAIRY: O.K., wise guy. So I granted myself parole. What's the difference?

WESLEY: Why, that's illegal!

WICKED FAIRY (*to* BEAUTY): Hey, what kind of brainy guys are you going with these days, sugar?

BEAUTY: What do you want, Tony?

WICKED FAIRY: I want to settle a little argument we never finished, baby. Remember the time the cops came, and you kept going to the window, said you felt hot? Sure you felt hot, you dirty double-crossing she-dog. Yeah.

BEAUTY (*nervous, not without reason*): Say what you have to, and beat it.

WICKED FAIRY: What I've got on my mind don't explain itself with words.

BEAUTY (*still more nervous*): What do you mean?

WICKED FAIRY: I'm so big, sweetheart, I've got a friend to do my arguing for me. (*He draws a gun.*)

WESLEY: Put that gun away.

WICKED FAIRY: Button your lip.

WESLEY: Have you a licence for that firearm?

WICKED FAIRY: Sure, bishop, I even got a diploma.

BEAUTY: You wouldn't dare shoot me!

WICKED FAIRY: No?

WESLEY: You'd be guilty of first-degree murder.

WICKED FAIRY: You're wrong, saint, I got me a good lawyer. I never get more than second degree.

WESLEY: You will this time.

WICKED FAIRY: How come?

WESLEY: I'll be right there in the courtroom.

WICKED FAIRY: You'll be a patch of grass, brother. I'll pump you both with lead. A guy can't die twice, and if I go, you're coming right along with me.

Pause. The WICKED FAIRY *sits down.*

Yeah, funny thing. I'm in a generous mood. I'll let the both of you kneel down and say your prayers.

WESLEY: It's not too late for salvation, Tony. Kneel down with us and be saved.

WICKED FAIRY: Are you kidding? I'll give you one more chance, sugar, and then it's curtains. I figure I've gotten to that time in a guy's life when he kinda wants something different, something solid. I'm going straight, kid.

WESLEY (*ecstatic, juggling with haloes*): You're going straight?

WICKED FAIRY: Sure, after I've bumped you off, I'm going straight. Going to run a gambling ship off the coast of Mexico. Strictly on the level. I've got dough. Plenty dough. A guy don't live for ever.

[229]

WESLEY: He may inherit the life everlasting, even at this late stage.

WICKED FAIRY: Don't give me that!

BEAUTY: Don't give us that, will you?

WICKED FAIRY: Listen, babe, I want a kid. A kid can take over the gambling ship when I'm cold.

BEAUTY (*livid*): Are you suggesting marriage?

WICKED FAIRY: Don't say it that way, it don't sound so good.

BEAUTY: Listen, louse, I go with guys, but I don't marry them. That's not me. I'm not made that way. That's not the way I tick. I'm one of the little people, that like little, simple things. I don't get big ideas, the way you do. I'm little, and I like little guys, guys that go to the ball-game Sundays and stand right there and shout and put their souls into their shouting, and love and cry and live and die down here by the railroad track. I don't want big ideas, Tony Carabosse, on account of they eat you up, like fire, from the inside. All that was once laughter and sadness gets like it was strictly business, and you get cold and hard and treat the human soul like it was real estate. It's guys like you that drive honest school-kids to crime and slaughter and all those other big things I only heard talk about, and it's guys like you try to smash the little things, and the beautiful deep things, and the U.S. Constitution. They ought to brand you right there on the forehead, where all the little guys can see, "This is the enemy," in letters of flaming red.

IKONENKO: Has she refused?

BEAUTY (*vastly superior*): And there's something else. Thomas Jefferson once said——

WICKED FAIRY (*breathing*): O.K., sister. You asked for this.

> *He is about to shoot, when* WESLEY *expertly knocks the gun out of his hand, and confiscates it.*

Why you——

WESLEY: Stay where you are.

WICKED FAIRY (*quavering*): Don't do it. Don't shoot me. I'll give you a partnership in the gambling hell, reverend. Fifty grand down, and I'll pay your taxes.

WESLEY: Why, you poor misguided child. I'm going to call the District Attorney, but first——

WICKED FAIRY: They got dames in Mexico. Swell dames.

WESLEY (*louder*): But first——

WICKED FAIRY: And dough.

WESLEY (*louder still*): But first——

WICKED FAIRY: Liquor.

WESLEY (*even louder*): But first——

WICKED FAIRY: Automobiles . . .

WESLEY (*shouting*): But first, I'm going to teach you a little Scripture lesson.

WICKED FAIRY (*falling to his knees*): Oh no, not that!

WESLEY: Sure. (*He places one hand pontifically on the* WICKED FAIRY'S *head, while with the other he holds the gun to his temple.*) Samson smote the Philistine host with the jawbone of an ass. "And he found a new jawbone of an ass, and put forth his hand, and took it, and slew a thousand men therewith." I'm not that ambitious. I take them on one at a time.

> *He throws down the revolver. After a moment of indecision, the* WICKED FAIRY *makes a dive for it.* WESLEY *is too quick for him, seizes him, lifts him into the air, and sends him reeling into the corner with a fierce uppercut. The orchestra helps the illusion. The* BEAUTY *encourages* WESLEY, *who rushes at the* WICKED FAIRY. *The* WICKED FAIRY *places his feet on* WESLEY'S *stomach and sends him tottering back. The* WICKED FAIRY, *with a superhuman effort, wrenches the top section off the juke box, and staggers towards* WESLEY *with it.* WESLEY *takes the juke box away from him easily with one hand, discards it, and then proceeds to deal the* WICKED FAIRY *some brutal, but apparently ineffectual blows, for the* WICKED FAIRY *always comes back for more. At length twelve tremendous uppercuts, accompanied by the orchestral drums, send the* WICKED FAIRY *uneasily to the ground. One writhe, and all is stillness.* WESLEY *smoothes his hair with his hand. The* BEAUTY *awaits his embrace.*

BEAUTY: O.K., feller, you win. When do we leave?

WESLEY: Leave?

BEAUTY: For Girls' Town. I never felt more religious in my life.

WESLEY: Then . . . you will come?

BEAUTY: You're a funny guy.

WESLEY: Why?

BEAUTY: You've been fightin' over me, haven't you?

WESLEY: In a way . . .

BEAUTY (*her arms open*): Then why don't you take me, you dope?

WESLEY: I wasn't fighting just for you, Rory, but for the forces of light and freedom all over the world.

BEAUTY (*seductive*): That's as maybe, but it's me you want.

WESLEY: Don't talk that way. That's horrible . . . (*A sudden realization.*) That's temptation!

BEAUTY (*very much in love*): It's just old man nature knocking at our door.

WESLEY (*powerful*): I have come to save you from the abyss, not to be dragged down myself!

BEAUTY (*sadly*): You got me wrong, butch.

WESLEY: My name is Wesley.

BEAUTY: I never lived like this. This is my first day's work.

WESLEY: Then you mean——?

BEAUTY: Yeah. I was in love with Tony, sure. He was going to be my man—and then . . . something inside me snapped, I guess.

WESLEY (*urgent*): You called the police?

BEAUTY: Yeah. I sent my man to the big house. He was going to be my first. After that, well, life was hard . . . I'd read books. I guess I took to it easy. Cut my dresses short. Got hold of eyeblack, lipred. Used my hips. I was all ready for the first guy to come along. And that guy had to be you!

WESLEY (*foolishly radiant*): Then I have saved you! Saved you from blemish!

BEAUTY: That's the way it looks.

WESLEY (*earnest*): What do you want out of life, Aurora-Mae?

BEAUTY (*much too fierce*): I want a guy I can *respect*!

WESLEY (*jaw rippling. Exaggeratedly manly*): I'm crazy about you, Rory, you must know that. I want you to marry me.

BEAUTY: But——?

WESLEY: I know what you're thinking. Listen, my dear . . . my darling—they only call me "Father". I'm an Episcopalian.

BEAUTY: Whoopee! Hold me tight. Tighter. (*Her eyes shut in ecstasy.*) My holy dreamboat! My Noah's ark!

> They are about to kiss when the GOOD FAIRY enters, bespectacled and grim.

GOOD FAIRY: So there you are, Wesley Breitenspiegel.

BEAUTY: Who's this?

WESLEY (*agonized*): Why do you follow me around?

BEAUTY (*ready for disenchantment*): Is she your girl?

WESLEY: No.

BEAUTY: Your wife?

WESLEY: No. My psychiatrist.

GOOD FAIRY: Now come away from that girl, Wesley, and just relax completely.

WESLEY *breaks away obediently, and sits down on the chair, which the* GOOD FAIRY *provides.*

BEAUTY: What's wrong with him? Is it a war wound?

GOOD FAIRY: He mustn't have excitement of any sort. Wesley, make your mind a complete blank. My dear girl, don't pursue this matter further. Take my advice.

BEAUTY (*fiercely*): But he loves me! He wants to marry me!

GOOD FAIRY: Illusion, my dear. Just a superimposition of the mother image onto you. *Very* unfortunate. He's always going round trying to marry girls. It's part of the illness.

BEAUTY: But . . . but Girls' Town . . . ?

GOOD FAIRY: Exactly, my dear.

The WICKED FAIRY *staggers to his feet. He seizes the revolver.*

WICKED FAIRY: O.K., wise guys . . . (*He sees the horror-struck* BEAUTY, *the grimly functional* GOOD FAIRY, *and the glazed-eyed* WESLEY, *and says, resignedly*—) Oh, what's the use. Curtain. Bring it down.

The curtain falls.

AIMÉ: Well, there's our great romantic, our Don Quixote who has to ask a policeman the way to the windmills.

IKONENKO: He demonstrated very clearly the hysterical undertones of contemporary Pluto-Fascist society.

DESMOND: No, I can't allow that, old man. He just showed evidence of a deeply moral upbringing at a school which was undoubtedly a sight too good.

IKONENKO: Too good? A school cannot be good or bad, it can only be accurate or inaccurate.

DESMOND: Oh, nonsense, old fellow. I went to a school which is generally considered the best there is. Well, it was far too good to produce really useful citizens.

AIMÉ: How about you?

DESMOND: I flatter myself that my one saving grace is that I was such a bad pupil. But thanks for the compliment.

The WICKED FAIRY *looks through the curtains.*

WICKED FAIRY (*depressed*): Next please. Colonel Ikonenko.

IKONENKO: I do not wish to take part in the experiment.

AIMÉ: What?

WICKED FAIRY: Don't you love the girl?

[233]

IKONENKO: What is the meaning of such a word? Is it a realistic approach to life to say that you are at any time in love?

DESMOND: Good gracious me. Realism can be carried too far, you know.

IKONENKO: No. People who have never seen a bath do not want a bath. That is realistic. Knowledge breeds desire, and desire breeds hatred.

WICKED FAIRY (*sly*): Yes, but you have seen the girl. You know her.

IKONENKO: Unfortunately.

WICKED FAIRY: Those flaxen curls, that freckled face, those strong arms and legs, that healthy, child-bearing body. Can you resist it?

IKONENKO (*after a pause. Rises*): I shall go just to see her again. For no other reason.

WICKED FAIRY: Which period do you wish to see her in?

IKONENKO: A period in which they had the rounded epaulettes with golden tassels on them.

WICKED FAIRY (*smiling*): Orchestra. Valse Pathétique.

> *The orchestra begins to play a sentimental waltz.* IKONENKO *and the* WICKED FAIRY *go.*

DESMOND: What an uncouth fellow.

AIMÉ: I wonder. I begin to see a little of his point of view.

DESMOND: Blowed if I do.

AIMÉ: Can we men really be in love with something so fragile, so unexplained, as an ideal? Didn't we go up there to show off to each other, because we've heard the girl is beautiful?

DESMOND: I thought she was beautiful, myself.

> WESLEY *enters, back in uniform.*

Bad luck, Galahad.

WESLEY: I want to go back, out of this dream-world.

AIMÉ: Why?

WESLEY: She's a great kid. A really swell kid. But I'm all tied up in knots.

AIMÉ: What knots?

WESLEY: I just want to go back and talk to Doctor Polgeister. (*With a wan smile.*) That's the worst of being a romantic.

> DESMOND *and* AIMÉ *exchange looks. The lights dim. The curtains part to reveal a Chekhovian garden. Croquet hoops on the ground. The* BEAUTY, *dressed in* 1900 *costume, and stouter than before, is idly playing croquet.* IKONENKO *enters. He wears a*

[234]

dark green uniform with epaulettes; he sits down on a garden swing, and begins knitting.

IKONENKO: So it is summer once again . . . who would have thought it.

BEAUTY: Summer seems to pass like a single hour when one is playing croquet . . . Anatol Lvovitch will be thirty-eight next birthday . . .

> *Pause.*

IKONENKO: Excuse me, I have not been listening to what you have been saying . . .

BEAUTY: It was nothing . . .

IKONENKO: It was something . . . it was something . . . "Golden words tumble from your lips like a waterfall lit by the midnight sun" . . . that was Pushkin, I believe . . . great man, Pushkin. Greatest poet Russia ever had . . .

BEAUTY: I don't read . . .

IKONENKO: None of us read. You play croquet . . . I knit . . . I am knitting a pair of mittens for Kolya, the medical orderly . . . why do we do it?

BEAUTY: Are we in love?

IKONENKO: In love?

BEAUTY: With life? It is so important not to give up hope. (*She hits the croquet ball with her mallet.*) There, I have scored a splendid point, and there was nobody here to see it.

> *Pause. A shot rings out.*

What was that?

IKONENKO: A woodman felling a birch tree . . .

BEAUTY: It sounded to me like——

IKONENKO: It was raining in Kharkov last Friday. I know, because Grischa left his umbrella at the barracks.

BEAUTY: Ever since Papa died, I have never carried an umbrella. There were so many at the funeral . . .

IKONENKO: Was it raining?

BEAUTY: No . . .

> *Pause.*

IKONENKO: Now I have dropped a stitch, and must undo it all.

BEAUTY: I was so looking forward to yesterday.

IKONENKO: Sadovsky's dance?

BEAUTY: Yes . . . but now that it is over, I cannot look forward to it any more . . .

IKONENKO: I did not go . . .

BEAUTY: Nor did I . . .

IKONENKO: I stayed here . . . in the drawing-room . . . mending the General's watch . . .

BEAUTY: I was here too . . . in the dining-room . . . thinking . . .

IKONENKO: We were in the house alone . . .

BEAUTY: Yes . . .

IKONENKO: And I never knew . . .

The WICKED FAIRY *enters, dressed in eccentric summer clothes, and with a long white beard.*

WICKED FAIRY: Boo! Do I interrupt an idyll? Are the lovebirds ruthlessly pecking one another? Have I chanced upon a courtship in the aviary?

BEAUTY: Uncle! Dear, darling Uncle!

WICKED FAIRY: What? Is my starling playing croquet, then? Ah, but only until evening, I'll warrant? Eh? Then, when the moon emerges from her starry retreat . . . ? Eh? Eh? Do I make myself clear?

IKONENKO: I must leave for Moscow to-night.

WICKED FAIRY: Eh? Eh?

BEAUTY: To-night?

IKONENKO: They have given me a regiment in Kazakstan.

WICKED FAIRY: What a disgrace! How you have upset me! There is no telling what the authorities will do. Only yesterday I heard from Sadovsky, the old rascal, that Ignaty Ivanovitch Bulkin, the Associate Assessor of an intermediary grade, in a temporary capacity from the Rural Board, a dear but foolish man, kind but despicable, as you might say, if . . . so . . . inclined . . . a man, mark you, who never travels by train because the noise of the engine frightens him, he believes the devil to be sitting inside it, boiling water for his tea, well— where was I? I'm getting old.

BEAUTY: Dear, dear Uncle.

WICKED FAIRY: Ah, yes—this man has been made Inspector-General of the local railway, if you please! If it were true, it would be absolutely scandalous. Fortunately Sadovsky is as unreliable as I am, may God and his saints forgive me, and there is no possibility of it being true. All the same, it has excited me somewhat. I really must sit down. (*He sits. Then pretends to shoot into the air with an imaginary gun.*) Piff! Paff! Pouff! (*He raises his imaginary rifle to shoot again*

[236]

when another shot rings out, off stage.) I enjoy shooting seagulls, but it is less cruel without a gun.

BEAUTY: There is that noise again . . . there cannot be many birch trees left . . . my poor, lovely birch trees . . .

WICKED FAIRY: That's no birch tree. It is Uncle Mischa trying to shoot himself. It really is degrading how he fails at everything he puts his hand to. So bad for the family's name. While, as an ex-officer, his inability to shoot straight is a direct reflection on His Imperial Majesty's Army. But there, I must not excite myself. If one took everything to heart, where would one be . . . where would one be . . . why, just exactly where one is . . .

BEAUTY: Dear, darling Uncle. Why does Uncle Mischa do it?

WICKED FAIRY: He is in love . . .

BEAUTY: With life . . . like me?

WICKED FAIRY: He is in love with . . . a certain party . . . a pretty little starling who passes her youth in playing croquet. But there, I talk too much, as always . . .

BEAUTY: In five or six hundred years . . . perhaps then I will be happy . . .

> *Pause. Suddenly the* WICKED FAIRY *gets up, furious, tears off his wig, and pushes his false beard up onto his forehead.*

WICKED FAIRY (*to* IKONENKO; *out of character.*) Damn it, you're just not trying!

IKONENKO: Why should I try? Haven't I seen what happened to the others?

WICKED FAIRY: I give you one last chance. Will you seduce her or not?

IKONENKO: No!

> *The* GOOD FAIRY *enters, much stouter than before, with a black wig and horrible bun. She is dressed from head to foot in black.*

GOOD FAIRY: D'you mean to say I've got dressed for nothing?

IKONENKO: Aha! You are my wife. I knew you would come if I tried to seduce her. What's the use? I'd rather sit quietly knitting in my Beauty's company than invoke you.

> *The* BEAUTY, *who has been idling with the croquet mallet, suddenly looks up, and sees her beloved Uncle without his hair, and with his beard apparently growing out of the top of his head. She screams, pointing at him, and swoons.*

GOOD FAIRY (*upset—to* WICKED FAIRY): Now look what you've done! (*She runs over to comfort the* BEAUTY.)

[237]

WICKED FAIRY (*furious*): The interlude is over! Curtain once again! For the last time!

> *The curtain falls.*

AIMÉ: Well, that's that.

WESLEY: What in hell's the matter with that guy?

DESMOND: Thoroughly cynical, if you ask me.

AIMÉ: No, I don't agree. I call him uncomfortably intelligent.

WESLEY: I don't feel I can work with any of you again after this.

DESMOND: I want to get back, and double quick. I'll have a word about it with Donovan. Funny, but I don't entirely trust the other fellow.

> *The* GOOD FAIRY *enters*, RIGHT. *She is in her A.T.S. uniform again.*

GOOD FAIRY: Well, have you decided? Do you want to stay?

CHORUS: No.

GOOD FAIRY: You realize you will never defile the Beauty while I prevent you.

AIMÉ: But you still want us to reach for the unattainable. You want us to stay.

GOOD FAIRY: How do you know what I want?

AIMÉ: Carabosse also realizes that the Beauty is incorruptible, so he——

WICKED FAIRY (*looking through the curtains*): What does he want you to do?

AIMÉ: Ah, there you are—you wish us to return to the wilderness of normal life, where we can deceive our wives at your pleasure.

> *The* WICKED FAIRY *and the* GOOD FAIRY *exchange glances.*

GOOD FAIRY: Stay—with perfection.

AIMÉ: Why do you make perfection sound so desirable?

WICKED FAIRY: Well, isn't it?

AIMÉ: Is it?

GOOD FAIRY: It's . . . it's very peaceful . . .

AIMÉ: Exactly. It's very boring.

WICKED FAIRY (*lively*): Very well, you know-all. Yes, I want you to return. But I'll be fair to Donovan. If you sin, you must sin with conviction. I'm sick of empty victories. So if you'll return to your seats, I'll show you what you may expect to return *to*.

> IKONENKO *enters, back in uniform.*

[238]

DESMOND: What are you driving at, sir? Nothing's happened in our absence, has it?

WICKED FAIRY: Oh, yes . . .

WESLEY: Well, tell us. There's not another war, is there?

WICKED FAIRY: Not yet.

IKONENKO: Has a superior arrived from Moscow, and I was not there to receive him?

WICKED FAIRY: You're getting warmer.

AIMÉ: Have we all got visitors?

WICKED FAIRY: Yes.

DESMOND: Well, show us, for heaven's sake. Stop insinuating.

WICKED FAIRY: Are you ready? Orchestra. (*He squats and talks among the palms, sotto voce.*)

The orchestra begins Chopin's Funeral March. The lights dim.

DESMOND: Good gracious, someone's died.

GOOD FAIRY (*sad*): Don't worry. It's only Carabosse's cynicism. The music is intended to be descriptive rather than elegiac.

The curtain rises slowly, and the WICKED FAIRY *comes back among the* COLONELS. *The scene is the set of Act I. Now* FOUR WOMEN *sit around in silence. One is gaunt, wears a shapeless hat, and regimental jewellery.* DESMOND *recognizes her immediately.*)

DESMOND: Mabel!

Another is terribly chic, wears a hat with vast feathers.

AIMÉ: Thérèse!

Another is tweedily smart, wears glasses.

WESLEY: Shirley!

Another is stout, and resembles the GOOD FAIRY'S *last disguise. She holds a newly-born baby.*

IKONENKO: Olga!

GOOD FAIRY: Yes, after two and a half years of negotiation, the four powers have reached agreement, and given your wives permission to join you.

DESMOND: And we weren't there to meet them!

WICKED FAIRY: Don't say you wanted to be there?

DESMOND: That doesn't enter into it, old man. It's *done.*

WESLEY: Why don't they say anything? They're not dead, are they?

WICKED FAIRY: No. (*Calls.*) Stop the music!

The music stops.

[239]

MABEL: We seem to have run out of conversation . . .

SHIRLEY: Yeah . . .

The baby starts yelling fitfully.

IKONENKO: What is that child doing here?

WICKED FAIRY (*laughing*): It's yours.

DESMOND: Don't be ridiculous, he's been away two and a half years.

WICKED FAIRY: Quite.

GOOD FAIRY: Oh, you cruel, cruel fairy.

IKONENKO: Am I to understand that I am not the father?

DESMOND: I'm terribly sorry, old chum.

IKONENKO: Such events are only to be expected in difficult times.

WESLEY: Do you mean to sit there and tell me you don't mind? Why, I'd divorce her, find the guy that's responsible and beat the living daylights out of him.

DESMOND: I will not conceal the fact that I am profoundly shocked at your attitude, sir.

IKONENKO: Why should I——?

Before he can finish his sentence, MABEL, *who has been consulting a jewelled watch, says:*

MABEL: Do you realize we've been here for two hours?

SHIRLEY: And no sign of the boys. Well, they can't say they didn't get the cables, because here they are, right on the table.

THÉRÈSE: What do you expect from men?

SHIRLEY: I demand a certain degree of courtesy. After all, I'm a hard-working woman. I have to fly to Frankfurt tomorrow, Rome Friday and back here Sunday.

MABEL: You won't see much of Rome in two days.

SHIRLEY: I don't go there to see it, Mrs Sparrow—I work. I'm the women's editress of a group of syndicated magazines, including *Wife*, a woman's magazine with a difference, *Urge*, which is a frank journal for children in the difficult age, and *Think*, a more mature publication dealing with the psychological aspects of marriage in general and matrimonial misfits in particular. I'm being advised in all this by Orlando Kisfaludy—

WESLEY: The bastard.

SHIRLEY: —one of the greatest alienists we have in the States.

WESLEY: Oh God, she talks an awful lot.

SHIRLEY: And then, of course——

[240]

THÉRÈSE: I don't understand what there is left to talk about on the subject of marriage.

AIMÉ: Bravo, Thérèse.

SHIRLEY: Oh, one hell of a lot. I'm just inundated with material. I've gotten very much more than I can use.

WESLEY: That's always been your trouble, honey. You use it all the same.

SHIRLEY (*shrewdly*): Of course, I am helped by having a husband who is psychologically unstable.

WESLEY: Hey!

THÉRÈSE: Aren't they all?

MABEL (*shocked*): I trust not!

DESMOND: Oh, shut up, Mabel dear.

SHIRLEY: Well, in a way, yes. We have statistics which show that the male sex has recourse to outlets on an average 4·8 times in a year, while the female sex has recourse to outlets only 1·9 times.

MABEL (*frigid*): What do you mean by outlets?

SHIRLEY: Unfaithfulness. "Outlets" is a technical term in our statistics office.

THÉRÈSE: 1·9 times? That means that every year you sleep with one man who is not your husband, and also with nine-tenths of another man?

MABEL: Really, what an extraordinary conversation.

THÉRÈSE: I think it's all nonsense. It proves nothing.

MABEL: Hear, hear.

THÉRÈSE: You can't dissociate a woman's behaviour from the man's. The human element is completely lacking in all these figures, and a study of the human heart will tell you much more.

SHIRLEY: I don't agree. Well, if you're in the mood for experimenting, let's conduct a little poll here and now.

MABEL: God forbid!

SHIRLEY: Dr Schultz says a healthy woman has nothing to hide.

MABEL: I don't care what Dr Schultz says. Even if a woman has nothing to hide, she should be at great pains to hide it.

SHIRLEY: Well, I'm modern! I don't mind telling you girls that I need an outlet, perhaps even more than others, because I am emotionally attracted by psychological work—and then, my husband is an unusual and interesting mental specimen.

WESLEY: That's enough, Shirley!

WICKED FAIRY: She can't hear you.

SHIRLEY: He's got a strong streak of the infantile, the backward, in him, his mother's fault, of course.

WESLEY: Well, knock me down.

SHIRLEY: This side of Wesley's character does not satisfy the deeply mature side of my nature, and there you have clear evidence of maladjustment. Naturally, I have to find an element to satisfy my maturity elsewhere. An outlet, in fact. It's as simple as that.

MABEL: You might call it painfully simple.

SHIRLEY: Why? Eradicate shame! Why be inhibited? Live, live, live.

MABEL (*shocked*): I do very well in my own way, thank you.

SHIRLEY: Yeah, I bet. Listen, I've had three outlets this year.

WESLEY (*shouting*): What?

AIMÉ (*to* WESLEY): How many have you had, Wesley?

WESLEY: Two, damn it.

SHIRLEY: I'm not ashamed. I wouldn't mind telling Wesley, he'd be interested to hear.

WESLEY: That's a lie!

SHIRLEY: He and I are friends.

WESLEY: That's a heresy!

SHIRLEY: But there, I've talked too much.

WESLEY: That's the first true thing you've said!

SHIRLEY: How about you, Mrs Frappot? After all, we're all girls together.

THÉRÈSE: Well . . . my husband is a typical man. Very kind; very thoughtful—except when he is in love with someone else; very cultivated; very intelligent; very handsome; a very nice man; not a wonderful husband.

AIMÉ: Her generosity is atrocious.

THÉRÈSE: He appreciates beauty perhaps too much, because he can never resist investigating it. He also adores intelligence, and an intelligent but ugly woman can make me more unhappy than a pretty face. To make matters more difficult, I like and admire his taste in these things. It is to me a little indiscriminate, but always discriminating. He always likes women, categorizes them, and if he flirts with them he knows exactly what he is doing, and can almost tell to a day how long an affair is going to last. I love him very much.

SHIRLEY: I see. A high intelligence quotient. And how do you respond? Passively?

THÉRÈSE (*after a second's reflection*): I have an agreement with a business man—a transport chief.

AIMÉ: Ah, if that were only true!

SHIRLEY: A steady date?

THÉRÈSE: Oh yes, for years.

SHIRLEY: And no divorce?

THÉRÈSE: I'm in love with my husband . . .

AIMÉ (*pained*): Oh . . .

SHIRLEY: I see. That brings our average to two. Now, Mrs Sparrow.

MABEL: I refuse to discuss the matter. I consider it absolutely scandalous.

SHIRLEY (*to* THÉRÈSE): There's a great deal of tact involved in my work. (*To* MABEL.) Won't you even tell us about your husband?

MABEL: He's a rattling good sort. There. Are you satisfied?

SHIRLEY: That is hardly data, Mrs Sparrow.

MABEL: It was never intended to be.

SHIRLEY: Is he virile and demanding?

MABEL: I'm sure I don't know what you mean. He plays cricket.

SHIRLEY: Athletic, huh?

MABEL: If you must know, extremely. (*Bitterly*.) Excessively. Whenever I want to talk to him, he's either shadow-boxing or skipping.

DESMOND: Oh, I say.

SHIRLEY: I see. Is he therefore intellectually a little dry, a little restricted?

MABEL: He's intellectually non-existent. But then, I like that. I loathe intellectuals of any shade or colour. In my opinion, they are responsible for half the world's present misery.

DESMOND: Oh dear, she's off.

MABEL: D'you think we would have acquired our Empire if we had kept asking the whys and wherefores of things? And d'you think my husband would be the first-class administrator he is if he bothered to find out what other people thought? And could I run my Guide Company so that it wins an honourable mention in every jamboree if I spent half the time on thinking that I do on doing? Certainly not.

SHIRLEY: So there is no intellectual starvation.

MABEL: I really don't know what you're talking about. Desmond is a regular officer. He's a bit of an amateur engineer, and he loves wild animals. And that's that.

SHIRLEY: Has he any other interests? Does he write or draw?

MABEL (*more deeply shocked than ever*): Certainly not!

[243]

SHIRLEY: And about him and women?

MABEL: You are being quite unnecessarily disgusting, Mrs Whateveritis.

SHIRLEY: And on the point of your infidelity, Mrs Sparrow?

MABEL (*terrible*): I am his wife!

SHIRLEY: I know that, but——

MABEL: That is quite enough of that!

WESLEY (*bitter*): Congratulations, old boy.

DESMOND (*sighing*): It isn't strictly true, you know. She gets drunk occasionally. At the Regimental dinner before last, she chased the Divisional Commander all over the Barracks . . .

SHIRLEY (*who has been doing a sum on an envelope*): The average is now 1·3. Now, Mrs Ikonenko.

No reply.

IKONENKO: She doesn't speak English.

SHIRLEY: Madame, voulez-vous . . .

No reply.

DESMOND: Your wife doesn't say much, Ikonenko.

IKONENKO: She doesn't speak French either.

SHIRLEY: Frau Ikonenko, Wollen Sie bitte . . .

IKONENKO: She doesn't even speak much Russian. In fact, she hardly speaks at all.

WESLEY: What a godsend!

At that moment, MME IKONENKO *decides it's time to feed the child. With her back to the audience, she bares her breast, and places the child to it, humming an ancient lullaby.* MABEL *gazes at her, horrified.* THÉRÈSE *is whimsically amused, but* SHIRLEY *is visibly taken aback.*

MABEL: Well, really, what a place to choose.

SHIRLEY: So insanitary!

THÉRÈSE: You really mean, so public, so uncomplicated!

IKONENKO: There! Olga has done the first decent and feminine thing, and all the others are shocked.

AIMÉ: Not Thérèse! Oh, Thérèse, if only I loved you!

SHIRLEY (*a little confused*): Well, anyway, there's evidence of an outlet there. That makes the average 1·25. Only ·65 of an error. You see, there is truth in figures.

The MAYOR *enters.*

MAYOR: Good evening. Good evening, ladies. No sign of the Colonels yet?

DESMOND: Oh, not this cove again!

WICKED FAIRY (*smiling*): Had enough?

CHORUS: Yes!

WICKED FAIRY: Curtain!

The curtain swings down.

Well, what is your decision?

WESLEY (*rising, livid*): I'm going to get a divorce, that's what I'm going to do.

AIMÉ: Why?

WESLEY: What d'you mean, why? Didn't you see?

AIMÉ: I saw, and I suffered, for myself and for us all.

DESMOND: Jolly decent of you.

AIMÉ: But remember, we only see them as we saw ourselves before we came here. Reverse the situation. What would they have thought if they had eavesdropped on one of our conversations? We don't know our wives. They don't know us. We are all alone, impenetrable jungles. How can we be happy?

GOOD FAIRY: Listen to me!

AIMÉ: No! You represent perfection. You don't know the difficulties of choice.

WICKED FAIRY (*bitter*): Difficulties? It's what we envy most in you.

AIMÉ: But how do we know what is right and wrong?

GOOD FAIRY: I am right.

WICKED FAIRY (*slighted*): So am I!

AIMÉ: Ah, but when it is all mixed, in that jungle! You are on rails, my friends—we have to walk a slippery road. We can't do right without not doing wrong, and we can't do wrong without not doing right. Every act is a renunciation of another. We must do one thing or the other, and when we do one thing, the other is undone.

DESMOND: I haven't your sort of architectural mind, Aimé.

AIMÉ: Donovan wants us to stay, because she knows the Beauty to be incorruptible. She wants us to reach for the unattainable in a vacuum. A cruel aim for such a pretty girl.

The WICKED FAIRY *laughs.*

AIMÉ: Carabosse wanted us to rape perfection, to make his victory complete, to end his awful immortality.

WICKED FAIRY (*furious*): I can never forgive God for having invented the French.

AIMÉ: He has just now seen that it is hopeless. Now he wants us to return, so that we may lose ourselves again in the morass, open to

[245]

temptation, wide-eyed and willing, the more so since we have just seen our wives.

DESMOND: I see. Well, whatever you may have to say, I'm going back.

The WICKED FAIRY *laughs quietly.*

There's one thing you've overlooked in my case, you see. I'm quite fond of Mabel, yes, but not in any special way, you understand— that was over a long time ago, just before I married her, to be precise. But I do badly want to see my dogs again—Ranger, Thunderbolt, and Black Havoc. And then . . . (*He laughs, shyly.*) . . . the Editor of *Field* said he was interested in a poem for the Christmas issue . . .

GOOD FAIRY (*sad*): So you're going back . . .

DESMOND: Yes. Sorry to let you down, Donovan, after all you've done. I'd have made you a Lance-Corporal if you weren't above all that.

IKONENKO: I too will return.

The WICKED FAIRY *cackles.*

GOOD FAIRY (*indignant*): Why?

IKONENKO: Colonel Sparrow——

DESMOND: Rinder-Sparrow.

IKONENKO: Colonel Desmond is right when he says that his love for his wife was over just before he married her. If we stayed, what would happen? We would awake in a hundred years, and try to seduce the Beauty again, and again we would fail. Then we would return to life. My friends . . . Comrades . . . You have seen my wife. I can't boast about her, but I can't complain. I leave ideals to fools, and return to my duties as a Soviet officer with relief. I am not interested in horizons, gentlemen, I am interested in breathing, and I wish to forget this as quickly as possible, and return to the life I know, with all its inequalities and suffering and welcome constriction.

WICKED FAIRY: Excellent!

AIMÉ: Yes, a surprisingly intelligent assessment, if I may say so, but I am staying.

WICKED FAIRY (*aghast*): What? You were the one I thought I could count on most!

GOOD FAIRY (*entranced*): Oh, Aimé!

AIMÉ: Listen. I have lived my life as an explorer in the world of women. It has been easy, fascinating, and often very beautiful, but it was all accessible, and therefore transitory. All that I have not experienced is the quest for the unattainable. I happened to marry Thérèse. I could as easily have married any of the others. If I had married one of the others, I should probably have loved Thérèse more. My dear fairies, you envy me my power to choose, but I am sick of choosing, for at the moment of choice, I always regret what I have not done. Therefore I long to give myself to the selfless and patient pursuit of a single elusive woman, whom, as a punishment, I shall never possess.

WESLEY: I guess I'm staying, too, though not from any clear motive. My whole life seems to me so incoherent and horrible that I just don't really know how to explain why I don't want to go back. There must have been a time I thought Shirley brilliant—just brilliant. But after being here, and seeing what made the four of us tick, she just seemed so damned pretentious, and . . . I don't know the word . . . insensitive ? . . . Yeah, that's it . . . insensitive . . . to my problems and everyone else's . . . well, what it boils down to, fellows . . . I need a rest.That's all, folks.

WICKED FAIRY: Two to you, and two to me.

GOOD FAIRY: An equitable score.

WICKED FAIRY (*wan*): It's something we have in common. (*Brisk.*) All right, we'll put you to sleep. We'll give you comfortable beds on the stage. Say your farewells, if you will.

DESMOND: Goodbye, Aimé. I think you're mad.

AIMÉ: I enjoy taking myself by surprise. *Bon voyage*, Desmond.

IKONENKO: Goodbye. (*He salutes.*)

WESLEY: It's been fun, and I want you to know it.

    General goodbyes.

WICKED FAIRY: Right. Now, Aimé and Wesley, will you go onto the stage ?

DESMOND: Any message to your wives ?

WICKED FAIRY: That is not permitted. We will have to arrange an accident.

WESLEY: An accident ?

WICKED FAIRY: Your disappearance will have to be explained. The police are so much more active than they were even a hundred years ago. Donovan, come with me.

    The TWO FAIRIES *go into the wings.*

DESMOND: Good-bye again, Wesley, old son.

WESLEY: Pitch right in there, Des. Yahoo!

    WESLEY *and* AIMÉ *disappear behind the curtain.*

DESMOND: Extraordinary. Wesley's like a fellow with a great load off his mind. I say, you don't think we're being fools leaving them ?

IKONENKO: No.

DESMOND: And we're not in any sense letting them down, I suppose. I'd hate to do that.

IKONENKO: We are right and they are wrong.

DESMOND: I hope so.

IKONENKO: I too . . .

IKONENKO and DESMOND go off into the wings, but stop and turn back as the WICKED FAIRY and the GOOD FAIRY return from the other side of the stage, dressed as a Doctor and a Nurse.

WICKED FAIRY: Ideal clothes, you see. We'll arrive at the Control Commission Office as a Doctor and Nurse straight from the scene of the accident. You'll have to put on grave faces though.

IKONENKO: Mine is always grave.

The curtains part. The décor is the first pastoral setting with two more beds, one on each side of BEAUTY. AIMÉ and WESLEY are lying on them. The WICKED FAIRY and the GOOD FAIRY go onto the stage.

GOOD FAIRY: Aimé . . . Wesley . . . sleep . . . a dreamless sleep . . . Orchestra—sleep in five minutes—but until then, play!

Soft music begins, the music of the beginning.

WICKED FAIRY: Come on, no time to lose, back to the cold winds of the living world . . . into the air . . . away . . . away . . .

The TWO FAIRIES, IKONENKO and DESMOND sweep out. The WICKED FAIRY's voice gets softer quickly.

AIMÉ (*quiet*): Wesley, are you asleep?

WESLEY: Not yet, brother . . .

Pause. Their two hands reach out, and almost touch the BEAUTY.

Aimé . . . I can't reach the Beauty . . . can you?

AIMÉ: No, not quite . . . it was arranged like this on purpose . . .

Slight pause.

WESLEY: Aimé?

AIMÉ: Mm?

WESLEY: Were we wrong not to go back?

AIMÉ: What is the use of asking such a question? At this precise moment, they are asking themselves if they were wrong not to stay . . .

CURTAIN

LONDON
27 November 1950

NO SIGN OF THE DOVE

A Play in Three Acts

No Sign of the Dove was presented at the Savoy Theatre, London, on 3 December 1953, with the following cast:—

Niobe D'Urt (Matthew D'Urt's daughter)	Beatrix Lehmann
Sir Mohammed D'Urt (Matthew D'Urt's son)	Raymond Huntley
Lord Basingstoke	Robin Bailey
Professor Lodegger	David Kossoff
Matthew D'Urt	Miles Malleson
Hope (the Girl)	Suzanne Cloutier
Lady Basingstoke	Alvys Maben
Buttress	Stanley Van Beers
Bone	Norman Pierce

Play produced by
PETER USTINOV
Décor and Costumes by
NADIA BENOIS

The action takes place at St Blodwen's, Country Seat of the D'Urts, but it could take place anywhere, in the future . . . or in the present?

ACT I

The Venetian room on the first floor. A room furnished with great care, and exuding an atmosphere of carefully contrived decadence. Negro slaves in wood hold up trays—tapestries depicting somewhat dusty pastoral orgies hang about—tables held up by anguished lions. Every chair leg seems to culminate in claws. It is as though an effeminate and exquisite mind had contrived a superb shop window ten years ago which had been lived in since. Archway LEFT, *giving on to a Chinese Regency room, the beginning of which is discernible. Archway* RIGHT, *giving on to a Roman chamber. A statue of a dying athlete is in view. There are no doors, but large windows at the back, now concealed by voluptuous curtains. The curtain rises to reveal this sumptuous scene, crowned by its brightest jewel, the poetess* NIOBE D'URT, *a large woman of epic and handsome appearance, dressed in the fantastic clothes of a Turkish janissary of the 18th century. A cluster of white feathers rises from her turban like a quivering exclamation mark. She is seated at a big chair, reading Mohammed's book. She laughs twice then sighs with the beauty of it.*

The telephone (*which is in the shape of a dolphin, gilt and ponderous*) *rings.* NIOBE *crosses to it.*

NIOBE (*lifting the receiver. Her voice is affected without being in any way effete. It is baroque*): Yes, yes, yes, no, no, no. Yes. (*Sitting on chair.*) Are we not lucky? My darling, I realise precisely how badly you wish to meet the Professor, but I have decided to be greedy, and claim him for my very own for this his first weekend in England . . . Well, of course he's fascinating, what a question . . . I'm surprised, Ethel, that you should be interested in mere appearances. I must say that when I curled up in bed with *Modern Man in Adam's Shadow*, I felt for practically . . . hold on a moment . . . (*She changes the telephone laboriously to the other hand.*) . . . I felt for practically the first time in my life that I held a man's soul in the palms of my hands . . . I did not even wish to meet him . . . the only other occasion I have experienced such a transcendental sensation of mingled subjection and elevation was with my brother's latest book, *Unicorns and White Wine* . . . Yes, fragrant is but a paltry word, is it not? . . . Just a minute . . . (*She changes the telephone to the other hand.*) What? . . . The weather? How painfully conventional of you to mention it . . . will it ever stop

raining? T. S. Eliot has something fairly good to say about rain . . .
I forget what it is . . .

> SIR MOHAMMED D'URT *enters. He is somewhat portly, balding,
> and in a velvet jacket.*

MOHAMMED: T. S. Eliot. Who is that?

NIOBE (*hand over mouthpiece*): Ethel Taplow.

MOHAMMED: Tell her I loathed her last book.

NIOBE: Mohammed has just come in. He's in a perverse mood.
He told me to tell you that he loathed your last book . . . What?
She says she loathes yours.

MOHAMMED: She is the past mistress of repartee. Tell her I hope
she makes a lot of money.

NIOBE: Mohammed, that is the cruellest of remarks to make to a
woman of Ethel's artistic aspirations.

MOHAMMED: That, dear sister, is precisely why I passed it.

NIOBE: You are incorrigible, dear genius.

MOHAMMED: Genius thrives in its own high latitude, and enjoys its
own concessions. It steps on the backs of the kneelers, and is irritated
by the uneven texture of the roadway.

NIOBE: Put that down before you forget it.

MOHAMMED: Have you not rather forgotten the envious talent at
the other end of the electric cable?

NIOBE: What? (*She regards the dolphin.*) So I have. (*Into the
mouthpiece.*) Goodbye, Ethel. (*She hangs up.*) Now.

MOHAMMED: Now I am silent.

NIOBE: I love to hear you think . . .

> *Pause.*

NIOBE: We were foolish to introduce the telephone into this
quattrocento dolphin. It's practically impossible to hold.

MOHAMMED: It puts a period to the flow of unnecessary conversation in which one is compelled to indulge . . . I approve of it.

NIOBE: It looks beautiful.

MOHAMMED: It looks dreadful, but I still approve of it.

> *Pause.*

NIOBE: Where's the Professor?

MOHAMMED: I don't know.

NIOBE: Don't pretend you don't care.

MOHAMMED: I left him in the Gothic room.

> *Pause.*

[254]

NIOBE: I do hope father will behave.

MOHAMMED: Forlorn hope.

NIOBE: Forlorn . . . what an exquisite word . . . (*Pause.*) Bill Basingstoke looks pale.

MOHAMMED: Barbara is sublime.

NIOBE: A little in love?

MOHAMMED: Toulouse-Lautrec.

NIOBE: What?

MOHAMMED: As stupid and as animal as a woman should be, with a gallery of disarming pretensions. She wears her many hearts on her crêpe-de-chine sleeve as though they were medals gained in conquest.

NIOBE: You're in form.

MOHAMMED (*weary*): Bravo.

> LORD BASINGSTOKE *enters. Young and feeble, the product of centuries of careful aristocratic marriages.*

BASINGSTOKE (*silly*): Hullo!

NIOBE: Bill! Come and hold my hand.

MOHAMMED: Where's Barbara?

BASINGSTOKE (*who has a slight nervous twitch*): I don't know.

MOHAMMED: She's a lioness.

NIOBE: Dear Bill. I'm afraid you've lost your wife to Mohammed.

BASINGSTOKE (*laughing*): I'm resigned to that.

MOHAMMED: Please don't be. The seduction will lose its savour.

BASINGSTOKE (*emotional*): Oh, it's heaven to be in a civilised house!

NIOBE: You are tinged with melancholia.

BASINGSTOKE: Yes. I never am at home, but when I come here I feel so miserably talentless.

NIOBE: Darling Bill. Some of us are born with a wealth of poetry—others are born with just wealth. You play your part just as we do.

MOHAMMED: We are the bricks in the temple of human achievement. You, Basingstoke, are the cement.

BASINGSTOKE: You're very kind, both of you.

MOHAMMED: I can assure you that is not the intention.

NIOBE: Of course it is, Bill. Mohammed is abominably rude.

BASINGSTOKE: That's his prerogative.

NIOBE: You know how grateful British thought is for your generosity. After all, you financed that immature but valuable little monthly magazine . . .

BASINGSTOKE: *Brain Pan.* Did you like it, Mohammed?

MOHAMMED: I didn't read it, but I hated the cover.

BASINGSTOKE (*with a bleak smile*): It lost eight thousand pounds in two weeks, which I'm told is a record.

NIOBE (*generously*): Long may it stand! How much did your other ventures lose? Or is that indiscreet?

BASINGSTOKE: *Counterpoint* lost eleven thousand, but then it ran to two issues. *Symbol* is still losing at the rate of about eight hundred pounds a month, so I think we can count it a moderate success.

NIOBE: They're so valuable as stimulants. Mohammed?

MOHAMMED: No opinion.

NIOBE: And what are your plans, Bill?

BASINGSTOKE: Well, I'm financing a new intellectual magazine, tentatively called *Midnight Oil*—

MOHAMMED: Midnight?

BASINGSTOKE: Oil. D'you like it as a title?

NIOBE: I have a vision of a profusion of weird moths and the vertical lines of a wrinkled brow rising into the darkness of the room like organ pipes. Mohammed?

MOHAMMED: Do you really want me to tell you what I think of it?

NIOBE: No. Go on, Bill.

BASINGSTOKE: Well, the atmosphere is going to be nocturnal—it is designed to be read at night, you see—

NIOBE: A decoration for insomnia.

BASINGSTOKE: Quite. It is printed in white print on black paper . . .

NIOBE: And who is writing for you?

BASINGSTOKE: I've got a rather curious piece on nightmares by Jean-Leopold Pichot.

> MOHAMMED *emits a kind of exasperated explosion, which the other two ignore.*

NIOBE: Pichot?

BASINGSTOKE: The Frenchman who killed his mother in order to analyse his own reactions to crime in general. He wrote a book about it—*Le Jeune Œdipe*—Young Oedipus—which created a furore in Paris.

NIOBE: Was he executed?

BASINGSTOKE: No. He won the *Prix Goncourt.*

NIOBE: Fascinating. What else?

[256]

BASINGSTOKE: Oh, a couple of dirges from the Chinese, a very brilliant comparison of Dali and Burne-Jones by Professor Dunstan—

MOHAMMED *emits another explosion.*

—and some frightfully interesting speculations on death by a teen-aged American drug addict, a little artless, perhaps, but they read like a breath of fresh air after the usual contemporary stuff.

NIOBE: It sounds too wonderful.

BASINGSTOKE: I suppose there's no chance of persuading the Professor to write a piece?

NIOBE: Well—

MOHAMMED: It depends how much you're willing to pay.

NIOBE: Mohammed!

MOHAMMED: Philosophers are more interested in money than are financiers, and for the very valid reason that they have less of it. There is even a phrase in the English language—"To be philosophical about it." That in itself suggests that to be a philosopher is to be perma-nently equipped to withstand the worst that can possibly occur. As a consequence, philosophers are invariably grateful for any little indulgences which will relieve them for a moment from their graceless state of philosophy. A word of kindness, an attentive ear, a pecuniary consideration will earn their eternal thankfulness.

NIOBE (*desperate*): Oh, Mohammed, it should be written, written, written! It is so agonising to hear the stuff flowing from you, un-recorded and passing into silence, to make way for the banalities of others.

MOHAMMED *sighs deeply.*

PROFESSOR LODEGGER *enters. Elderly and riotous, his face wears a mask of distinction which nature has not surrendered to him without a struggle. His face, as such, is undistinguished. He imitates importance.*

PROFESSOR: Hallo.

BASINGSTOKE *rises and backs* DOWN LEFT.

NIOBE (*to* RIGHT *of Professor*): Professor! (*Brings him* CENTRE.) A sherry?

PROFESSOR: After bathing in a maelstrom of the intangibles it is a relief to take in one's hand something so reassuring, something so visible and unmetaphysical as a glass of sherry. (*He laughs.*)

NIOBE: Mohammed!

MOHAMMED: Let him help himself. It always tastes better when one helps oneself. One acquires the brief illusion that one had a hand in its manufacture.

[257]

PROFESSOR (*wagging a finger*): Not without profound significance.

BASINGSTOKE: No, no.

NIOBE: Bill!

BASINGSTOKE (*in response to an appeal from Niobe*): I'll get it.

PROFESSOR: Aha. You wish to deprive me of that feeling of achievement which manual labour inspires. You are cruel, young man. (*He laughs.*)

BASINGSTOKE: If you'd rather . . .

PROFESSOR: No, no, no. My legs are tired. I shall sit down.

NIOBE: Bill!

BASINGSTOKE: Yes.

    Slight pause.

PROFESSOR: There cannot be many people called Mohammed.

MOHAMMED: Quite a few in Arabia, I believe.

PROFESSOR: One in particular! The Prophet. (*He laughs warmly at his perception.*) But you must admit that outside Islamic circles it is rare.

MOHAMMED: I spent a perfectly miserable childhood because of it—and a curiously pleasant maturity. People find it intriguing, and I do not even have to encourage them.

PROFESSOR: You have the honesty of the truly great man. Your vanity, which would be repellent in a lesser man, becomes in you a positive virtue . . . (*With terrific precision.*) A *lack* of affectation!

NIOBE: There's a compliment indeed.

MOHAMMED: This would seem to be the appropriate moment to tell you how much I enjoyed your book, *The It, the Ego, and the If.*

PROFESSOR (*cold*): You enjoyed it? I am surprised.

NIOBE: Surprised?

PROFESSOR (*terrible*): It was not written to be enjoyed, madam. It was written to be detested. Professor Gritzalbacher, a fine scholar and one of my pupils, has pointed out in an address to the University of Freiburg that it is the first book in the history of the written word which achieves its effect by an *adverse* reaction. The process of logic, as I call it, is as follows—the reader reads, and is repelled. By chapter six the repulsion has reached a stage of such inhuman pressure that the subsequent words are read in a hypnotic trauma of hatred. (*With weighty satisfaction.*) Thus my design is triumphantly realised.

MOHAMMED: I sincerely believe I am incapable of hatred. It's too tiring.

[258]

PROFESSOR: All of us are capable of hatred, my friend. It is only love of which we are incapable.

NIOBE: How melancholy and how true.

MOHAMMED: I am eminently capable of love.

PROFESSOR: You *think* you are! But here there is confusion of terms.

> *He lights an ancient pipe laboriously, in deep thought, placing the tobacco tin on the table.*

By love you mean the gratification of a physical need . . .

MOHAMMED: I—

PROFESSOR (*urgently*): Please, please! It is so. Do you love your sister? Think. Is it love?

MOHAMMED: I have the same affection for her as I would have for a friendly piece of furniture.

NIOBE (*moved*): Dear Mohammed.

PROFESSOR: Precisely. It is not that you love her more than others, but that you hate her less. A human is only capable of loving himself—as for the rest of humanity, his relationship to it can only be assessed in degrees of hatred.

MOHAMMED: I can't say I hate you, Professor. It's ridiculous. It's impolite.

PROFESSOR: Your hatred of me is dormant because you are educated to hide your feelings. But can you deny that you hate me more than you did when I started this conversation?

MOHAMMED (*reasonable*): No, I can't.

PROFESSOR (*in triumph*): Aha!

> MATTHEW D'URT *enters the room. He is the father of* NIOBE *and* MOHAMMED, *a gnarled and epic figure of a man in his early hundreds. He is dressed in wet waders, an equally wet black sou'wester, and he carries an assortment of bits of wood, stick, string. His white beard flows angrily down his chest. He walks straight through the room with a forced, rhythmic gait, the metronomic sound of which is emphasised by the plash of the boots.*

NIOBE: Father! At least be civil . . .

> MATTHEW *exits. A* GIRL *runs after him—about fourteen, barefoot, wet up to the waist and very thinly dressed. She too carries wood.*

NIOBE: Hope! Come here this instant, child!

> *The* GIRL *stops, intimidated, shy.*

Where have you been? Surely not out in the floods, dressed like that? Father's utterly mad.

MATTHEW (*off, roaring*): Hope!

    The GIRL *makes to go.*

NIOBE: Stay here! Answer my question!

    MATTHEW *appears, livid.*

MATTHEW: Hope! Don't stay and pollute your mind by listening to these deflated observation balloons.

NIOBE: Oh, Professor, this is my father.

PROFESSOR (*with a heavy effort at elegance*): A veritable King Lear!

MATTHEW: What's that? King Lear? Don't you dare to compare me to that self-pitying old ass. Who are you, anyway?

NIOBE (*hissing*): Behave, Father. (*Loud.*) This is the celebrated Professor Lodegger.

MATTHEW: Professor? Professor of what? Don't tell me, let me guess. Pornography. You've written books. You've that silly look of achievement about you.

PROFESSOR: What admirable hatred!

MOHAMMED: Father, you bore me.

MATTHEW: I'm in no mood for flattery, Mohammed. I only came back to rescue Hope from the pit of hell.

NIOBE: It's quite sinful to make the child go out into the floods dressed in practically nothing.

MATTHEW: Sinful? She's a cave-woman. Come here, show them. Fourteen years I've had her, and she's never had a common cold. I only wish I had been brought up as she has. Then I wouldn't have to burden myself with these cumbersome protective garments. (*He sees the* PROFESSOR'S *tin of tobacco.*) Have you finished with this tin?

PROFESSOR: You want it?

    MATTHEW *empties the remaining tobacco on to the table and pockets the tin.*

MATTHEW: Thank you.

NIOBE: Father collects tins.

PROFESSOR: They take up more room than stamps or butterflies.

MATTHEW: You are attempting to humour me. I refuse to be humoured. (*Remembering.*) Hope, go to my room and shut your ears to this degrading conversation.

    The GIRL *runs out.*

MATTHEW: I refuse to be humoured because I have passed through several childhoods and I can afford to ignore the patronising airs of one who is stuck pompously in the wasteland of his first maturity. My dear fellow, life begins after the second childhood.

PROFESSOR: May I lend you my book?

MATTHEW: I read nothing but the stars. They make infinitely more satisfying reading than do words, even if their message is unrelievedly and grimly prophetic. There is no time to lose. I am in a hurry.

He goes out.

PROFESSOR: Remarkable.

NIOBE: I wish we could agree. We've tried to have him certified, but he hummed the whole of the Art of the Fugue to the doctor, who, far from certifying him, made arrangements to meet every Wednesday for musical sessions. We have been forced to endure recitals for two recorders every Wednesday evening for nine years.

PROFESSOR: He appeared to me not only sane, but filled with a spontaneous and desirable hatred.

MOHAMMED: Professor, it is one thing to admire the Sistine murals in their proper setting. It is quite another to have them in your bathroom.

PROFESSOR: I do not follow.

MOHAMMED: Father will provide us with many affectionate memories . . . when he is gone.

PROFESSOR (*sharp*): Aha! The death wish!

MOHAMMED: What?

PROFESSOR (*to himself, but deliberately audible*): Der Todeswunsch. An almost perfect example.

MOHAMMED: You think me capable of murdering him?

PROFESSOR: Ideologically.

MOHAMMED: No, Professor. I would miss the delicious irritation he causes. The really civilised mind is of necessity so lazy that it must be continually stung into sparks, like the dull grey anvil under the hammer. I am grateful to Father for tempering my mind into the hard and resilient high-precision instrument it is.

NIOBE: Rest, Mohammed, rest your head, a crown of incalculable price, on its *petit point* cushion.

MOHAMMED (*smiling and stretching out a languorous hand which is not accepted*): Sister's in her poetry mood.

NIOBE (*with a mysterious serenity*): Just words at the moment, trying to find a place in the sentences, staking their claims like the fluttering pigeons on the tightrope ledges round Trafalgar Square . . .

BASINGSTOKE (*soft*): Shall I ask him now?

NIOBE: What?

BASINGSTOKE: About the article.

[261]

NIOBE: Boor. You have broken a mood. Seven years' bad luck.

BASINGSTOKE: I'm sorry.

NIOBE: Ask him.

BASINGSTOKE: Professor? Professor?

PROFESSOR: Who speaks?

BASINGSTOKE: Me. Bill Basingstoke.

PROFESSOR: You? I didn't notice you.

MOHAMMED: The insignificance-grise of the literary world.

NIOBE (*delighted*): Naughty brother!

BASINGSTOKE: I wanted to ask you a question.

PROFESSOR: That is not forbidden.

BASINGSTOKE: Good. Would you write an article for me?

PROFESSOR: An article?

BASINGSTOKE: Yes, for me. For my magazine.

PROFESSOR: I find it difficult to contain my ideas into a shape smaller than a book.

BASINGSTOKE: You might find it worth while—I mean we could, I am sure, *make* it worth while.

PROFESSOR (*terrible*): You speak of money?

BASINGSTOKE: Well . . . is that wrong?

PROFESSOR: You dare to mention the word to me?

BASINGSTOKE: Would you rather do it free?

PROFESSOR: Free? You wish to add insults to the injury?

BASINGSTOKE: No.

PROFESSOR: I would rather not do it at all.

BASINGSTOKE: Well—

PROFESSOR (*angry*): Hop! Hop! Final!

> MATTHEW *returns—opposite direction, accompanied by the* GIRL.

NIOBE: Father, you're not going out again!

MATTHEW: The stars which spoke of hours yesterday now talk of minutes.

NIOBE: At least leave the girl.

MATTHEW (*furious*): You expect me to do all the work by myself?

NIOBE: But what are you doing?

MATTHEW: Ah. (*Suddenly sad.*) Niobe, my daughter, why didn't you give me a larger room?

NIOBE: Your room is quite big enough, Father, and you know it.

MATTHEW (*roaring*): Twelve foot by eight!

NIOBE: It's beautifully furnished.

MATTHEW: The furniture's all broken up.

NIOBE (*horrified*): What? My Chippendale chairs!

MATTHEW (*irritated*): There was no room to move with furniture in the room. Niobe, mark my words, you will live to rue the day when you denied my simple request for a larger room.

NIOBE (*angry, hooting; rising*): Father, you're a menace.

MATTHEW (*to the* GIRL): Come on, Hope, before the floods rise above our necks . . . (*He makes to go out.*)

PROFESSOR: Sir.

MATTHEW: Don't be polite to me. It's far too late for that.

PROFESSOR (*amused*): I wish to be informed about something.

MATTHEW: Well, what's it to be? Make haste. Counterpoint? Jet propulsion? Hand weaving? Yogi?

PROFESSOR: I will sound like a cheap journalist.

MATTHEW: I expect nothing else.

PROFESSOR: To what single fact do you attribute your longevity?

MATTHEW: That's a far more intelligent question than I had expected. Congratulations. I attribute my relative longevity to having always made my own mistakes instead of those of other people. Do you understand?

PROFESSOR: It is not entirely convincing.

MATTHEW: No, because you are a suspicious strap-hanger in the overcrowded carriage of the intelligentsia.

PROFESSOR: May I hope to resume our conversation?

MATTHEW: Regrettably, there is no time.

PROFESSOR: Tomorrow, I mean.

MATTHEW (*with an enigmatic and troubling scoff*): Tomorrow . . .
    He exits with the GIRL.
    NIOBE *walks to the left-hand arch.*

MOHAMMED: Where are you going?

NIOBE: I intend to force his door.

MOHAMMED: In order to weep over the wreckage of your Chippendale chairs? But you gave them to him because you disliked them so intensely.

NIOBE: It's the principle of the thing.

MOHAMMED: Maybe he disliked them as much as you did.

NIOBE: He has no right to have taste at his age.

MOHAMMED: But his room is padlocked. Sit down!

NIOBE: It is my duty to make a gesture. Mohammed, I am extremely upset.

BASINGSTOKE: Let me come with you!

> NIOBE *holds out her hand. They go out. Pause. A man in a bowler hat looks out from behind the curtains. His eyes narrow. He disappears. For the sake of future reference, his name is* BONE.

PROFESSOR: Who is the girl?

MOHAMMED: I don't know.

PROFESSOR: The girl. The girl in the wet clothes?

MOHAMMED: Exactly. I don't know.

PROFESSOR: But . . . does she live here?

MOHAMMED: Father found her.

PROFESSOR: I don't understand.

MOHAMMED: Nor do I. Let's leave it at that. Energy must be saved for thought. (*Aimlessly humming.*) Ah . . . thought . . . thought . . . thought-thought . . . thought-thought . . .

> LADY BASINGSTOKE, BARBARA *to her lovers, enters dressed eccentrically in trousers and a backless top. Her eyes are half shut as she affects short sight.*

BARBARA: Where is everybody?

MOHAMMED: Barbara, I have been singing your praises.

BARBARA: To anyone in particular?

MOHAMMED: To your husband.

BARBARA (*bored*): Oh, him.

MOHAMMED: I told him I intended to seduce you.

BARBARA: Don't let's talk about him, Mohammed.

MOHAMMED: Let's talk about you, my sweet.

BARBARA: I'm sick of myself.

MOHAMMED: Help yourself to a cigar.

BARBARA: After dinner.

PROFESSOR (*who has risen*): May I . . . ahem . . .

MOHAMMED (*who has not*): Oh, Professor. I beg your pardon. I rather forgot you were in the room. How delightful—you've even risen to your feet. There's no need to, you know, with Barbara. She'll join you in your chair willingly.

BARBARA: Don't give away secrets.

MOHAMMED: Barbara, this is Professor Lodegger.

BARBARA: I am disappointed.

[264]

PROFESSOR (*stung*): Disappointed?

BARBARA: I saw you as a much younger man. You see, I read your last book, and adored it.

MOHAMMED: Don't insult him.

PROFESSOR (*with weighty gallantry*): Sir Mohammed, a beautiful woman is allowed to react to my book as she pleases.

BARBARA: I do so agree with you about hatred, but I still thought you were a much younger man.

PROFESSOR (*stiffly*): I am sorry.

BARBARA: So am I.

MOHAMMED: Barbara.

BARBARA: Mm?

MOHAMMED: Nothing. Just Barbara.

   Slight pause.

BARBARA: Do sit down, Professor.

PROFESSOR (*whose feelings have been hurt*): I prefer to stand.

MOHAMMED: Barbara.

BARBARA: Do stop saying that.

MOHAMMED: It's an infinitely rhythmic and fruity name.

BARBARA: Fruity?

MOHAMMED (*dreamily*): Rhubarbara. (*Slight pause.*) What are you doing? Come where I can see you.

BARBARA: You're the laziest seducer I've ever come across.

MOHAMMED: Portrait of Mohammed waiting for the mountain.

BARBARA: Ass.

MOHAMMED: Professor. Could you leave us for a while?

PROFESSOR (*ice*): Where do you wish I should go? To help your father find some tins, perhaps outside in the rain?

MOHAMMED (*laughing*): You mustn't mind the way I talk. It's personal.

   The hysterical voice of NIOBE *is heard.*

NIOBE (*off*): Mohammed!

MOHAMMED: Oh, damn. Professor, would you be so kind as to see what she wants?

PROFESSOR: I can hear what she wants. She wants you.

NIOBE (*off*): Mohammed!

   BASINGSTOKE *appears at the archway.*

BASINGSTOKE: Mohammed. Niobe wants you.

MOHAMMED: What is the matter? Has she forced the door?

BASINGSTOKE: It's far more serious than that. The floods have risen by several feet, and cut off the servants in the garage.

MOHAMMED: What are the servants doing in the garage?

BASINGSTOKE: I don't know. They went over to play cards with the chauffeur—at least, that's Niobe's theory.

MOHAMMED: Well?

NIOBE (*off*): Mo-ha-mmed!

BASINGSTOKE: It's a question of food, I gather. It means we'll have to serve ourselves.

> MOHAMMED *rises languorously from the position he has occupied for the entire act.*

MOHAMMED: Oh, the responsibilities of being a gentleman! The fact that I served for several months as a junior officer in the Horse Guards makes everyone consider me as a leader of men. (*Calling out.*) Coming, Niobe!

MOHAMMED (*quiet*): Barbara, your knight is riding to the wars. Throw him the rose of your approval.

> BARBARA *takes a flower out of a bouquet, and throws it at* MOHAMMED.

MOHAMMED. Thank you. (*To* LORD BASINGSTOKE.) Pick it up, would you?

> *He goes.* LORD BASINGSTOKE *picks up the flower and replaces it in the bouquet.*

BARBARA: God, how I hate you.

BASINGSTOKE: You are indifferent to me, Barbara, which is worse.

BARBARA: Go away.

BASINGSTOKE: Please don't make a scene.

BARBARA: Go away.

> LORD BASINGSTOKE *goes. Pause. The* PROFESSOR *watches* BARBARA *like a hawk.*

Well? Tell me about myself.

PROFESSOR: You are . . . I would say . . . unhappy.

BARBARA: Unfulfilled. Do you find me attractive?

PROFESSOR (*bitterly*): I am too old to judge.

BARBARA: Yes, I suppose you must be. It's extraordinary how many intellectuals seem to be permanently waiting for something to happen. They never seem to do anything themselves.

PROFESSOR: Your dreams are filled with boxers and football professionals.

BARBARA: Nothing as concrete as that. I loathe muscle.

PROFESSOR: You fascinate yourself.

BARBARA: Who doesn't? You said in your book . . .

PROFESSOR: Books are for the mind. They . . . they control not the body.

BARBARA: Hm. (*Brief reverie.*) What would you do if I told you I thought you madly fascinating?

PROFESSOR: I would warn you that you are playing with fire.

BARBARA: I love playing with fire, and I loathe being warned.

PROFESSOR (*military*): Which means?

BARBARA: I do find you vaguely fascinating. You're so repellent.

PROFESSOR (*sharp*): Aha?

BARBARA: You smell so hideously of old pipes, of nicotine.

PROFESSOR: Aha?

BARBARA: You're so hopelessly inelegant, and a little phoney, I would say.

PROFESSOR: So?

BARBARA: Your eyes are like pebbles.

PROFESSOR: Yes?

> *He is entirely immobile and stiff while she circles him vaguely and lazily.*

BARBARA: I can't think of much else.

PROFESSOR: No?

> *There is a pause.*

BARBARA: Well, say something interesting.

PROFESSOR: You wish me to be angry? You wish to play with me as you do with all men? To submit me to the slavery of your smallest caprices? (*Pause—shouting.*) Answer me!

BARBARA (*surprised*): Yes. You're quite right. So you should be—after all, you're a Professor.

PROFESSOR: This submission I do not intend to make!

BARBARA (*a little alarmed*): All right. Let's forget the whole thing.

PROFESSOR (*with vehemence*): We will not forget it. Women are like horses. They must be broken in, trained, and taught obedience.

BARBARA: Nonsense. You talk like a male suffragette.

PROFESSOR (*same tone*): Is not nonsense. You have already made up your mind to have an *affaire* with me.

BARBARA: How dare you!

PROFESSOR: I dare! That's where I am different to others. I agree to have an *affaire* with you, but on my conditions!

BARBARA: Shall I call my husband?

PROFESSOR: By all means. Call Sir Mohammed. It will not alter an indestructible *fact*!

BARBARA: You are annoying me.

PROFESSOR: The horse objects to being broken in. The cowboy is confident. Come here.

BARBARA: Certainly not.

PROFESSOR: Aha! You are frightened.

BARBARA: I very certainly am not frightened.

PROFESSOR: You are, because your heart is beating faster. You are afraid of my hypnotic eyes. They may make demands of you which you are not used to concede.

BARBARA: Look, if I flirted with you, it was out of force of habit and . . .

PROFESSOR: I care not for reasons. It is too late. Now, I demand obedience. Like a dog in the circus, you will jump through the loop at a whispered word of command. Hop!

BARBARA (*annoyed*): Shut up.

PROFESSOR: If you are not afraid, come here. I challenge you to a duel of our eyes. Meet your master, and bow your head in subservience!

> BARBARA *approaches him and stares at him.*

BARBARA: There. Here I am. Entirely unafraid. Are you satisfied?

PROFESSOR: Open your eyes wider.

BARBARA: I can't. I'm short-sighted.

PROFESSOR: Tremble!

BARBARA: I refuse.

PROFESSOR (*furious*): I order you to tremble!

BARBARA: Oh, how idiotic!

PROFESSOR (*transcendental*): Idiotic!

> *He seizes her and forces her to kiss him in the most ungraceful and unromantic manner imaginable. The second lot of curtains part and another bowler-hatted head peers out. For the sake of reference, this man is* BUTTRESS. *He disappears.* BARBARA *is desperately trying to free herself when* MATTHEW *enters carrying a tree under his arm. He is followed by the* GIRL.

[268]

MATTHEW (*not bothering to look*): Parlour games.

The couple break. MATTHEW *and the* GIRL *go out.*

BARBARA: You revolting old man.

PROFESSOR: Forgive me. I love you.

BARBARA (*walking away*): Ha. Love me.

PROFESSOR: Please put something over your back. It is so provocative.

BARBARA: Who is the master now?

PROFESSOR: You, always you.

BARBARA (*leaving the room*): Now sit down and read a scholarly book.

She exits.

PROFESSOR (*following her*): Barbara. Be cruel, yes, but not so cruel . . .

They go. BUTTRESS *emerges from the curtains on tiptoes. He is a very small sharp-featured man in a raincoat which shows signs of wear. He briefly re-enacts the love scene we have just witnessed in mime, at the same time making copious notes on a pad.*

Suddenly MATTHEW'S *voice is heard roaring.*

MATTHEW (*off*): Who's been tampering with my door? How dare you . . . (*Etcetera, etcetera.*)

BUTTRESS *disappears behind his curtain.*

NIOBE *and* LORD BASINGSTOKE *appear.*

NIOBE: Oh, it's all so awful.

BASINGSTOKE: How can I console you, Niobe?

NIOBE: Floods on an unprecedented scale, a lunatic father, an irritable genius of a brother, and no servants. Name me one Greek tragedy with a more valid reason for moaning.

BASINGSTOKE: Tell me I am a redeeming feature.

NIOBE: Dearest Bill, of course. The white moth in my Pandora's box. Always there, a friendly pressure of the hand. Bless you for being you.

BASINGSTOKE: Bless you too, for being you.

NIOBE (*eyes shut*): The chain-mail of words which wind themselves ivywise round the lingering lovers. Oh, Romeo.

BASINGSTOKE (*eyes shut*): Juliet.

NIOBE: Troilus.

[269]

BASINGSTOKE: Cressida.

NIOBE: Leander.

BASINGSTOKE: Hero.

NIOBE: Pelléas.

BASINGSTOKE: Ossa.

NIOBE: Try again.

BASINGSTOKE: Mélisande.

NIOBE: Kiss me.

BASINGSTOKE: With pleasure.

NIOBE: No, not with pleasure. With love.

BASINGSTOKE: With love, then.

NIOBE: So be it.

> *They kiss.* BONE *enters silently by the left arch. He makes a quick note on a pad and rejoins his set of curtains. He is a large and melancholy man. The kiss goes on.* MOHAMMED *enters.*

MOHAMMED (*irritated*): Where's Barbara?

> *The kiss goes on.*

You have the entire weekend before you. Would you kindly do me the charity of telling me where Barbara is?

BASINGSTOKE: Who's Barbara?

> *He resumes the kiss.*

> MOHAMMED *wanders out right, calling:*

MOHAMMED: Barbara!

BASINGSTOKE: Why did I ever marry?

NIOBE: It is good that you are married, my darling. Great love always has impenetrable obstacles to face. Great love is wonderfully unproductive and negative.

BASINGSTOKE: This, then, is great love.

NIOBE: It is, oh, it is.

> MATTHEW *enters.*

MATTHEW: Did you try to force my door?

NIOBE (*in ecstasy*): Guilty!

MATTHEW: You fool.

BASINGSTOKE: Don't talk to Niobe like that!

NIOBE: Galahad!

MATTHEW: Can you swim?

BASINGSTOKE: As a matter of fact, no.

MATTHEW: The Lord is indeed merciful.

BASINGSTOKE: I beg your pardon?

NIOBE: I trust you will change for dinner, Father?

MATTHEW: I am not having dinner.

NIOBE: I can't say I'm sorry.

MATTHEW: There's no time.

NIOBE: What?

MATTHEW: About the door.

NIOBE: Yes?

MATTHEW: I forgive you.

NIOBE: Thank you.

MATTHEW *goes out the same way he came, calling out:*

MATTHEW (*off*): Hope! Preserve it all. Every twig has its value.

BARBARA, *the* PROFESSOR *and* MOHAMMED *come back.*

MOHAMMED (*stopping before the dying athlete*): This was discovered in the water off Naples. No doubt if it had no arms or legs it would be as highly thought of as the Venus de Milo.

PROFESSOR (*somewhat chastened*): Most interesting.

BARBARA: I love this house.

NIOBE (*who is sitting now*): We used to play hide-and-seek in these rooms when we were children. It was ideal for it.

MOHAMMED: Can we induce Father to serve at dinner?

NIOBE: Oh, Mohammed.

MOHAMMED: He has a passion for manual labour which none of us share. Hope, perhaps?

NIOBE: They're not having dinner.

MOHAMMED: Oh. Just as well, perhaps. What's that noise of hammering?

NIOBE: He's probably breaking up more furniture. (*Gripping* LORD BASINGSTOKE'S *hand.*) And frankly, I don't care . . .

MOHAMMED: Shall we go in?

NIOBE: Yes, let's.

MOHAMMED: While I'm standing up I feel like moving. If I sit down I know I shall want to stay recumbent. Perhaps, Professor, you will take my sister in. I shall take Barbara. And Basingstoke, if you wouldn't mind following.

They move off.

[271]

(*Formally.*) We insist on these little formalities. They still stamp every thought and action with quality . . .

> *The cortège moves into the next room. Pause.* BONE *emerges and tiptoes after them.* BUTTRESS *stops as he sees* BONE, *and inadvertently upsets a glass.* BUTTRESS *hears the noise, and wheels round.*

BUTTRESS (*soft*): Mr Bone!

BONE (*soft*): Mr Buttress!

> *They shake hands fervently. Suddenly* BONE *stops shaking and says darkly, quietly, suspiciously:*

Well, well—(*Curtain in pause.*) What are you doing here?

CURTAIN

ACT II

The second floor. A landing in the form of a rotunda. Door extreme LEFT. *Door* LEFT *centre. Door* RIGHT *centre. Door extreme* RIGHT. *In the centre, an alcove with a potted palm and a circular seat running round it. There is a small door on the extreme* RIGHT, *which is the bathroom.*

Entrance LEFT *from the head of the stairs. It is dark at curtain rise. Women's voices are heard.* NIOBE *and* BARBARA *enter.* NIOBE *is holding a lantern.*

NIOBE: It's too dreadful that the lights should have failed. It is lucky, however, that we usually eat by candlelight. There.

> *She places the lamp on a small occasional table, and begins to light candles, which stand in candelabra round the wall.*

It must be the floods. Whatever man invents for his convenience and befuddlement, nature always produces a sly reply, does it not?

BARBARA: I think human beings stink.

NIOBE: An ugly Anglo-Saxon word. Thank God for the Normans. Without them, our language would be unspeakable.

BARBARA: I sometimes wish I were an animal.

NIOBE: Good gracious me. An animal? I would so miss the clothes. (*Lights up.*) Ah.

BARBARA: Which is my room?

NIOBE: Now here—(*she indicates the left door*)—is Mohammed's room. (*She opens the door.*)

BARBARA (*impatient*): Which is my room, though?

NIOBE: Oh. Did I misunderstand? Over there—(*she indicates the extreme right-hand room*)—is *my* room, then over here—

BARBARA (*annoyed*): Is there a room set aside for me?

NIOBE: Well, but surely. Do you wish to be alone?

BARBARA: Is that unreasonable?

NIOBE: We did rather consider you as a married woman when we were making the arrangements.

BARBARA: I've no objection to that.

NIOBE (*incredulous*): Surely you don't wish to share a room with your husband?

[273]

BARBARA: Why not?

NIOBE (*dramatic*): Traitress!

BARBARA: No, Niobe, just fed up.

NIOBE: I am not thinking of myself so much as of Mohammed. You know he loves you desperately, and as he is now working on the sequel of *Unicorns and White Wine*, it is of the utmost importance that he be kept happy.

BARBARA: He loves me desperately? Even the Professor has the courtesy to stand up when I enter a room.

NIOBE: Surely you don't lay any store by such silly gestures. You know Mohammed. He's in the clouds, searching, searching. His silences are the colour of candle flames reflected in claret—burgundy. In times when the little white phosphorescent light is burning blindingly, he must be comforted. Barbara, he has been looking forward to this.

BARBARA: How revolting. And in any case, it's all insincere. You want Bill to yourself.

NIOBE (*shutting her eyes*): William and I are walking, hand in hand, to the very pinnacle of platonic possibilities, a realm where you, Barbara, have no place. Bill has this room.

BARBARA: Next to yours. Very convenient.

NIOBE (*hissing*): Low woman!

BARBARA: Bluestocking!

NIOBE: Ha! Ha!

> MATTHEW *passes with a piece of garden gate. It is dripping wet. The* GIRL *follows with a bush.*

NIOBE: Father. The carpet.

MATTHEW (*sadly*): Daughter. The mind.

NIOBE: And it's ages past Hope's bedtime.

MATTHEW: And dear people, you are quivering on the very brink of yours. Come, Hope . . .

> *He goes out with* HOPE.

BARBARA: Who's in this room?

NIOBE: The Professor.

BARBARA: There's another room over there.

NIOBE: That is the bathroom.

BARBARA: I'll sleep in the bath.

NIOBE: You will do no such thing. You have behaved in a profoundly unreasonable and ungrateful way. I shall expect you to do the honourable thing. (*Emotional.*) Please, Barbara, for the sake of literature. I shall retire. I know I can rely on you.

> *She goes coyly to her room. A pause.* BARBARA *looks around furtively.* BONE *enters from behind the palm.*

BONE: Psst!

BARBARA: Oh, there you are, Bone. Well, you must have overheard that. What shall I do?

BONE: Lie low for the moment, Lady Basingstoke.

BARBARA: Yes, but where?

BONE: Let me see. (*Enumerating rapidly.*) When the gentlemen come up, it is to be presumed that Sir Mohammed will enter his own room. Right? The Professor will go in here. Right? Lord Basingstoke will go in here. Right? And Miss D'Urt is in there. Right. Leaving—

BARBARA: The bathroom.

BONE: —the bathroom.

BARBARA: Shall I go in there?

BONE: For the moment.

BARBARA: But someone may wish to have a bath.

BONE: Too bad. Lock the door. If I knock three times—a rapid tattoo—knock—knock-knock—it's all right to come out.

BARBARA: But when will it be all right to come out?

BONE: When I have the evidence we want, Lady Basingstoke.

BARBARA: Have you noticed anything yet?

BONE: Love scene in the drawing room. Big stuff. I timed the kiss at the thirty-one seconds by my stop-watch, and—(*He taps the watch.*) —this old thing has never let me down.

BARBARA: I could kill Basingstoke.

BONE: May I advise against that, milady?

BARBARA: I wouldn't really. It's just so humiliating. I'm relying on you, Bone.

BONE: As well you may. I regret to say that Lord Basingstoke—

> *There is the crash of a door.*

Sssh! Into the bathroom.

> BARBARA *rushes into the bathroom.* BONE *disappears into the shadows.* NIOBE *peeps out of her room. Her hair is let down to resemble a girl of sixteen. She has a Juliet-like shift on. She gathers confidence, and tiptoes into the room laid aside for* LORD BASINGSTOKE. *She shuts the door behind her.* BONE *re-emerges and tiptoes to the bathroom door. He stops as he hears a noise. He takes refuge again. The* THREE MEN *enter.*

[275]

MOHAMMED: I often stay up until the small hours, spinning the ball of conversation round the roulette-table of the mind, but tonight, for some unaccountable reason, I am tired.

BASINGSTOKE: Yes.

PROFESSOR: I, too, find the atmosphere unsympathetic to argument.

BASINGSTOKE: I do hope the floods abate by the morning.

MOHAMMED: That, Basingstoke, is something we all hope, and therefore is in no need of utterance. Too many carpets and exquisite bric-à-brac have already been damaged for me to take lightly to the subject as a pretext for banter.

BASINGSTOKE: I'm sorry. I realise—

MOHAMMED: You realise very little. My wines are entirely submerged under water of the wrong temperature.

BASINGSTOKE: It was tactless of me.

MOHAMMED: You know, you apologise too readily. I derive very little enjoyment from scolding you as a consequence.

BASINGSTOKE: I beg your pardon.

MOHAMMED: Defend yourself, man!

PROFESSOR: This conversation is altogether too superficial for me. Will you kindly indicate to me the location of my chamber?

MOHAMMED: You have been irritated by some strange internal pressure all the evening, Professor. May I give you an American pill which is warranted to inspire in you a feeling of aggressive well-being?

PROFESSOR: Pills can cure the body, not the mind.

MOHAMMED: Good gracious me. You look like a kind of superannuated Hamlet.

PROFESSOR (*wanly*): Sein oder nicht sein, das ist der Frage . . .

MOHAMMED: I am so used to the phrase in translation, I am hardly receptive to it in the original of Unser Shakespeare.

PROFESSOR: To exist or not to exist, so is the problem.

MOHAMMED: Thank you.

PROFESSOR: Shakespeare was an optimist. He could still ask himself such a question. Now, please, my chamber.

MOHAMMED (*throwing open the door*): There. I hope it is warm enough.

PROFESSOR (*bitterly*): Warm enough? To soothe the heart? (*He vanishes enigmatically.*)

BASINGSTOKE: He certainly seems very upset about something.

MOHAMMED: Your perspicacity is extraordinary for one of your age.

BASINGSTOKE: I know I'm a fool.

MOHAMMED: I'm sorry. You'd be much happier if you didn't.

BASINGSTOKE: Where's my room?

MOHAMMED: My room is here, if you understand me.

BASINGSTOKE: Yes.

MOHAMMED: Niobe's is at the end.

BASINGSTOKE: Yes.

MOHAMMED: And the bed in that adjacent room is made up.

BASINGSTOKE: I see.

MOHAMMED: Good night.

BASINGSTOKE: Good night.

> MOHAMMED *enters his room, saying:*

MOHAMMED: Barbara . . .

> MOHAMMED *closes the door.* LORD BASINGSTOKE, *who seemed about to enter his own room, now quickly moves to* NIOBE'S, *and enters furtively, saying:*

BASINGSTOKE: Niobe . . .

> BUTTRESS *emerges from the shadows, and makes for* NIOBE'S *door with the intention of listening—he hears a noise, and retires silently.* MOHAMMED'S *door opens. He emerges, and looks down the corridor.* NIOBE'S *door opens, and* LORD BASINGSTOKE *emerges.*

MOHAMMED } She's not there . . .
BASINGSTOKE }

MOHAMMED: Where can she be?

BASINGSTOKE: You are looking for Barbara?

MOHAMMED: Naturally.

BASINGSTOKE: She must be there.

MOHAMMED: She isn't.

BASINGSTOKE: Can I help you look? She's awfully like a chameleon, you know, she rather dissolves into her surroundings. Have you a balcony?

MOHAMMED: Certainly. Can you imagine a room without a balcony?

BASINGSTOKE: Have you looked there?

MOHAMMED: It is raining.

BASINGSTOKE: Barbara loves the rain. She stands out in it for hours, feeling sorry for herself.

MOHAMMED: What exquisite sensibility.

> *They enter* MOHAMMED'S *room.* NIOBE *furtively emerges and tiptoes to her own room again.* BUTTRESS *watches from the confines of the shadows. A pause.* MOHAMMED *and* LORD BASINGSTOKE *emerge.*

[277]

BASINGSTOKE: You're quite right. She's not there.

MOHAMMED: She may be with Niobe. There's really no need for you to follow me round like this. I am quite capable of finding your wife by myself.

He goes to NIOBE'S *door.*

BASINGSTOKE: Well, you won't find Niobe in there.

MOHAMMED: How do you know? Have you tried?

BASINGSTOKE: Yes.

MOHAMMED: My poor sister. There's no reason why she should be anywhere else.

BASINGSTOKE: Try my room.

MOHAMMED: What vanity!

They knock and enter LORD BASINGSTOKE'S *room.* NIOBE *looks cautiously and disappointedly round her door.*

The PROFESSOR *looks warily out of his door. They see each other.*

NIOBE (*affable*): Good night, Professor.

PROFESSOR: Good night, madam.

They shut their doors. LORD BASINGSTOKE *and* MOHAMMED *emerge.*

MOHAMMED: Well, they can't both be with the Professor.

BASINGSTOKE: The bathroom!

MOHAMMED *strides over to the bathroom.*

MOHAMMED: Barbara!

There is silence.

Barbara!

He tries the door. It is locked.

Barbara!

BARBARA (*off*): Go away. I'm in my bath.

MOHAMMED: I shall be in my room, most dear one . . . don't knock . . . it will lose a second of sainted time . . .

The TWO MEN *withdraw from the door.*

BASINGSTOKE: But where is Niobe?

MOHAMMED (*self-satisfied*): I haven't the faintest notion. I give you a good night, Basingstoke. Good night.

BASINGSTOKE: Good night, Mohammed . . .

MOHAMMED *retires to his room. A pause.* LORD BASINGSTOKE *looks around vaguely. He plucks up courage and knocks at the Professor's door. The door opens immediately. The* PROFESSOR *looks out. He is in a dressing gown.*

[278]

PROFESSOR: Yes?

BASINGSTOKE: I do hope I haven't woken you up, Professor.

PROFESSOR: No. I always work for several hours before retiring.

BASINGSTOKE: I wonder—have you by any chance got Miss Niobe with you?

PROFESSOR (*angry*): For what you take me?

BASINGSTOKE: No offence intended, I do assure you. Have you any idea where she could possibly be?

PROFESSOR: As a matter of fact, yes. I greeted her a moment ago with a wish of good night.

BASINGSTOKE: Oh? Where was she?

PROFESSOR: Where a lady should be at this time of night. In her room.

BASINGSTOKE: Oh, really? Thanks. She must have been hiding, dear soul. Good night, Professor.

PROFESSOR: One moment, young man. Was it my imagination, or did you ask me to contribute to a magazine?

BASINGSTOKE: Oh, please forget that, Professor. I realise now that it was an insult.

PROFESSOR (*with ebullient good nature*): An insult? Why? Did not Voltaire, Kierkegaard, Hegel and Schopenhauer have to earn a living? Is there one great intellect in the history of culture who did not, at one time, have to come down to earth from the zenith of his capabilities in order to gather the humble crumbs for the next meal?

BASINGSTOKE: I suppose not. I'll think about it.

PROFESSOR: There is nothing to think. It is a fact. The brain, like the body, is fed by way of the mouth.

BASINGSTOKE: Yes. Tomorrow. At the moment—

PROFESSOR (*menacing for a second*): Now. Now. At the moment as you say. How much you pay?

BASINGSTOKE: I really don't know.

PROFESSOR: A shilling a word?

BASINGSTOKE: That sounds reasonable.

PROFESSOR: One shilling sixpence.

BASINGSTOKE: Very well, yes.

PROFESSOR: How many words?

BASINGSTOKE: I can't tell yet.

PROFESSOR: Two thousand.

BASINGSTOKE: Yes.

PROFESSOR: Two thousand five hundred.

BASINGSTOKE: It depends.

PROFESSOR: Three thousand.

BASINGSTOKE: No.

PROFESSOR: Two thousand five hundred?

BASINGSTOKE: All right.

PROFESSOR: I believe not in contracts. Here is my hand.

They shake hands. The PROFESSOR *smiles amiably.*

I like you, young man. You have talent. Good night.

BASINGSTOKE: Good night.

The PROFESSOR *disappears.*

LORD BASINGSTOKE *walks quickly to* NIOBE'S *door. Before he can enter,* BUTTRESS *emerges from the shadows.*

BUTTRESS: Ppsst!

BASINGSTOKE: Yes? Good lord—Buttress.

BUTTRESS: Don't go in. You're walking right into a trap.

BASINGSTOKE: A trap?

BUTTRESS: I can't talk louder. I'm being watched.

BASINGSTOKE: Watched?

BUTTRESS: Sssh!

BASINGSTOKE: By whom? By Lady Basingstoke?

BUTTRESS: I'm not the only detective in the house.

BASINGSTOKE: D'you mean Barbara—?

BUTTRESS: Exactly. Go to your own room. I'll explain later.

BASINGSTOKE (*petulantly*): Damn her! Damn her!

He goes into his room. A pause.

BONE *emerges from the shadows.*

BONE: That was quick of you.

BUTTRESS: Your move, Bone.

BONE: Brainy Buttress they used to call you in the Frontier Force. Damn clever, no denyin' it—but I'm not done yet.

BUTTRESS: Do your worst, Bone, do your worst. I'm ready for you.

MATTHEW *enters.*

MATTHEW: Who are you?

The DETECTIVES *start.*

Burglars? If you are, don't touch the Chinese pottery, it's nearly all fake.

BONE: We're not burglars.

[280]

MATTHEW: No, of course not. Dull of me. You're detectives.

BUTTRESS: How do you know?

MATTHEW: By your uniform. It's so carefully chosen to look inconspicuous. Shall I bring you a cup of tea?

BONE: Not while I'm on duty, thank you, sir.

BUTTRESS: I wouldn't say no, sir. There's no rule against it in my firm.

BONE: Who do you work for, by the way, Buttress?

BUTTRESS: Styles and Chivers, Shaftesbury Avenue.

BONE: Good people. Good people. You couldn't . . . I mean, I'm not a greenhorn at the game . . . seven years, Hong Kong Police . . . four years City of Hull Vice Squad as you know . . . you couldn't . . . the point is, I'm not happy where I am . . .

BUTTRESS: Certainly, Bone. I'll have a word with old Chivers. He's more amenable than old Styles. By the way, where are you now?

BONE: Lingfield, Lennox and Green.

BUTTRESS *draws in his breath in disapproval.*

MATTHEW (*who has been waiting patiently*): Well, have you decided?

BONE (*grinning sheepishly*): Well, I'll stretch a point, sir. I could do with a cuppa.

MATTHEW: With sugar?

BUTTRESS: One lump.

BONE: I acquired a sweet tooth in the tropics, sir. I'll take two.

MATTHEW: I can only spare one lump apiece. It may have to last for days. No milk, I'm afraid. We'll have to learn to be without.

He goes.

BONE: Rum old codger, eh?

BUTTRESS: I don't know, we meet all sorts in this game.

BONE: I'll say. Did you understand any of that conversation downstairs?

BUTTRESS: Why, didn't you?

BONE: Not a word of it.

BUTTRESS: You surprise me, Bone.

BONE: Why, did you?

BUTTRESS: Well, I have always had an intellectual inclination, you know. I've read a great deal. I must say I thoroughly enjoyed the conversation.

BONE: Ah, there were bits of it I enjoyed.

BUTTRESS: I enjoyed all of it.

A pause.

[281]

If you'd care to let me lend you a book or two . . .

BONE (*piqued*): I've got my own books.

BUTTRESS: There are books and books, old man.

BONE: I've got those as well.

BUTTRESS: The Brontë Brothers are my particular favourites.

BONE: They were sisters.

BUTTRESS: We must be talking about different people.

There is a noise.

BONE: Cave!

They retire into the shadows.

MOHAMMED *emerges from his room in a fantastic dressing gown worthy of Genghis Khan. He goes to the bathroom door.*

MOHAMMED: Barbara! . . . (*He hisses.*) Barbara! Are you still there?

The PROFESSOR'S *door opens slightly.*

Barbara, say something. A word, a sound. I must know that you are still in there before I liberate the flow of my finer feelings through the keyhole.

BARBARA (*off*): I'm in my bath.

MOHAMMED: You surprise me. I have tried the taps in my sink, and observe that the hot water is off. Am I to presume that you, of all people, are enjoying the rigours of a cold bath?

BARBARA (*off; after a momentary hesitation*): I always take cold baths.

MOHAMMED: Come out. Let me take your dear blue body in my arms.

BARBARA (*off*): Go away.

MOHAMMED: Barbara, you're an inveterate liar. You are standing up, fully dressed, and blushing with pride at your own perversity.

BARBARA (*off*): How do you know?

MOHAMMED: Your voice is the voice of a well-covered, irritated and unrecumbent woman. Can it be that you are frightened by the prospect of my passion?

BARBARA *lets out a peal of laughter.* MOHAMMED *is taken aback for a moment.*

MOHAMMED: The hollow laugh of a Carmen before she has read her destiny in the cards. Come out this instant, before I take the door off its hinges.

MATTHEW *enters with two cups of tea.*

MATTHEW: You can't do that, my son. I have expropriated all the tools.

MOHAMMED: Father, go to bed.

MATTHEW: Dawn is at six-twenty-three. Where are they?

MOHAMMED: In their rooms like civilised people.

MATTHEW: Not them. (*Bellows.*) Tea's up.

MOHAMMED: Father, are you mad? Madder than usual, that is? This is no time for afternoon tea.

MATTHEW: It is no time for evoking the splendours of the Golden Horde either, my son. Which of us is madder?

MOHAMMED: My clothes are picturesque, as picturesque as my name, for which you are entirely responsible.

MATTHEW: Yes, you were born at a time when I had just been converted to Islam, and I actually believed that one religion was better than, and different from, another.

MOHAMMED: And do you actually believe that a Chinese wrap is more eccentric in the bedroom than a sou'wester?

MATTHEW: Well, look at yourself in the mirror, and you will see that if Marco Polo had discovered you on his travels, he would have had the good taste to keep quiet about it. D'you want a cup of tea?

MOHAMMED: No, thank you.

MATTHEW: You'll stick to opium.

BARBARA (*off*): Who are you talking to?

MOHAMMED: Come out, Barbara, and join the conversation.

MATTHEW: Who's in there? That pin-headed nymph?

MOHAMMED: I forbid you to talk like that!

BARBARA (*off*): What did he say?

MOHAMMED: Father called you a pin-headed nymph.

BARBARA (*off*): Tell him he's a maladjusted cave-man.

MOHAMMED: Barbara says—

MATTHEW (*grimly*): I heard her.

> *He goes to the bathroom door, and roars:*

Can you hear me?

BARBARA (*off*): Go away.

MATTHEW (*roaring*): Sphinx without a Secret. Oracle without a Clue. Lust's Waste-Paper Basket. Dust-Bin of Desire. Voluptuous Jellyfish. I'm going before I say something offensive.

> *He exits down left, livid, with his tea.*
>
> *The bathroom door opens and* BARBARA *appears, furious.*

MOHAMMED (*tenderly*): My Barbara!

> *The bathroom door shuts again.*

[283]

MOHAMMED: I shall spray my room with the rarest perfume, and light the incense burners. Come to me, all fire and anger, and make my night an elegant misery. I shall be waiting for you, *ma bien-aimée.*

> *He enters his room.* BONE *and* BUTTRESS *emerge from the shadows.*

BUTTRESS: Now we've missed our tea.

BONE: I could have done with a cup.

BUTTRESS: Look out!

BONE: What?

BUTTRESS: Door handle.

> *He indicates the bathroom door. They retire. The bathroom door opens.* BARBARA *appears, angrily. The* PROFESSOR *launches out of his half-open door.*

BARBARA: Bone!

PROFESSOR: Barbara!

BARBARA: Oh, no! (*She locks herself in in time.*)

PROFESSOR: Open the door, my angel, and set your hatred free!

BARBARA (*off*): I shall do no such thing.

PROFESSOR (*sinks to his knees*): Barbara. I will be the carpet upon which you may walk, even into the room of another man.

BARBARA (*off*): I don't like garrulous carpets.

PROFESSOR: If you will not appear, I must stimulate your desire by my words alone. Barbara, I am on my knees, before the profane altar of my lust, like a were-wolf, respectable and honourable by day, but by night a reversion to a primitive brute.

BARBARA (*off*): Go and prowl on the roof.

PROFESSOR: What delicious cruelty! Your words fall on my ears like the sting of adders, each one filled to overflowing with poison which I drink, drink avidly.

BARBARA (*off*): Is there any hope of your dying soon?

PROFESSOR (*triumph*): Ach! The death wish! My theories are given life—the marble breathes—like Pygmalion, I see my statue flushing with blood. Come out, statue, and claw my breast with your stone fingers! Carry me, like a dying Adonis, into your pastoral bed, and weep a single tear on me, which will turn to a dagger as it falls, and plunge, quivering, into my heart! (*Tender.*) Can you hear me, Barbara?

> *There is no reply.*

Barbara, I command you to come out! You will dance to my fiddle! You will be like a marionette in the hands of the master! Come out,

Coppélia, and be my slave! (*Clutching his head.*) Oh, the spirit is torn between the extremes of erotic possibility, both egos are alter-egos! Mother, why did you have to die so soon?

    MOHAMMED *appears.*

MOHAMMED: What are you doing here?

PROFESSOR: Is it a sin to wish to enter the bathroom?

MOHAMMED: Is it your habit to go on your knees before a door you wish to open?

PROFESSOR: The door is locked.

MOHAMMED: The room is probably occupied.

PROFESSOR: It has been occupied for hours.

MOHAMMED: Then I suggest that you return to your room.

PROFESSOR: I refuse.

MOHAMMED: You refuse to return to your room? It is uncomfortable?

PROFESSOR: I refuse because, if I surrender my position at the door, you will occupy it.

MOHAMMED: Then you know who is inside?

PROFESSOR: You do also. I overheard your obscene speeches.

MOHAMMED: How dare you!

PROFESSOR: I am destroyed by love!

MOHAMMED: A charming way to return my hospitality.

PROFESSOR (*writhing*): I don't want your hospitality. I want love.

MOHAMMED (*pushing him*): You ridiculous satyr . . .

    The PROFESSOR *falls to the ground.*

I didn't even get halfway through your last book.

PROFESSOR: You would strike a kneeling man?

MOHAMMED: It's considerably less risky than striking a standing one.

    The PROFESSOR *rises with agility.*

PROFESSOR: Now repeat your insult.

MOHAMMED: I wouldn't dream of it.

PROFESSOR: And what did you say of my book?

MOHAMMED: It had one sin I can never forgive, that of dullness.

PROFESSOR: I may have acquired finesse, but I was educated at Heidelberg.

    He pushes MOHAMMED.

MOHAMMED: You savage! You pushed me!

PROFESSOR: Honour is only partially satisfied.

    He pushes MOHAMMED *again.*

MOHAMMED: Take that!

He pushes the PROFESSOR.

PROFESSOR: Force must be met with force.

He pushes MOHAMMED. *They push each other several times in a laborious and ineffectual manner.* MATTHEW *has entered with the cups of tea.*

MATTHEW: Thus did the knights of old enter the lists and do courtly combat for the hand of the lady of their fancy.

MOHAMMED: Silence, father.

MATTHEW: You ridiculous people. No wonder Divine warmth is exhausted, no wonder the rain is falling in troughs and buckets and reservoirs. (*Calls out.*) Tea's up! Come out from behind the curtains, you idiots. There's no time left for discretion, or for strategy. Come out.

BONE *and* BUTTRESS *emerge.*

MOHAMMED (*amazed*): Who are you?

BUTTRESS: Detective Buttress, Sir Mohammed.

MOHAMMED: Detective? Who let you in?

BONE: My name is Bone, Sir Mohammed. We entered the premises in the course of duty.

PROFESSOR: I am an American citizen, and wish to speak to my Consul.

BONE: We're private detectives, Professor, not regular dicks.

MOHAMMED: Private detectives?

MATTHEW: Oh, don't waste your breath talking to him—take your tea. It's practically ice-cold, as I've been carrying it around absent-mindedly for some time. One lump in each.

BUTTRESS
BONE   } : Thank you very much.

MOHAMMED (*recovering from his surprise*): Just one moment—

MATTHEW: Have you not even the grey matter to realise these gentlemen's functions?

MOHAMMED (*to* BONE): Who employed you, sir?

BONE: It is a breach of professional etiquette to say, sir.

MOHAMMED (*terrible*): Was it Lady Basingstoke?

BONE: Em . . .

BUTTRESS: It was, yes, sir.

BONE (*fiercely*): I shan't forget this, Buttress.

BUTTRESS: The game's up, Bone, can't you see that?

[286]

MOHAMMED (*majestic*): Am I to understand that you were employed by Lady Basingstoke in order to acquire grounds for divorce owing to the adultery of her husband? I must warn my poor sister. Pray heaven it will not be too late.

PROFESSOR (*restraining him*): Sir Mohammed—a process of deduction leads me to the conclusion that the other gentleman was employed by Lord Basingstoke in order to acquire grounds for divorce against Lady Basingstoke.

MOHAMMED (*arrested in his progress*): Is that so?

MATTHEW: Obviously.

MOHAMMED (*to Buttress*): I'm asking you.

BUTTRESS: Yes.

MOHAMMED: How dare you?

BUTTRESS: It is the nature of my employment, sir. It takes all sorts to make a world.

MOHAMMED: You will leave my house this instant.

MATTHEW: The water is ten feet high.

MOHAMMED: Can you swim?

BUTTRESS: No, sir.

MOHAMMED: Excellent. Kindly leave the house.

PROFESSOR (*nervously*): Sir Mohammed, there must be no scandal. My reputation is of quite a different sort. (*To the detectives.*) Promise me you will forget what you heard.

BONE: The truth is inflexible, Professor. I have my notes.

PROFESSOR: At least, represent me as a positive character—violently by all means, but forget that I ever pleaded with a woman, it would do me great damage.

BONE (*reading from his notes*): "Carry me, like a dying Adonis, to your pastoral bed, and weep a single tear on to me—"

MOHAMMED (*disgusted*): You said that?

PROFESSOR: I am a passionate man.

MOHAMMED: You are pathetic.

BONE: Sir Mohammed said, "I shall spray my room with the rarest scent—"

MOHAMMED: I must have said "perfume"—the word "scent" has always seemed to me entirely inadequate to its purpose.

BUTTRESS (*consulting his notes*): He's right, Bone.

BONE: Is he? Lend me your rubber, will you? (*He makes an alteration.*)

[287]

PROFESSOR (*desperate*): Are you open to bribes?

BONE: No, sir.

BUTTRESS: It depends.

BONE: Buttress!

BUTTRESS: Don't be a fool, Bone. We're not millionaires, are we?

BONE: All the same—

BUTTRESS (*pleasant*): He'll see reason, Professor. The question is, how much?

PROFESSOR (*with an effort*): Ten pounds.

BUTTRESS: Oh, come, Professor, we're not children.

PROFESSOR: Ten guineas.

BUTTRESS: I suggest, and this is generous, mind you, one hundred pounds from each of you to each of us, making four hundred pounds in all.

PROFESSOR (*passionately*): Agreed!

MOHAMMED: But you tell everyone that you're penniless.

MATTHEW (*suddenly roars with laughter and calls out*): Hope!

MOHAMMED: Why are you calling the girl?

MATTHEW (*delighted*): I was wrong to send her out of the room before. Hope! If she is to survive, let her know what she is leaving behind.

MOHAMMED: What are you talking about?

HOPE *enters.*

MATTHEW: Wash your ears, child—make them stand on end like a terrier's, and digest what man has done with life.

HOPE, *left of Mohammed, looks at him, then takes his hand.*

MOHAMMED: You are quite insupportable, father.

MATTHEW: Here endeth the first lesson in filial gratitude. (*Pushes* HOPE *to the others.*) Now the others.

HOPE *goes to each in turn.*

PROFESSOR *is counting money and can't speak properly.*

MATTHEW: Well, go on.

MOHAMMED: Father.

MATTHEW: Very well, I'll set the ball rolling again.

NIOBE (*off*): Come in!

The door opens as MATTHEW *enters.*

At last, my love! Oh!

MATTHEW: You're wanted by detectives.

[288]

NIOBE: What? What have I done?

MATTHEW: You have entertained licentious thoughts. Come out.

He comes back, followed in a moment by NIOBE, *who has made up voluptuously, with white ribbons in her hair.*

NIOBE: Why are you all still awake?

MOHAMMED: Do you mean to say you heard nothing?

NIOBE: The ear was attuned to the mind's lyre. Who are these men?

MATTHEW: Detective Bone was employed by Barbara Basingstoke to acquire incriminating evidence for a divorce. Watch for fireworks, Hope.

NIOBE: She did that? Where is she?

MATTHEW: She has taken up diplomatic residence in the bathroom.

NIOBE (*her claws out*): Does Bill know?

MOHAMMED: I hardly think—

NIOBE: Quite! Where is he?

MATTHEW: In that room.

NIOBE: Father, send the child to bed.

She bursts in on LORD BASINGSTOKE, *who screams.*

BASINGSTOKE (*off*): Don't come near me! There's a detective in the house.

NIOBE: You knew! (*Tender.*) So that explains your reticence, my heart's darling.

BASINGSTOKE (*off*): Do be careful!

NIOBE (*reappearing*): So she's in the bathroom, is she? I'll teach her.

MATTHEW (*delighted*): Throw fine phrases to the wind.

NIOBE: Father! (*To the bathroom door.*) Come out of there this instant, Barbara.

LORD BASINGSTOKE comes out of his room, looking more feeble than ever.

MOHAMMED (*advances menacingly*): You swine!

NIOBE (*taken aback*): Mohammed!

PROFESSOR (*equally menacing*): You provocateur!

NIOBE: Professor, what on earth—?

MOHAMMED: That detective was employed by Basingstoke for precisely the same reason as that one was employed by Barbara.

NIOBE: You don't mean to say so. Oh, Bill—

MATTHEW *laughs.*

BASINGSTOKE (*pale*): Don't come near me, any of you. I'm a man of peace. It's all Barbara's fault. She started it.

The bathroom door flies open.

BARBARA: I started what?

BASINGSTOKE (*petulant*): My God, how I hate you.

BARBARA: Because I prevented you from lying? What did I start? I've never sent a detective after you before.

BASINGSTOKE: You could so easily have done. As for you, Buttress, I shall never forgive you for betraying a confidence.

Suddenly NIOBE *screams dramatically.*

MOHAMMED (*calm*): Why do you elect to scream now?

NIOBE: If the Montagues and the Capulets had employed detectives . . .

MOHAMMED: What then?

NIOBE: I don't know, but it's a fascinating speculation.

BASINGSTOKE (*with as much power as he can muster*): I only did what I did out of love. I wanted my freedom, in order to lose it again to you, darling heart.

NIOBE: No, Bill, no.

HOPE *crosses to left of* NIOBE.

NIOBE: To be the other woman is to hold the initiative. To be a wife of a free man is to be on the defensive all day, and more especially all night. Hope, go to bed.

NIOBE *tries to push* HOPE *up the stairs, but she rushes to* MATTHEW *and* NIOBE *follows.*

BARBARA: You blind fool, Niobe, to try and insult me so.

NIOBE (*surprised*): Insult you?

BARBARA: You class me as a wife. Oh, I can see your intention quite clearly.

MATTHEW: She was talking of herself, she never talks of anything else.

NIOBE: Father! Stop adding pepper to the salad!

BARBARA: Don't confuse me! I'm not intelligent like the rest of you, but I'm pretty damn shrewd when there's another woman about. I'm a wife, Niobe. I'm not on the defensive, I'm on the attack.

NIOBE: What are you suggesting?

BARBARA: I loathe Basingstoke's methods, but then I loathe Basingstoke. If you wish to marry him, I will not stand in the way.

NIOBE: I have no intention of marrying him. Did I not make that clear?

BARBARA: Why not? You're obviously ideally suited to one another. You talk the same language, which no one else can understand.

NIOBE: I may have loved Basingstoke in the silent avenues of sin—

BASINGSTOKE: Ha!

NIOBE: —but I like him even less than you, Barbara.

BARBARA: D'you expect me to stand by and listen to you insulting my husband?

NIOBE: Barbara, be consistent!

BARBARA: I am! You are trying to cast an aspersion on my taste in men. After all, I did marry the man, which is more than you ever did!

NIOBE: You married him for his money! There, the foul words are liberated from the bitter heart!

BARBARA: There was no need to marry him, for crying out loud. I've lived with men twice as rich as he, and been damned happy.

NIOBE: The title! The title!

MOHAMMED: It seems to me that the conversation has become somewhat out of hand. I haven't said a word for a full minute.

BARBARA: Let me answer her.

MOHAMMED: No. Barbara, there is to be no scandal.

BARBARA: Why not? Your whole existence has been one long scandal.

MOHAMMED: Admittedly, but it has never been sordid, it has always been literary. Therefore, silentium.

BARBARA: Therefore what?

MOHAMMED: Pas devant les detectives.

BASINGSTOKE: Buttress, have we any evidence at all?

MOHAMMED ⎫
BARBARA   ⎬ : No!

BUTTRESS: It depends.

NIOBE: Father, take Hope away!

BASINGSTOKE: On what does it depend?

BUTTRESS: Evidence is as relative as anything else. I don't doubt that with a somewhat coarse phraseology tonight's little gymnastics can be made to resemble a Roman orgy, while by the use of a more elegant style, it can be made to seem like a harmless charade.

BASINGSTOKE: You're a horrible cynic.

BUTTRESS (*agreeable*): About everything, sir—

[291]

BONE: Mr Buttress.

BUTTRESS: Quiet, Bone. About everything, sir, except my house in Maidenhead, my flat in Park Lane and my Rolls-Royce.

BONE: Rolls-Royce!

PROFESSOR: One moment. You have already accepted a bribe!

BUTTRESS: In principle, but then I always do in principle.

PROFESSOR: A specific financial figure was mentioned.

BUTTRESS: Was it?

PROFESSOR: And agreed!

BUTTRESS: Show me the agreement!

PROFESSOR: You are a villain.

BUTTRESS (*pleasant*): No greater villain than a reformed policeman, sir.

MOHAMMED (*calm*): In any court of law it would only be the evidence of one man against another.

BUTTRESS (*sinister*): No, sir. Of two men against one.

MOHAMMED: Two men?

BUTTRESS *indicates* BONE.

BUTTRESS: Our evidence would, of course, tally exactly. We never met in the course of our duty, naturally. This conversation never took place, equally naturally. Did it?

BONE: No—no, it didn't.

BUTTRESS: We stand to gain or lose nothing by our impartiality, whereas you will, if you dare to appear in court, be accusing each other within five minutes.

BONE (*sweating*): Mr Buttress—

BUTTRESS: Shut up, Bone. And there's another thing in our favour. We've both got distinguished records of public service. Nothing more likely to melt a Judge's heart than a record of selfless and dangerous service in the public interest at a low salary. (*Shakes Bone's hand.*) Besides I'm experienced. I know which evidence they'll trust. (*Going behind Barbara.*) Lady Basingstoke's been married three times, and was once arrested for trying to go through the Customs with bottles of French scent strapped to her corset.

BARBARA: How d'you know that?

BUTTRESS: We're nothing if not thorough. Lord Basingstoke . . .

BASINGSTOKE: But you're on my side.

BUTTRESS: No, sir, I'm on my side. Lord Basingstoke was once fined for trying to travel to Edinburgh on a platform ticket.

BASINGSTOKE: But that was years ago, before I'd inherited.

BUTTRESS: Basic characters don't alter—at least, only in religion, not in law. Sir Mohammed wrote a book of dubious spoonerisms, which were almost banned in France, of all places.

MOHAMMED: I'm not ashamed of them. They are of exquisite sensibility and positively Apuleius-like abandon.

BUTTRESS: No doubt, and I'm sure that I'd personally very much appreciate them, but you know how old-fashioned these judges are. The Professor once wrote a telegram of good wishes to Hitler.

PROFESSOR: It's a lie!

BUTTRESS (*drawing a cutting from his pocket*): I found the press cutting.

PROFESSOR: My appointment at the University depended on it. It was only a birthday wish.

BUTTRESS: Quite innocent, I'm sure.

PROFESSOR (*very nervous*): I have sent birthday wishes to people of all classes and tendencies. Birthdays have always been to me entirely free from political significance. If I find anyone who has a birthday, I immediately wish them the best wishes for it. It is a religion with me.

BONE (*meek*): It happens to be my birthday today.

PROFESSOR: You! (*Recovering his balance.*) I wish you the very best of returns and a happy wish. There! You see!

BUTTRESS: But it won't be his birthday on the day this case comes up, or anyone else's for that matter. As for Miss D'Urt, I can see nothing at all reprehensible in her records.

NIOBE (*suffering*): Oh, how degrading! How can I ever live this down!

BUTTRESS: Still, one clean record among so many will hardly sway the balance.

MOHAMMED: Now. The time for decisions is upon us. I am your host, and I address you all in a spirit of calm determination. Barbara and you, Lord Basingstoke. I ask you to withdraw your charges against each other, and to dismiss your employees.

BARBARA: I'm willing.

BASINGSTOKE: I am too. Barbara, perhaps we could make a fresh start.

NIOBE: Bill! I forbid it!

MOHAMMED: Niobe, take refuge in tears, not in words.

BARBARA: No, Bill. I'm not starting again. But we were wrong and silly to do this to each other. I forgive you.

BASINGSTOKE: Thank you, Babs.

MOHAMMED (*to* BUTTRESS): Now, sir, do your worst.

BONE: I told you you'd go too far.

BUTTRESS (*unruffled*): I don't think you understand me, sir. This need not be a legal matter at all.

MOHAMMED: What?

BUTTRESS: Sunday can be an awfully dull day without interesting reading. Do I make myself clear?

MOHAMMED: Explain yourself.

BUTTRESS: The revelations of Ex-Inspector Buttress and his Watson, Ex-Constable Bone of the Hull Vice Squad. How the English aristocracy live. An inquiry into vice in Hertfordshire. Are your womenfolk safe while licentious orgies take place not sixty miles from Leicester Square? A professor who enjoyed Hitler's confidence seeking to abduct titled smuggler at door of bathroom, while husband, who once cheated London, Midland and Scottish railway of fare, chases poetess through marbled halls. Does that sound good to you?

MOHAMMED: I could sue you for libel!

BUTTRESS: But then we'd be back in court again, and I think I've explained the drawbacks to you.

NIOBE: Mohammed, do something!

BONE: I don't like blackmail.

BUTTRESS: We don't call it that, not in the trade. We prefer to call it private enterprise . . . Now, sir, I'm quite sure the figure I mentioned, four hundred pounds, against the loss of your reputation . . .

MOHAMMED: And you say you can't swim?

BUTTRESS (*nervous for once*): Eh?

MOHAMMED: Accidents take place in floods.

PROFESSOR (*terribly sinister*): Masterly! Masterly, not since the days of Cesare Borgia has such an idea seriously crossed the mind of an intellectual.

NIOBE: Oh no, not murder! Mohammed!

MOHAMMED (*quiet*): The house is full of windows low enough for a negligent man to slip, just as they slip off ocean liners, and nobody notices until it's too late.

BUTTRESS: Let's talk this over.

MOHAMMED: We shall go to court all right, with melancholy faces and a nice garnishing of black, but it will be a coroner's court, and the verdicts will be accidental death. Come on, Basingstoke, outnumber them. Barbara, open the window. Niobe, go away, and compose an ode.

[294]

BONE (*desperate*): I've come to see the truth! I've come to see reason.

MOHAMMED: Then give us a hand.

BUTTRESS (*vicious, as he is lifted off his feet*): I shan't forget this, Bone.

> MATTHEW, *who is standing left by the banisters, suddenly laughs loud and long. The entire group gazes at him in surprise.*

MATTHEW: Fools, concerning yourselves with trivialities, while the real danger's creeping up on you. Come over here, Niobe. Look over the banisters.

NIOBE (*doing so*): Why? I can see myself.

MATTHEW: Quite clearly?

NIOBE: Like Narcissus. I look pale and old. But how . . .?

MOHAMMED (*disturbed, as they all are*): Niobe, what are you talking about?

NIOBE (*agitated and mysterious*): Mohammed. The water. It's climbing the stairs!

> *They drop* BUTTRESS *to the floor, and line the banisters, looking down in silence.*

CURTAIN

ACT III

The roof. It is a grey and wistful morning. On the roof, there is a turret in the shape of a small fortress, crowned by a weathercock. It has in it a wooden door in the unnecessarily severe mediaeval style. The numerals "1837" are visible above the door, grimly and in-eradicably engraved on the stone. Baleful trees screen the confines of our vision. There is a horizon, with one or two isolated roofs and turrets standing like lonely sentinels in the water.

Pause.

The door opens. MATTHEW *emerges with* HOPE.

MATTHEW (*with satisfaction, his arm round* HOPE): As I thought, as baleful a morning as one could wish for the final act. The elements haven't much of a sense of humour, but they have a miraculous sense of occasion. Whenever wars are declared, the sun shines brightly. With what irony are we reminded that we are about to destroy! Still, the sun would be out of place today. It would only reflect in the water and give us two suns to regret, while this—well, it's tactful weather, as tactful as black at a funeral, as reticent as a muttered prayer. Yet somehow we must find the courage, you and I, to giggle during the service, to drop our umbrellas during the supreme moment of stillness. Think of a joke for me to laugh at, my darling, and save one for the journey. Our conversation must be rationed like our food. No sighing. No humanity. Keep your eyes on the distance, and block your ears against the wailing—there'll be plenty of it. Oh, they'll be fighting for Bibles today, searching among the dusty pages for instructions. There's no salvation in a book, my love, there's salvation in the eye and head and heart. Well remembered. Well . . . every second lost is a century squandered, so come along, come along . . . we can say goodbye later . . . easy does it . . . You go first . . .

HOPE *lets herself over the side and drops.* MATTHEW *looks over the parapet.*

Steady . . . steady now . . .

BARBARA'S *voice:* "Goodness, these stairs are narrow."

MATTHEW *lets himself over the side and disappears. Pause. The door opens and* BARBARA *enters, followed by* MOHAMMED. *She is in pyjamas, and he wears the grotesque Chinese dressing gown.*

BARBARA: I didn't wake up until the water was well over the sofa.

[296]

My God, it's freezing. If you were a gentleman, you'd give me your dressing gown.

MOHAMMED: Don't you realise, Barbara, that I wish to give you far more than a mere dressing gown?

BARBARA: It's the dressing gown I want.

MOHAMMED: The man goes with it.

BARBARA: Can't you see I'm cold?

MOHAMMED: I'm older than you. I suffer oppressively from lumbago.

BARBARA: How romantic you have become.

MOHAMMED: I have always suffered from lumbago, it has nothing whatsoever to do with age. Sometimes lying in the cradle was an absolute agony.

BARBARA: Good heavens, look at the water!

MOHAMMED: Barbara, don't change the subject. I say, it is higher. The Westerbys' house seems to have disappeared altogether. Thank goodness Alma's away at the seaside.

BARBARA: What's that over there?

MOHAMMED: The Bishop of Luton's place.

BARBARA: But what are those black dots on the roof?

MOHAMMED: Probably clergymen. He has frequent ecclesiastical weekends. They must be in the same position as we are.

BARBARA: One of them seems to be waving.

MOHAMMED: Then look away quickly. They're frightfully boring and equally frightfully friendly, and a mere sketch of a smile would be enough to have them all swimming over here for a glutinous gossip.

BARBARA: There's another house over there, with towers.

MOHAMMED: In normal times that mansion has a moat around it, but that's a little difficult to imagine today. I hope you can see no signs of activity there.

BARBARA: None whatever.

MOHAMMED: I'm glad. They are captains of industry, by which I mean manufacturers of domestic disinfectant, and about as pleasant as people can be whose comfort is based on an antiseptic smell.

BARBARA: There's a chimney over there, among the trees.

MOHAMMED: It's a great shame that England's small enough for one to have to tolerate neighbours.

BARBARA: There seems to be a man sitting on the chimney.

MOHAMMED: An elderly man of quite unnecessary dignity?

BARBARA: He's reading a book, I think.

[297]

MOHAMMED: Can you see which book?

BARBARA: Give me a chance. He's about three hundred yards away.

MOHAMMED: It's not important. I just thought it might be one of mine.

BARBARA: Who is he?

MOHAMMED: Lord Justice Walberswick. He probably feels quite at home on a chimney.

BARBARA: Why?

MOHAMMED: Well, it's a high hard seat.

BARBARA: Ha! You don't seem a bit surprised or alarmed at the level of the floods.

MOHAMMED: I am English. Nothing surprises me. That is, you surprise me, Barbara—

BARBARA: Yes, yes, I know about that. But aren't you even alarmed?

MOHAMMED: Nothing alarms the English until it is far too late for them to do anything about it. We have already won because we've never realised when we've been defeated. Nobody tells us. In war, as in politics, we are deaf to the umpire's whistle.

BARBARA: This is water, Mohammed, not foreigners.

MOHAMMED: Oh, it's all one. We're permanently geared to look disaster square in the face.

> *He touches her leg with his umbrella.* BARBARA *mutters:* "Oh", *and breaks* UP CENTRE.

It is in those moments of disaster that we begin to believe seriously in victory—and it is for that reason also, Barbara, that every refusal to my advances brings me nearer my ultimate goal. You seem unmoved.

BARBARA: I haven't been listening.

MOHAMMED: That, Barbara, is a lie.

BARBARA: What if it is?

MOHAMMED: Ah. Then there is no need for me to repeat it.

BARBARA: Mohammed, I'm bored to tears by you.

MOHAMMED: Excellent. The advance continues. You will soon lose your temper.

BARBARA: No, I won't.

MOHAMMED: Yes, you will.

BARBARA (*very calm and accurate*): No, I won't.

MOHAMMED (*cajoling*): You will.

BARBARA (*angry*): I won't!

MOHAMMED (*very quiet and smiling*): Yes, you will.

BARBARA (*losing her temper*): I won't.

MOHAMMED (*quiet, wagging his finger*): Ha ha.

BARBARA: I hope you drown!

MOHAMMED: What if everyone else drowns, Barbara, but us? (*He sings softly.*) If you were the only girl in the world, and I was—

BARBARA: What a sordid imagination you've got.

MOHAMMED: How long would you resist my caresses in an empty landscape with not a neon sign or a friendly cocktail for miles?

BARBARA (*frightened*): Don't joke about such things . . .

MOHAMMED: Why not? What is life and love but an appallingly unfunny joke, made tolerable by high conversation and the body's rapture?

BARBARA: You're repellent.

MOHAMMED: Barbara, you're cold.

BARBARA: I've told you that myself.

MOHAMMED: Take my dressing gown.

BARBARA: Why didn't you offer it to me before?

MOHAMMED: I had no reason.

BARBARA: What's your reason now?

MOHAMMED: I could help you on with it.

BARBARA: Well?

MOHAMMED: And steal a kiss?

A pause. They look at one another.

At least I'm honest, Barbara.

BARBARA (*vicious*): I'm beginning to enjoy being cold.

MOHAMMED: Why must we torture one another?

BARBARA (*starting suddenly*): Good heavens, I'm sure the water's risen since we came out. Go and warn the others.

MOHAMMED: No.

BARBARA: D'you mean you're too lazy?

MOHAMMED: I do not wish to go.

BARBARA: Then I'll go.

MOHAMMED: And I shall prevent you from going, by force if necessary.

BARBARA: But they may all drown!

MOHAMMED: Then we will be alone, Barbara, at last, without eavesdroppers, without alternatives.

BARBARA: You're mad!

MOHAMMED (*amorous*): And you, my darling, are the cause.

NIOBE'S *voice*.

BARBARA: Look out!

MOHAMMED (*melodramatic*): Oh, drat!

They hide behind the turrets as the door opens, and NIOBE *emerges in her nightdress.* LORD BASINGSTOKE *follows her. He wears pyjamas, and a dressing gown with a coronet on the pocket.*

BASINGSTOKE: Aren't we criminals?

NIOBE: Yes, my own dear sensitive heart, but on a grand classical scale. We are sacrificing all to love, just as the heroes of mythology were wont to do.

BASINGSTOKE: Shouldn't we at least wake Mohammed? He'll drown.

NIOBE: What matter? It is a poet's death. Bill, I have but thoughts of you. How silly was our lovers' tiff.

BASINGSTOKE: I thought you meant it when you said—

NIOBE: The mind spoke, and sought to stab the heart, not knowing of that organ's immortality. I recant. I swallow the words of treachery I uttered. (*Precipitately.*) Take my hand.

They hold hands.

BASINGSTOKE (*nervously*): I feel a certain obligation towards—

NIOBE: Tush!

BASINGSTOKE: After all, she is my wife.

NIOBE: Let them all drown. What matters it?

BASINGSTOKE: You were so squeamish before.

NIOBE: What could not any of us do if we felt we were for once unobserved! The floodgates of violence which lie within us all and are the oldest part of nature are so guarded, dear Bill, by the fear of scandal, that even in our baths we sit as though spied on by a watch committee. Have you never felt murder in your heart as an obvious solution to even the tiniest problem? Have you never felt like turning up naked at a large reception?

BASINGSTOKE (*miserable*): No, I haven't.

NIOBE: There. You have made the blushes rise to my cheeks, by uttering the words of a civilised conscience. But I won't let you do it, Bill, for this is freedom. Let them drown, for they are the ears and eyes which make us be what we are not. In a world without mirrors I am beautiful, and young, and infinitely desirable. Their faces are worse than mirrors. Worse, Bill. Their faces are the reflection of their

[300]

horrid thoughts, all satire, irony, sarcasm, spite, all the little twinklings of the eye and subtle puckerings of skin which shout out to me, "You're ugly, and ridiculous." (*Quieter.*) That's why I like you, Bill. You seem to like me.

BASINGSTOKE (*frightened*): I do like you, it's only . . .

NIOBE: I'm grateful. (*Closing her eyes.*) Oh, to dance to a flute without causing embarrassment. Oh, to admit to a love of liquorice and Bakewell tart without a lack of intellectual integrity. Oh, to be a mother without any outside help. (*Opening her eyes and smiling.*) I couldn't say such things unless I was alone with you, Bill, because you're so dear and insignificant. You see, this time I have conquered my blushes.

BASINGSTOKE: All the same—

NIOBE: No, no. No all-the-sames. Stand there and smile at me like a young Greek shepherd beloved of an ageless goddess. Think hard, and you will hear the pastoral pipes.

> *She hums and dances in the neo-Greek fashion.* LORD BASING-STOKE *consults his watch.*

Oh, don't look at your watch, cruel-fair! (*Appealing.*) Don't! Our wings have beaten the life out of time. We are living legends.

BASINGSTOKE: Ssh! Listen!

NIOBE: Uh?

BASINGSTOKE: There's someone coming.

NIOBE: What?

BASINGSTOKE: There's someone coming up the stairs.

NIOBE (*with a heartfelt moan*): They have survived! The human mirrors follow me like furies.

BASINGSTOKE: They'll be furious if they find out we didn't wake them. Better hide.

NIOBE: Not just hide, Bill, but hide like guilty lovers.

> *She takes his hand, and they tiptoe out of sight, like caricatures of Renaissance lovers.* MOHAMMED *and* BARBARA *move round to another side of the turret.* BONE *and* BUTTRESS *appear through the door.* BUTTRESS *is carrying the back of a bed.*

BONE: They've done a bunk, and it's all your fault, Buttress.

BUTTRESS: Easy to be wise after the event, Bone.

BONE: All the same, I think we ought to have woken the Professor. (*He looks at the water, and whistles.*) Look at the water. This is more than just floods. This is something out of science fiction.

BUTTRESS: Exactly. We've got to keep our heads and make a plan.

[301]

BONE: I don't altogether trust your plans, Buttress.

BUTTRESS: Why not?

BONE: Because you're a self-confessed criminal, that's why.

BUTTRESS: You don't understand that without people like me about, there'd be no need of police.

BONE: What?

BUTTRESS: Think it over. It's people like me that's helping to solve the unemployment problem. Come on, let's push off.

BONE: But what about the Professor, snoring down there?

BUTTRESS: This bedstead would never hold the three of us.

BONE: Oughtn't we to draw straws out of a hat?

BUTTRESS: Don't be silly, we've got two hats, but no straws.

BONE: No, you're right. Why did you wake me up, and not him?

BUTTRESS: You're bigger than he is. I wouldn't like you to get nasty. You might have woken up of your own accord.

BONE: Mr Buttress, I'll be free with you. I am an ex-policeman. I've got honour. I don't like it.

BUTTRESS: But you'll lump it.

BONE: I don't know.

BUTTRESS: Who saved your life by waking up?

BONE: You did.

BUTTRESS: Who's the brains?

BONE: We've both got those.

BUTTRESS: Who's got the honour?

BONE: I have!

BUTTRESS: Who's got the Rolls-Royce?

BONE: You have.

BUTTRESS: Who's the boss?

BONE (*reluctantly*): You are.

BUTTRESS: Come on then, and help me launch this.

BONE: Pss!

BUTTRESS: What is it?

BONE: There's someone coming up the stairs. I'll tell you what—

BUTTRESS: You leave this to me. Hide behind the tower. Get behind here. I'll flatten him.

> *They hide.* NIOBE *and* BASINGSTOKE *move round. So do* MO-HAMMED *and* BARBARA, *who emerge on the other side. The* PRO-FESSOR *enters, distraught, dressed in pyjamas, the trousers of which are wet up to the knees. He wears an ornamented skull-cap.*

NO SIGN OF THE DOVE

PROFESSOR (*shouting*): Help! . . . Help! . . . Help! (*He turns round and sees* MOHAMMED *and* BARBARA.) Ach! There you are. I thought I had been left alone!

MOHAMMED: Come out, Niobe, and you, Basingstoke.

NIOBE *and* BASINGSTOKE *emerge.*

MOHAMMED: And you, too . . . Come on, I know you're there!

BONE *and* BUTTRESS *emerge.*

BONE: I told you I didn't like it, Buttress.

MOHAMMED: And bring that bit of wood with you, sir.

In angry mood, BUTTRESS *brings it out and lets it drop onto the stage.*

A pretty state of affairs, I will say.

NIOBE: Tell me you didn't overhear.

MOHAMMED: So you wish to dance to a flute, do you, and become a mother without assistance, do you?

NIOBE (*really suffering*): Oh, no, no, don't.

MOHAMMED: And you wish to let us drown? Bravo, Basingstoke.

BASINGSTOKE: I disapproved of the idea from the outset.

MOHAMMED: But you did absolutely nothing to prevent it. And you, sir, thought to float to safety on a fragment of stolen bedstead, did you? Not content with blackmail, you and your crew hoped to emulate the rats by leaving the foundering galleon, did you?

BUTTRESS: We thought you'd left, didn't I say so, Bone?

BONE: I never liked the way you said it, though. It didn't ring true.

BUTTRESS: Bone! That's the second stab in the back.

MOHAMMED: It is the most disgusting . . .

BASINGSTOKE: Anyway, you must have been out here first, Mohammed. Why didn't you wake us up?

ALL *murmur agreement.*

MOHAMMED: I was on the point of doing so.

NIOBE (*violently*): Then why did you hide when we appeared, and make of my flights of innocent fancy a vile psychiatric ambush?

MOHAMMED: What? Do you shout at me, sister?

NIOBE: Yes, I shout at you, for you have unveiled my mind, and must pay the hideous consequences.

MOHAMMED: Let me assure you, Niobe, and indeed all of you, that I was bent on rescue, but a leader's brain needs quiet to hatch ingenious plots with which to cheat the elements. I hid for the purpose of calm reflection.

[303]

BARBARA: Liar! When I wanted to wake them up, you barred my way. You're the worst of all, because you woke up first.

MOHAMMED: I have always been a notoriously light sleeper. I was only teasing you. (*Powerful.*) And in any case, which one of you has not expressed a wish to be rid of all the others? Answer me that?

LORD BASINGSTOKE *and* BONE *hold up their hands.*

You two miseries acquiesced out of weakness, which is worse than all the villainies, for it makes villainy possible the world over.

LORD BASINGSTOKE *and* BONE *look at each other and withdraw their hands sheepishly.*

PROFESSOR (*in a sudden fury*): Nobody made any effort to wake me up, who am the most of value from you all!

MOHAMMED: Why should we? Your theory of hatred has been carried to its logical conclusion. You should be intellectually satisfied even if you are physically uncomfortable.

PROFESSOR: I am not satisfied! I am too important a person to be so easily satisfied! My life must be saved at all costs!

MOHAMMED: Reserve a seat on the bedstead.

BUTTRESS: You damn fool, Bone, holding us up with your arguments. We'd have been well away by now.

MOHAMMED: Do you boast of your attempted treachery, sir?

BUTTRESS: Yes. I've got a healthy respect for my own grey matter. I'm of more value than that crackpot professor.

PROFESSOR (*pacing agitatedly*): I was the last to be woken. Ach. It is enough to give a man persecution mania.

BASINGSTOKE (*calm*): You weren't the last, Professor.

PROFESSOR: I not? Then who?

BASINGSTOKE: What about your father, Mohammed?

NIOBE (*who has been sitting on the ground, her head between her hands, brooding*): Father!

MOHAMMED: He . . . he would not have survived much longer.

BASINGSTOKE (*quiet*): And Hope?

MOHAMMED (*suddenly resolute*): Basingstoke. Do the first useful act of your wizened life. Go and rescue them.

BASINGSTOKE: Buttress.

BUTTRESS: And let you get away on the bedstead while I'm away? Not likely.

BONE: I'll go.

NIOBE: Oh, thank you, Bone.

[304]

BONE (*heroic*): Where are they?

NIOBE: Paddle down the corridor—Just a moment. Mohammed, who's that on the garage roof? Isn't that them?

MOHAMMED (*a cursory glance*): Those are the servants.

NIOBE *waves*.

(*Shocked.*) Don't wave at them, Niobe. Are you forgetting who you are?

NIOBE (*intimidated again*): But they waved at me.

MOHAMMED (*sad*): Oh, Niobe, Niobe.

He bows coldly at the servants, who start singing "Keep the Home Fires Burning."

NIOBE: They're singing.

MOHAMMED (*irritated*): I know. Ignore them.

BONE: I'm still awaiting instructions, ma'am.

A small sail suddenly rises with the air like a fan from beyond the crenelations. A great cheer is raised by the servants.

NIOBE: Why are they cheering?

BUTTRESS (*dry*): Look.

They all turn as MATTHEW stands up with HOPE. They are behind the battlements.

MATTHEW: There's no need to fetch us, Bone. Thank you all the same.

NIOBE: Father! What are you doing?

MATTHEW: Saying goodbye.

NIOBE: But where are you standing? On the water?

MOHAMMED (*looking over the side*): On an ark.

NIOBE: An ark? (*Hysterical.*) Rescue!

MATTHEW (*holding up his hand with the sad serenity of an ancient prophet*): I'm afraid not, my dear. I built this Ark as best I could, with the wholly inadequate means at my disposal. It has room for only two.

NIOBE: But we could stand!

MATTHEW: Look at the horizon. Can you see an island in sight? Will there be anything left of England but the peak of Ben Nevis by this evening, or anything of Europe but the Alps by tomorrow, or anything in the world but the pimple of Everest by the day after? Rescue, did you say? Rescue where to? To a nice cup of tea in a warm canteen served by a titled lady with a bedside manner? That's a thing of the past.

[305]

NIOBE (*hotly*): Why didn't you let us into your plan?

MATTHEW: Because I was mad, Daughter.

NIOBE: Then why didn't you build a bigger Ark?

MATTHEW (*slowly and sadly*): Why didn't you give me a bigger room?

A pause.

MOHAMMED (*in a dead voice*): Oh my God. (*Very quiet.*) Father, you're very old.

MATTHEW: And not quite clear in the head?

MOHAMMED: I wouldn't say that.

MATTHEW: I collected tins, didn't I? I gathered twigs, and little boxes you had thrown away. I scavenged your wastepaper baskets and your dustbins like a pariah dog. Well, I manufactured my Ark largely out of the things you had rejected as useless.

NIOBE *moans.*

I followed the instructions given to Noah but on a very much humbler scale, owing to the dimensions of my room, and I found that by divine providence the contraption floats. If you had allowed me to set up my workshop in the ballroom, I could have accepted you all as passengers—but on second thoughts I'm glad to leave you behind.

NIOBE: Glad, Father?

MATTHEW: There is not time to be squeamish or sorry now. (*To* MOHAMMED.) You said I was old. Why?

MOHAMMED: Isn't the duty of a parent towards his children?

MATTHEW: You wish me to deny my triumph, and to give you the boat?

MOHAMMED: Not necessarily me.

MATTHEW: Who, for instance?

MOHAMMED: Barbara?

MATTHEW: The Goddess of Love in this arid Olympus? Yes, it would be a Christian action, but I am no saint, no paragon of self-denial. I wish to benefit by my foresight.

MOHAMMED: But if you survive, Father, and you find yourself alone on Ararat, how will humanity begin again? Noah took precautions.

MATTHEW: If I give any of you the Ark, it will give humanity the worst start I can imagine. Think of a child of Niobe's as father of the human race, and sired by Basingstoke at that.

NIOBE: No, father. (*She hides her head in shame.*)

BASINGSTOKE: Steady, sir.

[306]

MATTHEW: Steady. It would be born as tentative and as gormless a weed as imagination can conceive to scatter the feeble seed over the empty continents of the earth. Think of a rejuvenated Africa hammering to the rhythms of black Niobes, or of a revived Asia, with mystic Basingstokes searching out the truth from mattresses of pins. No, Mohammed. There is a limit to my cruelty. I'd rather not.

MOHAMMED: But Barbara—?

MATTHEW: With you?

BARBARA: I prefer death.

PROFESSOR (*his chance*): Barbara! You—me!

BARBARA (*looking at the Professor*): I much prefer death.

MATTHEW: Even if the lady were willing, think of the world kicking off to a new dawn of empty pedantry and complicated language, the councils of plump Red Indians you would father, yawning their war cries, and think of the Eskimos who would call Barbara the Goddess of Creation, without enough wits to know the use of blubber, holding mannequin parades on the ice.

PROFESSOR: But me! My brain! Convince her!

MATTHEW: Your brain is the ultimate in human confusion. How could a parasite live in the emptiness, with nothing to feed upon?

PROFESSOR *moves* DOWN RIGHT.

MATTHEW: No. I shall take the Ark, but I shall not be alone. Hope will be with me, blessed and aptly named. You thought me criminal to harden her resistance by forcing her to wear only those clothes which modesty requires, but I knew what would happen. I foresaw the hardships we would have to face. And now she is ready, in all her simplicity, to be the mother of a younger world and its wise old grandmother on the evening of its first day.

MOHAMMED (*spluttering*): But she's illiterate—or dumb!

MATTHEW (*furious*): Who said so? Say something, Hope. Say something. Don't be afraid.

HOPE *is silent*.

MOHAMMED: There!

MATTHEW: She's shy, that's all.

MOHAMMED: And are you the new Adam, Father?

MATTHEW (*quiet*): No. I don't doubt I could be. But no.

NIOBE: But who is she?

MATTHEW: I found her.

NIOBE: Where?

MATTHEW: In a pram.

[307]

NIOBE: You stole her!

MATTHEW: She was being delivered to a convent and had a note attached to her, written illiterately by the tear-stained woman who was pushing the conveyance. She wished to consign this sweet innocence to the tender care of nuns. I bought Hope from her for two and sixpence.

NIOBE: Where did you acquire such a sum of money?

MATTHEW: Well may you ask. I borrowed it from Mayhew the butler, and paid him back a penny a week out of the sixpence pocket-money you graciously accorded me for my private needs.

MOHAMMED: As soon as the floods abate sufficiently to communicate with the garage in a dignified manner, I will ask Mayhew to seek other employment.

MATTHEW: Normally I would be angry with you, but as I know that the floods will not abate—

MOHAMMED: Nonsense.

NIOBE: No, I think Father's right. Alas, I do, I do, I do.

MOHAMMED: Even if he is, I shall dismiss Mayhew with the last breath in my body.

MATTHEW: Why?

MOHAMMED: Why? For conspiring with you to purchase a domestic animal, and for placing his capital at the disposal of your folly.

MATTHEW (*sharp*): Folly?

MOHAMMED: Folly. Who will father this new race of cave-men?

MATTHEW: Listen, Mohammed, we don't know any more than you do. We will set out with our eyes scanning the horizon and if all it holds for us is disappointment and death we are ready, because let me tell you that if, in the wide expanse of the globe, there is not a single youth who has found in himself the guts to survive, then the world's not worth saving, and will be happier empty.

> BUTTRESS *has surreptitiously picked up a shovel and is creeping up on* MATTHEW. NIOBE *screams.* "Look!" MATTHEW *turns on him.*

There's murder in your eye, Mr Buttress.

> *As* BUTTRESS *stops his advance,* NIOBE *gasps.*

You could easily kill an old fellow like me with a blow from that shovel, do you know that?

BUTTRESS (*snarling*): Of course I do. Why d'you think I've picked it up? What d'you think I'm going to do with it?

MATTHEW: You will do nothing at all, because you will be over-powered.

All move in.

If you create a vacancy in the boat, you will create a stampede.

BONE: Stand back. It's his Ark.

BUTTRESS: Stand back. I'm warning you.

MATTHEW: Stand back, Basingstoke. Mr Bone, you may proceed.

BONE *advances.*

BUTTRESS (*to* BONE): Don't be a fool, Bone, this is our chance, yours and mine ... I hadn't forgotten you ... I was going to take you, remember? ... I'll hit you! Bone, don't be a fool!

BONE: You said you was frightened because I was bigger than you ... well, I am ... and stronger ...

BUTTRESS (*sharply*): Bone!

With a deft movement, BONE *expropriates the weapon from* BUTTRESS *and throws it over the parapet.*

BUTTRESS: Bone! ... Bone!

BONE: There, I feel better. Now there's no more temptation. When there's no temptation I feel strong. I'm weak when I'm being tempted. Now get away, old man, while the going's good.

MATTHEW: I deeply regret that there's no room for you, Bone—you have a degree of delightful weakness and stupidity that the world can ill do without.

BONE: No, sir, I wouldn't come. I don't deserve it. On the other hand, I'll keep them in order till the end, trust me. Did I tell you that I'm a V.C.?

MOHAMMED: You're joking.

BONE (*humble*): No, sir. When I can see the enemy, and there's no arguing, I'm all right. I know my duty. It's when there's talking that I get muddled.

PROFESSOR *starts to talk.*

No, no! I can see clear now. Push off, sir, and that's an order.

NIOBE: Leave us some food, Father. You must have some with you, and I see no prospect at all of breakfast.

MATTHEW: What can I leave you? A tin of baked beans? No, dear, starvation is more dignified.

NIOBE (*a moan*): I'm sick of dignity!

BONE: Come on, come on, pull yourself together, miss.

NIOBE *looks at him, amazed and resentful.*

Push off, sir.

BARBARA: Just a moment. How did you know this would happen?

MATTHEW: How did I know? My dear, how could the state of affairs continue?

BARBARA: State of affairs? I was having a good time.

MATTHEW: The vultures always do when the explorers lie about in lifeless heaps.

MOHAMMED: Father, you have gone too far.

MATTHEW: I went too far long ago, and thoroughly enjoyed it. Unrestricted by the niceties of the drawing room, I didn't become confused. I observed the heat waves in midwinter and the cold spells in autumn, and saw the signs of mounting anger in the sky. "It's the bombs they're bursting" was on everyone's lips. And they were righter than they knew. Every bomb they burst, shattering colonies of inno-cent monkeys in mushrooms of smoke as a dress rehearsal to a human tragedy, was a slap on God's face. (*Heartcry.*) What have we done with those miraculous gifts of mind and body which grow in us as we move from birth to death through the subtle seasons of life? Look at you, Niobe, and you, Mohammed, enslaved by your own useless niceties of mind, forever adding perfume to the scandalous pot-pourri of lifeless intellect; and look at you, Professor, desperately seeking standing room in the long dark corridors of advanced opinion; and you, poor Basingstoke, trying so hard to buy intelligence with your rich inheritance; and you, Barbara, who have made of your proud body a sterile altar for sensual delights; and you, Buttress, who use your native wits to push those weaker than yourself into the drink, and to flatter those stronger with the sanctimonious smile of uprightness; and you, dear Bone, who have allowed your strength to be harnessed by anyone with an argument you haven't the brains to understand, and who barks like a police dog to a whistle.

MOHAMMED: Why should we be specially villainous?

MATTHEW: You're not. I just know you well owing to our un-fortunate proximity over the years. Look at the other roofs. (*Points his finger.*) The Bishop of Luton has organised games. The clergy is playing hide-and-seek among the chimney pots. A resilient man, you see, with the gift of cheerfulness, but what has the Church done but to split hairs, and to divide itself into teams as for a party game? How many good bodies the hungry flames have devoured owing to the profane differences of witch-doctors with personal superstitions to decorate the agonisingly simple symbol of the cross? The battle of crooks and mitres, of palaces and plate, could only end in deluge. With every faith a true faith, and every cross a true cross, we come to lunacy. (*He gazes in another direction.*) And over there, a Judge, old

Walberswick, still sitting in judgement on the floods, ready to sentence the offending water to a long and dreary term of prison, with a final word of sour sarcasm to rankle in the cell; and over there, the empty roof of those who have inherited the richness of the earth, and dream of accumulating more. Their comfort is more important to them than the quality of their products, just as the law is more important than justice, just as the Church is more important than religion. To love God, one must be an amateur, my friends, unpretentious, gay and child-like, and this is a professional world which is sinking to its doom, a world of irritable one-track men, who know their business, and wear blinkers in order not to see too far, for it is dangerous and unprofitable.

MOHAMMED (*angry*): Go away, Father, and let us die in peace.

BONE (*angry*): Don't talk to your guv'nor like that!

MATTHEW (*sadly*): There is the born disciple . . . of any old creed.

BONE (*earnest*): I think I understand, sir.

MATTHEW: You'd be a grand storm-trooper, Bone.

BONE (*pleased*): Would I, sir?

MATTHEW: Come on, Hope, shove off.

MOHAMMED: Goodbye, senility and ignorance!

BUTTRESS: I hope you sink!

PROFESSOR (*suddenly hysterical*): Stop! Stop! At least, take my book with you!

> *He produces it from his pyjamas.*

MATTHEW: What for?

PROFESSOR: Posterity! I *must* be remembered!

MATTHEW: Poor lonely soul. We already have our complement of books, most of them comic. They will produce an agreeable reminiscence.

MOHAMMED: Who have you got?

MATTHEW: Shakespeare, Voltaire, Gogol, Dickens, Rabelais, and —someone else.

HOPE: Boccaccio.

> *Stupefaction.*

MOHAMMED: Did you say something?

MATTHEW (*laughing loudly*): She said Boccaccio. Shove off, my darling little encyclopaedia, no time to lose.

> *As the boat moves off, he continues:*

I have attended to her education. Come on, Hope, to the tiller, steer where the sacred spirit moves you—if possible, away from the clergy—

They move off. NIOBE *waves.*

MOHAMMED: Don't wave, Niobe! Where have you picked up that ridiculous middle-class habit?

NIOBE: Boccaccio, at her age! (*She waves.*)

MOHAMMED: Niobe!

NIOBE: Well, he is my Daddy . . . (*She breaks into fitful tears.*) Oh, I can't bear it!

PROFESSOR (*in a trance*): He refused to take my book!

BONE: Right, now come on, sit down here, in lines.

MOHAMMED: What are you talking about?

BONE: I'm organising community singing, like I did in Tunisia when I won my V.C.

MOHAMMED: I refuse to sing.

BONE (*violent*): You'll do as you're told! Sit down. Come on, Buttress.

BUTTRESS: You won't get me to sing.

BONE (*furious*): I won't what?

BUTTRESS *sits down obediently.*

MOHAMMED (*sitting down*): You haven't said much, Basingstoke.

BASINGSTOKE: I hadn't much to say.

MOHAMMED: I am glad you are becoming selective.

BONE (*grim*): Now I suggest "Three Blind Mice". Buttress and you, Lady Basingstoke, will start off. Then the Prof and Miss D'Urt, and finally Sir Mohammed and Lord Basingstoke.

MOHAMMED: What are you going to do?

BONE (*grimmer*): I'm going to conduct. And I want to see a great deal of spirit and liveliness in your singing. Think of it as an inspirin' regimental march, not just a nursery rhyme. I want you to sing every word as though you meant it, is that clear? I want to actually be able to see them mice. Now, before we start. Any questions?

NIOBE (*emotional*): I can't help feeling we should sing a hymn—but then I don't remember any.

BONE: I select the music fitting to the occasion, lady, and being a serious moment, I want a lot of gaiety from you, like the old man said. A lot of gaiety and vigour and real class in your singing. Ready. One—two—

NIOBE: Shouldn't we forgive each other? Make some gesture?

The sun comes out, blindingly. They sit and look up. There is silence. Then NIOBE speaks, hushed.

The sun! It was my suggestion that brought it out . . . (*In ecstasy.*) I forgive you all!

She looks at the sun, and indeed it seems brighter. They all stare at the sky.

Bill!

BASINGSTOKE: I forgive you!

NIOBE: All, all.

BILL: All.

NIOBE: Mohammed.

MOHAMMED (*soft*): I say, this is embarrassing. I forgive you all.

NIOBE: Barbara.

BARBARA: I forgive you all.

NIOBE (*with rising emotion*): Professor!

PROFESSOR: I forgive you all.

NIOBE: Bone!

BONE: Eh? Oh. I forgive you all.

NIOBE: Buttress!

BUTTRESS (*automatic*): I forgive you all.

NIOBE: Now we are all united in love and in forgiveness! The sun is out, look at it, it has never looked so young. The dove should be here soon . . .

MOHAMMED (*hushed*): The dove . . .

NIOBE: The dove with the olive-branch . . .

Distant cheers. NIOBE waves at the clergymen and the servants.

MOHAMMED: Niobe!

He bows at the clergymen and at the servants.

BUTTRESS: Look, the level of the water's falling fast. It must have dropped an inch while we were talking.

NIOBE: Hurrah! Bill, kiss Barbara . . .

BASINGSTOKE: Should I?

NIOBE: She is your wife.

BASINGSTOKE: Barbara. May I?

BARBARA: Remember Capri, Bill? The Green Grotto.

BASINGSTOKE: The grotto's blue, but never mind.

[313]

BARBARA: The grotto's green, I remember it.

BASINGSTOKE: Darling Babs, you're always right. Of course it was green.

They kiss. NIOBE *is exercising super-human control.*

MOHAMMED: Just a moment, Basingstoke, before you settle down. If you have any spare copies of your magazine, I would be only too delighted to read the lot.

NIOBE: I will read them aloud to you, Mohammed.

PROFESSOR: I have been unreasonable in the past, young man. Perhaps I will write your article for no money—perhaps almost no money. Sir Mohammed, I hope I did not hurt you.

MOHAMMED: When?

PROFESSOR: When I made my most brutal attack to you last evening.

MOHAMMED: My dear fellow, it was entirely my fault. I misunderstood you. If I do have a few bruises this morning I have only myself to blame.

BONE: I suggest three hearty cheers for Miss D'Urt!

MOHAMMED: Later, Mr Bone, we've had quite enough excitement for one morning. Ah! The sun!

NIOBE: The great heartbeat of the world has returned to normal.

MOHAMMED: Normal's ugly.

NIOBE: I have a harvest of time to think of a better word.

MOHAMMED: How ridiculous father will look when he sinks to the middle of the countryside in his Ark. It shouldn't be too difficult to have him certified now.

NIOBE: Oh, no, Mohammed, we mustn't, we can't.

MOHAMMED: Why not? He practically sentenced us to death, leaving us here to die with an expression of odious satisfaction on his face. He's mad as a hatter, and the sooner that girl's handed over to an institution, the better. Boccaccio, indeed.

NIOBE: Perhaps you're right. We can talk about it later.

Suddenly BUTTRESS *slaps* BONE *on the face.*

BUTTRESS: So you'd have us singing "Three Blind Mice", would you? Blithering idiot.

BONE: There's no need to hit me, Buttress.

BUTTRESS: No? You want me to do it again?

NIOBE: Don't, Buttress! Please! We must all be linked in love.

BUTTRESS: Love? Did I hear right? My dear lady, your troubles aren't over yet.

NIOBE: What d'you mean?

BUTTRESS: There's a little matter of blackmail.

MOHAMMED: You wouldn't dare now!

BUTTRESS: I wouldn't? Why not?

MOHAMMED: Have you forgotten what we so nearly did to you before?

BUTTRESS: Ah, but we're in public now, and in broad daylight. A scream would have all the clergy looking in this direction, or the Judge, or the servants. I've got you where I want you now.

BARBARA: Bone will testify against you now.

BUTTRESS: Will he?

BONE: I don't know.

BUTTRESS: You'll do as you're told. The floods'll be all gone in a few hours, and we'll be back to normal. Back to Maidenhead. It's lovely by the river at this time of the year. Not too much water.

BONE: Sounds very tempting, Mr Buttress.

BUTTRESS: That's better. Now let's talk money.

BASINGSTOKE: I'll give you a thousand pounds to keep quiet, Buttress.

BUTTRESS: You shouldn't have started out so high, Lord Basingstoke. It makes me want to ask for more.

BASINGSTOKE: D'you accept it?

BUTTRESS: No.

PROFESSOR: I will give you an autographed first edition of my masterwork. It will have great value in a hundred years.

BUTTRESS: I can't wait that long.

NIOBE: Buttress, may I appeal to your humanity?

BUTTRESS: I haven't got any, and I don't want any. I consider it anti-social.

BARBARA: Buttress, you're a rather attractive man.

BUTTRESS: No use, Lady Basingstoke. I can get as many as I want with the money.

NIOBE: Mr Bone!

BUTTRESS: Bone!

BONE: I'm muddled, Miss D'Urt. I've always wanted to better myself.

NIOBE: But surely, Bone, humanity—

BUTTRESS: It's an expensive luxury, isn't it, Bone?

BONE (*quite lost*): It's certainly expensive.

NIOBE: Mr Bone!

MOHAMMED: It's hopeless, Niobe, the man's a deadhead. Anyway, we're no longer in charge.

BUTTRESS: Ah, the voice of reason. Well, what's the sum to be . . .?

A pause. It gets darker again.

NIOBE (*hushed*): The sun. It's going in.

BARBARA: I felt a drop of rain.

NIOBE (*calling*): I forgive you all! (*Louder.*) I forgive you all! (*A great universal shout.*) I forgive you all!

There is a rumble of thunder.

MOHAMMED (*calm*): They've changed the password.

BASINGSTOKE: The water's rising again. You can see it with the naked eye.

BUTTRESS (*nervous, looking around him*): I'll take a thousand, and we'll say no more about it.

NIOBE: Oh, idiots, fools!

PROFESSOR (*hissing*): You have tempted the elements, Buttress.

BUTTRESS: A thousand pounds.

A louder rumble of thunder.

MOHAMMED: You look wonderful in the rain, Barbara.

NIOBE: Don't say such things, Mohammed.

MOHAMMED: Oh, it's too late to be anything but courageous.

NIOBE: Courageous?

MOHAMMED: Yes, Niobe. The glory of the human race is that it has never shown as much courage as when it is destroying itself. Father may be mad and Hope too young to understand, but we must find it in ourselves to wish them luck, for the simple reason that they are alive.

NIOBE: Then Father was right!

MOHAMMED: I don't know, but I do know that I would have been undignified to admit that he was right to his face.

NIOBE: Dignity! That terrible word again!

MOHAMMED: What have we left but dignity and breeding, Niobe? We are not equipped for survival in a world where the arts are the precious toys of the few and where stupidity and science are linked in opposition to us. Therefore, be brave, like me. Sing "Three Blind Mice" as though it was the divinest music ever written, until the notes turn to bubbles.

NIOBE: I don't want to sing.

[316]

MOHAMMED: You will have to. We are no longer in charge. Basingstoke, I believe we're singing together.

BASINGSTOKE: Should be rather fun.

BONE (*slaps* BUTTRESS): So you'd interrupt my community singing, would you, in order to do a bit of blackmail? That's what comes of it. (*Taking charge.*) Right. Everyone back to their original places. At the double, move, move, move.

NIOBE: We'd much better pray.

BONE: You will do as I say. Come on, Buttress—like an old woman about ninety.

NIOBE: Bone, I appeal to you. Lead us in prayers.

BONE: I'll do as I think best.

A huge thunder clap.

They're shelling our position, lads. Now show them that we're not frightened.

There is lightning.

That's our artillery, lads. Keep your peckers up, and show them what we're made of.

NIOBE (*a great cry*): The sun! It's peeping through the clouds over there!

MOHAMMED: For heaven's sake surrender gracefully.

BONE: Ready now. Good and loud now, lads. One—two—

NIOBE: Look, look, it is the sun!

BARBARA: It is!

NIOBE: And yet, there's absolutely no sign of the dove . . .

The largest thunder clap of all is heard.

(*A cry.*) Whoever you are, whatever you are, drown us or let us live, but please, please, make up your mind!

A flash of lightning, and a beam of sunshine as well.

BONE: I'm not going to stand any more interruption, is that clear? One more of them, and I'll have you all doubling round the roof, got it . . . ?

PROFESSOR (*desperate*): I don't know the words!

BONE: Pick 'em up, pick 'em up as you go. Come on, show them you don't care. One—two—Come on.

They begin to sing "Three Blind Mice", encouraged by BONE, who conducts with the violence, if not with the subtlety, of a Toscanini.

[317]

(*Roaring.*) You've got more voice than that, Lady Barbara! If you can't sing, shout, Buttress!

There is a terrific thunder clap.

That's the spirit, Sir Mohammed. Lovely tenor you've got there, Lord Basingstoke. Stick at it, Prof, we'll make a Caruso of you yet . . .

As they sing with increasing strength, their eyes gaze at the trace of sunlight which lights their faces. The world is very dark . . .

CURTAIN